English Grammar Drills

English Grammar Drills

SECOND EDITION

Mark Lester

McGraw
Hill
Education

New York   Chicago   San Francisco   Athens   London   Madrid
Mexico City   Milan   New Delhi   Singapore   Sydney   Toronto

2 3 4 5 6 7 8 9   LHS   23 22 21 20 19

ISBN   978-1-260-11617-5
MHID   1-260-11617-4

e-ISBN 978-1-260-11618-2
e-MHID   1-260-11618-2

McGraw-Hill Education books are available at special quantity discounts to use as premiums and sales promotions or for use in corporate training programs. To contact a representative, please visit the Contact Us page at www.mhprofessional.com.

McGraw-Hill Language Lab App

Interactive quizzes and flashcards are available to support your study of this book. Go to www.mhlanguagelab.com to access the online version of this application or to locate links to the mobile app for iOS and Android devices. Alternatively, search "McGraw-Hill Education Language Lab" in the iTunes app store or Google Play store.

Contents

Preface

This book focuses on the grammatical problems that prevent speakers at your level from achieving a native-like command of English grammar. While the book covers most areas of English grammar, it has a heavy concentration on those aspects of grammar that have proven to be the greatest obstacles for intermediate and advanced nonnative speakers.

The book has an unusual format. Most topics are broken into small mini-units, most of them no more than a page or two. Each of these mini-units is supported by an exercise covering just the material in that mini-unit. The explanations help you understand the material, but it is the exercises that enable you to gain active control over it. All of the exercises have complete answers in the back of the book. It is very important for you to work through these exercises. There is a world of difference between the passive knowledge gained by reading the explanations and the active command gained by writing out the exercises.

English Grammar Drills is organized into three parts: Part 1 covers noun phrases, the first of the two fundamental building blocks of English grammar. Noun phrases function as the subjects of sentences, the objects or complements of verbs, and the objects of prepositions.

Part 2 explores verb phrases, the second of the two fundamental building blocks of English grammar. Verb phrases contain three components: the verb, the complement, and the optional adverbs.

Part 3 examines sentences. The main topics are how to form and use active and passive sentences, how to form questions and negatives, and how to change direct quotations to indirect quotations.

Each chapter is self-contained. Unlike a conventional textbook, you do not need to start on page 1. You may begin with whatever topic you would like to gain more active control over.

The book concludes with a Final Review chapter, containing exercises that test your comprehension of all lessons in the book. New to this edition, 40 interactive quizzes are available in the McGraw-Hill Education Language Lab app for convenient review on-the-go.

Part 1

Noun Phrases

1

Nouns

Proper and common nouns

There are two basic types of nouns in English: **proper nouns** and **common nouns**. Proper nouns are the names of specific individuals, places, and things; common nouns are the names of classes of persons, places, and things.

For example, *Ruth Ginsburg*, *Texas*, and *Microsoft Corporation* are proper nouns. *Woman*, *state*, and *company* are common nouns. The most obvious distinction between proper nouns and common nouns is that proper nouns are capitalized. Compare the proper nouns and corresponding common nouns in the following list:

Proper noun	Common noun
Gregory House	doctor
Florence Nightingale	nurse
Mayo Clinic	hospital
Mississippi	river
Atlanta	city
Washington Post	newspaper
The Tempest	play

Exercise 1.1

The following pairs of nouns contain one uncapitalized proper noun and a related common noun. Put the two nouns in the correct columns as in the list above and capitalize the proper noun.

	Proper noun	Common noun
movie, star wars	*Star Wars*	*movie*
1. hamlet, play	Hamlet	play
2. neighborhood, soho	Soho	neighborhood
3. car, ford	Ford	car
4. ocean, atlantic	Atlantic	ocean
5. everest, mountain	Everest	mountain
6. actor, harrison ford	Harrison Ford	actor
7. dixie, song	Dixie	song
8. ship, titanic	Titanic	ship
9. hotel, the ritz	The Ritz	hotel
10. planet, mercury	Mercury	planet

From this point on, we will focus only on common nouns.

Count and noncount nouns

Common nouns are divided into two groups: count and noncount. **Count** means that we can make the noun plural and use number words with the noun. Using the noun *dog*, for example, we can make the noun plural:

> The *dogs* are in the park.

We can also use number words with *dogs*: *one dog, two dogs, three dogs*, and so on. Most nouns that refer to concrete objects are count nouns.

However, nouns that refer to abstractions and nouns that are used to label things that occur in undifferentiated masses (as opposed to individual persons, places, or things) are often non-count nouns. The term **noncount** means that we cannot count these nouns with number words or make them plural. For example, the abstract noun *luck* cannot be counted: we cannot say **X** *one luck*, **X** *two lucks*, **X** *three lucks*. Also we cannot use the noun as a plural. For example:

> ***X** They have had really bad *lucks* over the last few years.

---

*Throughout the book, **X** signifies an incorrect choice or answer.

Count nouns

Most count nouns in English form their plural by adding a sibilant sound written as *-s* or *-es*. Plurals formed this way are called **regular plurals**. Some nouns form their plural in other ways. They are called **irregular plurals**.

The spelling of a regular plural is determined by its pronunciation. If the plural is pronounced as a single sibilant sound pronounced either as /s/ or /z/, then the plural is spelled *-s*. However, if the plural is pronounced as a separate unstressed syllable /əz/ rhyming with "buzz," then the plural is spelled *-es*. Here are some examples of each type:

Spelling of plural

-s (**pronounced /s/**):	hats, cops, tricks, paths
-s (**pronounced /z/**):	rugs, cabs, rings, keys, shoes
-es (**pronounced /əz/**):	wishes, glasses, catches, buzzes

Sometimes the spelling of regular plurals is disguised by the spelling rule that governs the use of a final silent *e*. The basic rule is that we add a final silent *e* to show that the preceding vowel is long. For example, compare the following words:

Short vowel:	cap (*a* is a short vowel /æ/ as in *ask*)
Long vowel:	cape (*a* is a long vowel /ey/ as in *grape*)

We make both of these words plural by adding a single sibilant sound:

Singular	Plural
cap	caps /-ps/
cape	capes /-ps

The final silent *e* in the word *cape* makes the plural look like the *-es* is pronounced as a separate syllable /əz/, but it is not. We have merely added a single sibilant sound, /s/, to the end of the singular form. *Caps* and *capes* have the same plural /s/ sound because although the silent *e* makes the *a* long, it plays no role in the pronunciation of the plural ending. Just pretend that final silent *e* is not there when you pronounce the /s/.

The pronunciation of the plural in regular nouns is determined by the final sound of the singular form of the noun according to the following three rules:

1. If the noun ends in a voiceless consonant sound (except a sibilant), then the plural is formed with the voiceless sibilant /s/, which is spelled *-s*. Here are examples of all the consonant sounds that this rule applies to:

/p/ cap-caps; cop-cops; snap-snaps; shape-shapes; hope-hopes

/t/ hat-hats; boat-boats; beast-beasts; fate-fates; rebate-rebates

/k/ back-backs; leak-leaks; trick-tricks; bike-bikes; lake-lakes

/f/ cliff-cliffs; cough-coughs; laugh-laughs; cuff-cuffs; sniff-sniffs

/θ/ path-paths; lath-laths; monolith-monoliths, bath-baths

2. If the noun ends in a voiced consonant sound (except a sibilant) or any vowel (all vowels in English are voiced), then the plural is formed with the voiced sibilant /z/, which is also spelled -*s*. Here are examples of all the consonant sounds that this rule applies to:

/b/ lab-labs; web-webs; blob-blobs; globe-globes; tube-tubes

/d/ bed-beds; fluid-fluids; flood-floods; code-codes; shade-shades

/g/ bug-bugs; rag-rags; flag-flags, pig-pigs; hog-hogs

/v/ wave-waves; hive-hives; love-loves; live-lives; cove-coves

/l/ girl-girls; pill-pills; wheel-wheels; role-roles; rule-rules

/m/ ham-hams; farm-farms; room-rooms; flame-flames; home-homes

/n/ hen-hens; teen-teens; moon-moons; loan-loans; tune-tunes; throne-thrones

/ŋ/ ring-rings; thing-things; throng-throngs; rung-rungs; song-songs

Since all vowels are voiced in English, this rule also governs the plural of all words ending in a vowel sound. For example:

sea-seas; zoo-zoos; cow-cows; bee-bees; show-shows; tree-trees

Words ending in the letter *y* are little more complicated. When the singular form of a word ends in a consonant + the letter *y* (that is, when the letter *y* represents a vowel sound), we form the regular plural by changing the *y* to *i* and adding -*es*. (There is a schoolroom saying that goes like this: "Change the *y* to *i* and add -*es*.")

The plural -*s* is pronounced /z/ in the expected way. The change of y to ie does not affect pronunciation—it is a graphic change only. Here are some examples (all with a /z/ pronunciation):

Singular	**Plural**
baby	babies
family	families
lady	ladies
sky	skies
story	stories

When the letter *y* is combined with a vowel, a different spelling rule applies. To see the difference, compare the spellings of the plurals of the words *fly* and *toy*:

Singular	Plural
fly	flies
toy	toys

In the word *fly*, the *y* by itself represents a vowel sound. That is why the spelling rule that changes the *y* to *i* states that the *y* must be preceded by a consonant—this is just a way of ensuring that we are talking about *y* used by itself to represent a vowel sound.

In the word *toy*, the vowel sound is represented by a combination of the two letters *o* + *y*, which is sometimes called a **blend**. Think of the *oy* spelling as a fixed unit that cannot be changed. To form its plural we merely add an *s* (pronounced /z/) as we would with any other vowel spelling. Combinations of other vowels with *y* follow the same rule. Here are some more examples of *oy*, *ey*, and *ay* plural spellings:

Singular	Plural
boy	boys
key	keys
subway	subways
tray	trays

Exercise 1.2

All of the nouns in the following list form their plural in the regular way with a single sibilant sound spelled -*s*. Depending on the nature of the final sound in the singular form of the noun, the -*s* can be pronounced either /s/ or /z/. Write the entire plural form of the noun in the /s/ or /z/ column that shows the pronunciation of the plural -*s*. (Hint: Say the words out loud. If you whisper or say them to yourself, voiced sounds will be automatically de-voiced so they will sound the same as voiceless sounds.)

Singular form	/s/	/z/
flame		*flames*
1. three	_____	_____
2. trick	_____	_____
3. stool	_____	_____
4. history	_____	_____
5. wall	_____	_____
6. rake	_____	_____
7. play	_____	_____

8.   stove   _____   _____

9.   cough   _____   _____

10. moth   _____   _____

11. day   _____   _____

12. note   _____   _____

13. delay   _____   _____

14. hike   _____   _____

15. tire   _____   _____

16. rain   _____   _____

17. plate   _____   _____

18. grove   _____   _____

19. show   _____   _____

20. pipe   _____   _____

3.   If the noun ends in a sibilant sound, either voiceless or voiced, then the plural is pronounced as a separate unstressed syllable /əz/ rhyming with "buzz," spelled -es. (Of course, if
the singular already ends in a silent e, we would add just an -s as in *horse-horses*, or else we would
have crazy spellings like **X** *horse-es*.) Here are examples of the most common consonant sounds
that this rule applies to:

   /s/ (often spelled -ce) glass-glasses; bus-buses; face-faces; prince-princes; rinse-rinses;
      fox-foxes

   /š/ (often spelled -sh) wish-wishes; rash-rashes; McIntosh-McIntoshes; bush-bushes

   /č/ (spelled -ch or -tch) watch-watches; switch-switches; bunch-bunches

   /ǰ/ (spelled -ge or -dge) rage-rages; page-pages; dodge-dodges

   /z/ buzz-buzzes; phase-phases; blaze-blazes; nose-noses; cruise-cruises

Exercise 1.3

All of the nouns in the following list form their plural in the regular way with a single sibilant
sound spelled -s (pronounced /s/ or /z/) or with a separate unstressed syllable spelled -es (pronounced /əz/). Write the entire plural form of the noun in the /s/, /z/, or /əz/ column depending

on the pronunciation of the plural *-s* or *-es*. (Hint: Say the words out loud. If you whisper or say them to yourself, voiced sounds will be automatically devoiced so they will sound the same as voiceless sounds.)

Singular form	/s/	/z/	/əz/
beach	_____	_____	*beaches*
1. race	_____	_____	_____
2. bay	_____	_____	_____
3. box	_____	_____	_____
4. clock	_____	_____	_____
5. rose	_____	_____	_____
6. mist	_____	_____	_____
7. dish	_____	_____	_____
8. try	_____	_____	_____
9. cottage	_____	_____	_____
10. colleague	_____	_____	_____
11. clause	_____	_____	_____
12. clash	_____	_____	_____
13. hedge	_____	_____	_____
14. phone	_____	_____	_____
15. freeze	_____	_____	_____
16. share	_____	_____	_____
17. duty	_____	_____	_____
18. patch	_____	_____	_____
19. allowance	_____	_____	_____
20. sheet	_____	_____	_____

For a variety of historical reasons, English has some plurals that are formed in an irregular way.

Seven words form their plural by a vowel change alone:

Singular	Plural
foot	feet*
goose	geese
louse	lice
man	men
mouse	mice
tooth	teeth
woman	women**

Notes: *In addition to the usual plural form *feet*, the noun *foot* has a second plural form *foot* when we use the word to refer to length or measurement. For example:

I bought a six *foot* ladder.
He is six *foot* three inches tall.

**Despite the spelling of *women*, it is the pronunciation of the first syllable rather than the second that changes: *woman* is pronounced /wo mən/; *women* is pronounced /wɪ mən/; the second syllables, -*man* and -*men*, are pronounced exactly alike with an unstressed vowel /mən/.

Two words retain an old plural ending, -*en*:

Singular	Plural
ox	oxen
child	children

The long vowel in the singular *child* also changes to a short vowel in the first syllable of the plural *children*.

Some words ending in *f* form their plurals by changing the *f* to *v* and adding -*es*. Here are the most common words that follow this pattern:

Singular	Plural
half	halves
knife	knives
leaf	leaves
life	lives
loaf	loaves
self	selves

thief	thieves
wolf	wolves

Some words have a plural form that is identical to their singular form. Most of these words refer to animals or fish. For example:

Singular	Plural
a cod	two cod
a deer	two deer
a fish	two fish
a sheep	two sheep
a shrimp	two shrimp
a trout	two trout

Since the singular and plural forms of these nouns are identical, the actual number of the noun can only be determined by subject-verb agreement or by the use of an indefinite article. For example:

Singular:	The *deer* was standing in the middle of the road.
Plural:	The *deer* were moving across the field.
Singular:	I saw a *deer* in the backyard.
Plural:	I saw some *deer* in the backyard.

If one of these words is used as an object with a definite article, then the number is ambiguous. For example:

Look at the *deer*! (one deer or many deer?)

Exercise 1.4

The following sentences contain one or more incorrect irregular plurals. Draw a line through each incorrect plural and write the correct form above it.

loaves   knives
I sliced the ~~loafs~~ and put the ~~knifes~~ back in the drawer.

1. My niece has a farm where she raises disease-resistant varieties of ~~sheeps.~~ *sheep*

2. Like all farmers, she has a constant problem with ~~mouses~~ and rats. *mice*

3. She and her husband run the farm by ~~themselfes,~~ so it is a lot of work for them. *themselves*

4. There are coyotes and wolfs [wolves] in the area, but their dogs help keep them away.

5. The coyotes in particular are like thiefs [thieves], always waiting and watching.

6. If a coyote gets just a few feets [feet] inside the fence, the horses will drive it away.

7. Once they lost some sheeps [sheep] when some childs [children] left a gate open.

8. Their valley is full of deers [deer], which also support a large population of coyotes.

9. The river in the valley is full of salmons [salmon] in the fall.

10. Farming is terribly hard work, but we all choose the lifes [lives] we want to live. ✓

Noncount nouns

The types of noncount nouns that you are most likely to encounter fall into the semantic categories listed below:

Abstractions:	beauty, charity, faith, hope, knowledge, justice, luck, reliability
Food:	butter, cheese, chicken, pepper, rice, salt
Liquids and gases:	beer, blood, coffee, gasoline, water, air, oxygen
Materials:	cement, glass, gold, paper, plastic, silk, wood, wool [Wolle]
Natural phenomena:	electricity, gravity, matter, space [Seide]
Weather words:	fog, pollution, rain, snow, wind

With certain exceptions that are discussed below, these noncount nouns are ungrammatical if they are used in the plural. For example:

X Please get some more *butters*.
X We need to stop and get *gasolines*.
X The *cements* on the garage floors are cracking.
X The *electricities* have been turned off in all the apartments.
X Everyone has noticed the worsening *pollutions* around major cities.

Many noncount nouns can be used as count nouns with a predictable shift in meaning to something like "different kinds of." Here are some examples:

gasoline (noncount):	The price of *gasoline* is outrageous. (liquid)
gasoline (count):	The station sells three *gasolines*. (different kinds or grades of gasoline)

cheese (**noncount**):	I love *cheese*. (food)
cheese (**count**):	The store sells a variety of *cheeses*. (different kinds of cheese)

Some words can serve as either a noncount noun or a count noun with a slightly different meaning. For example, the noncount noun *chicken* refers to chicken as a food. As such, we cannot use it with number words or in the plural. However, if we use the word *chicken* to refer to the living animal, then it is a count noun. For example:

chicken (**noncount**):	*Chicken* is a heart-healthy meat. (food)
chicken (**count**):	There were a dozen *chickens* in the yard. (living animals)

Exercise 1.5

All of the underlined nouns in the following sentences are in the plural. Some plurals are correctly used with count nouns. However, many plurals are incorrectly used with noncount nouns. Draw a line through each incorrectly used noncount noun and write the corrected form above it. If the plural is used correctly with a count noun, write OK above the noun.

Please be careful of the ~~woods~~ [wood] on the desks. [OK]

1. The roads [ok] were closed because of the dense ~~fogs~~. [fog]

2. We had to go shopping because we were out of ~~milks~~ again. [milk]

3. The team's ~~disappointments~~ [loss WRONG: ok] at their ~~losses~~ was obvious.

4. During the operation, the patient needed six pints of ~~bloods~~. [ok] [blood]

5. The recent storms [ok] have caused us to lose ~~powers~~ [power] for days on end.

6. Many household products [ok] are recycled, especially ~~papers~~ [paper] and ~~glasses~~ [glass].

7. You need to allow a lot of time so that the ~~paints~~ [paint] will dry between coats [ok].

8. Most Americans eat pancakes [ok] and waffles [ok] with ~~syrups~~. [syrup]

9. Most people seem to have an inborn ~~fears~~ [fear] of snakes [ok].

10. Many breads [ok] in the Middle East are made without ~~yeasts~~. [yeast]

Possessive nouns

Virtually all languages have some way of indicating that a noun is the owner or possessor of another noun. For example, in the phrase *John's book*, John is said to own or possess the book.

Of course the possessive forms of nouns can signal many things besides ownership. Often we use the possessive form with inanimate nouns to indicate that something is a part or a component of something else. For example, consider the following sentence:

> The computer's screen is flickering.

Here the possessive form tells us that the screen is a component of the computer.

In this section, however, we are going to focus solely on how English forms the possessive.

Before Shakespeare's time the possessive form of nouns was spelled exactly the same as the plural form: with an -s. By Shakespeare's time, however, writers had began to distinguish the possessive -s from the plural -s by the use of an apostrophe with the possessive: -'s. For example, they could distinguish the possessive form of the noun *friend* from the plural form:

Possessive:	friend's
Plural:	friends

The use of the possessive apostrophe after the -s to indicate that a noun is both plural and possessive did not become standard until the beginning of the nineteenth century. So today we have a three-way distinction between the three -s forms: the plural -s, the singular possessive -'s, and the plural possessive -s'. For example:

Plural:	friends
Singular possessive:	friend's
Plural possessive:	friends'

While it is correct to call -s' the "plural possessive," it is a little confusing to think of the -'s as just the "singular possessive." The problem with this definition arises with the possessive forms of irregular nouns that become plural by changing their vowels rather than by adding a plural -s. For example:

SINGULAR		PLURAL	
Noun	**Possessive**	**Plural**	**Possessive**
man	man's	men	men's
woman	woman's	women	women's
child	child's	children	children's

As you can see, -'s is used with these plural possessive nouns, not -s'. This is not really an exception to the general rule. At first glance, we might think we should use -s' with these irregular nouns in the same way we use -s' with regular nouns. This is not correct because it would mean that the -*s'* with these nouns is what makes them plural. What actually makes them plural is the change in their vowels or ending. We must use *'s* because we are only making these nouns (which already happen to be plural nouns) into possessive nouns.

A much better way to think of plural and possessive -*s* is given below. There are three types of -*s* endings:

Plural only	**Possessive only**	**Plural possessive**
-s	-'s	-s'

The -*'s* tells us is that whatever noun the -*'s* is attached to is now possessive. If -*'s* is attached to a singular noun (as is usually the case), then that noun has become a singular possessive noun. If -*'s* is attached to an irregular plural noun, then that noun has becomes a plural possessive noun.

This analysis will help you to always use the right form for both regular and irregular nouns.

One of the nice things about writing the different forms of the possessive -*'s* is that the spelling is completely regular. For example, here is how we spell the possessive forms of irregular nouns that change *f* to *v* in the plural:

Singular:	wolf
Possessive:	wolf's (note that the *f* does not change to *v*)
Plural:	wolves
Plural possessive:	wolves'

Here is how we spell the possessives of nouns ending in consonant + *y*:

Singular:	spy
Possessive:	spy's
Plural:	spies
Plural possessive:	spies'

Notice that the plural *spies* is spelled differently than the possessive singular *spy's*. In the singular possessive, the *y* does not change to *i* and we do not add -*es*. We just add the normal -*'s*.

Here is how we spell the possessive nouns ending in vowel + *y*:

Singular:	boy
Possessive:	boy's
Plural:	boys
Plural possessive:	boys'

Remember, the *y* is part of the spelling of the vowel and therefore nothing happens to it.

Exercise 1.6

Fill in the following chart with all of the forms for each noun.

Singular	Singular possessive	Plural only	Plural possessive
wife	*wife's*	*wives*	*wives'*
1. dog	dog's ✓	dogs ✓	dogs' ✓
2. horse	horse's ✓	horses ✓	horses' ✓
3. tree	tree's ✓	trees ✓	trees' ✓
4. lady	lady's ✓	ladies ✓	ladies' ✓
5. fox	fox's ✓	foxes ✓	foxes' ✓
6. tooth	tooth's ✓	teeth ✓	teeth's ✓
7. play	play's ✓	plays ✓	play's" ✓
8. worker	worker's ✓	worker(s) X	worker's X workers'
9. shelf	shelf's ✓	shelves ✓	shelves' ✓
10. man	man's ✓	men ✓	men's ✓
11. studio	studio's ✓	studios ✓	studios' ✓
12. place	place's ✓	places ✓	places' ✓
13. fly	fly's ✓	flies ✓	flies' ✓
14. child	child's ✓	children ✓	children's ✓
15. woman	woman's ✓	women ✓	women's ✓

The pronunciation of the possessive -*'s* (whether singular or plural) or -*s'* is governed by the same rules that govern the pronunciation of the plural -*s*:

/s/ if the noun ends in a voiceless consonant sound (except a sibilant)
/z/ if the noun ends in a vowel or voiced consonant sound (except a sibilant)
/əz/ if the noun ends in a sibilant sound

Here are some examples:

/s/:   cat–cat's, cats'; Kate–Kate's, Kates'; Smith–Smith's, Smiths'
/z/:   company–company's, companies'; officer–officer's, officers'
/əz/:   church–church's, churches'; horse–horse's, horses'

Exercise 1.7

Write the plural possessive form of each noun in the /s/, /z/, or /əz/ column depending on the pronunciation of the plural -s. The first question is done as an example.

Singular form	/s/	/z/	/əz/
beach			*beaches'*
1. face			faces' ✓
2. bridge			bridges' ✓
3. fox			foxes' ✓
4. chief	chief's' ✓		
5. boy		boys' ✓	
6. navy		←	navies' ✗
7. daughter	daughters' ✗ →		
8. carriage			carriages' ✓
9. play	plays' →		
10. college			colleges' ✓

2

Adjectives

The term **adjective** can be used broadly for any word that modifies a noun. In this book, however, we will divide all noun modifiers into three smaller groups and address each group in a separate chapter. In this chapter we will cover what we will call "true" adjectives. In Chapter 3 we will cover articles, and in Chapter 4 we will cover all post-noun modifiers, modifiers that follow the nouns they modify.

"True" adjectives

True adjectives have three distinctive features:

1. They immediately precede the nouns that they modify.

2. They have comparative and superlative forms.

3. They can be used as predicate adjectives.

To see the difference between a true adjective and another common type of noun modifier, let us compare the true adjective *slow* and the article *the*. Both *slow* and *the* are adjectives in the broad sense because they both modify nouns. For example, they modify the noun *cars* in the following sentences:

> *Slow* <u>cars</u> should stay in the right lane.
> *The* <u>cars</u> in the left lane passed me.

However, as a true adjective, *slow* has three characteristics that *the* does not have:

1. It always immediately precedes the noun being modified. We see in the preceding example sentences that both *slow* and *the* can be used immediately in front of the noun they modify. But what happens if we use both *slow* and *the* to modify the same noun? We can say this:

> *The slow* <u>cars</u> moved into the right lane.

But we cannot say this:

> **X** *Slow the* <u>cars</u> moved into the right lane.

There is a strict left-to-right rule that says that articles (and other types of noun modifiers as well) must precede true adjectives when they both modify the same noun. In other words, no other noun modifier can come between a true noun and the noun it modifies.

2. It has comparative and superlative forms. We can use *slow* in the comparative and superlative forms, but there are no comparative and superlative forms for the article *the*:

Base form	Comparative form	Superlative form
slow	slower	slowest
the	**X** ther	**X** thest

3. It can be used as a predicate adjective. The term **predicate adjective** refers to adjectives that function as predicates of linking verbs. (These terms are explained in detail in Chapter 10.) For now, let's just look at some examples of predicate adjectives:

> The Tower of London is *ancient*.

> The children are *quiet*.

> Our dinner is *ready*.

The verb *be* is by far the most common linking verb. The predicate adjective in linking verb sentences is used to give information about the subject. In the three example sentences, *ancient* gives information about the Tower of London, *quiet* gives information about the children, and *ready* gives information about our dinner.
We can use *slow* as a predicate adjective, but we cannot use *the*:

> The clock in the hall is *slow*.

> **X** The clock in the hall is *the*.

Exercise 2.1

Here are three exercises in one. Following are pairs of noun modifiers; one member of the pair is a true adjective, and one is not. Fill in the blanks to see (1) which adjective always immediately precedes the noun, (2) which adjective has a comparative and superlative form, and (3) which adjective can be used as a predicate adjective. The noun modifier that fulfills these three criteria is the true adjective.

some/strong

	Comparative	Superlative
some:	**X** *somer*	**X** *somest*
strong:	*stronger*	*strongest*

Order of modifiers: *Some strong* coffee keeps me awake at night.
X *Strong some* coffee keeps me awake at night.

Predicate adjective: **X** The coffee is *some*.
The coffee *is strong*.

True adjective: *strong*

1. true/two

	Comparative	Superlative
true:	_____	_____
two:	_____	_____

Order of modifiers: _____ stories are in the book.
_____ stories are in the book.

Predicate adjective: The stories are _____ .
The stories are _____ .

True adjective: _____

2. his/sweet

	Comparative	Superlative
his:	_____	_____
sweet:	_____	_____

Order of modifiers: _____ cupcakes were the hit of the party.
_____ cupcakes were the hit of the party.

Predicate adjective: The cupcakes were _____ .
The cupcakes were _____ .

True adjective: _____ .

3. fast/all

	Comparative	Superlative
fast:	_____	_____
all:	_____	_____

Order of modifiers: _____ boats have two engines.

_____ boats have two engines.

Predicate adjective: The boats were _____ .

The boats were _____ .

True adjective: _____ .

4. these/hungry

	Comparative	Superlative
these:	_____	_____
hungry:	_____	_____

Order of modifiers: _____ cats need to be fed.

_____ cats need to be fed.

Predicate adjective: The cats were _____ .

The cats were _____ .

True adjective: _____ .

5. bright/a

	Comparative	Superlative
bright:	_____	_____
a:	_____	_____

Order of modifiers: _____ moon was rising in the eastern sky.

_____ moon was rising in the eastern sky.

Predicate adjective: The moon was _____ .

The moon was _____ .

True adjective: _____ .

Comparative and superlative forms of adjectives

English is unusual in that it has not one but two ways of forming the comparative and superlative forms of adjectives. One way, as we have seen, is by adding *-er* and *-est* onto the **base form** of the adjective. The other way does not change the form of the adjective itself (the base form), but instead uses *more* + adjective for the comparative form and *most* + adjective for the superlative form. For example:

Base	Comparative	Superlative
reluctant	*more* reluctant	*most* reluctant
foolish	*more* foolish	*most* foolish
vicious	*more* vicious	*most* vicious

The reason why English has two different sets of comparative and superlative forms is historical. Adjectives of native English origin usually form their comparative and superlative forms with *-er* and *-est* endings. Adjectives borrowed from French usually form their comparative and superlative forms with *more* and *most*. Adjectives of English origin tend to be one and two syllable words. Adjectives of French origin tend to be polysyllabic, that is two, three, and even four syllables.

Over time, English speakers tended to forget about historical origin and instead associated the *-er* and *-est* endings with short adjectives and *more* and *most* with long adjectives. As a result, nearly all adjectives of one syllable use *-er* and *-est* and adjectives of three or more syllables use *more* and *most*.

Two-syllable adjectives pose a problem because they can form their comparative and superlative forms either way. A few adjectives can even use both ways. For example, the two-syllable *polite* can be used in either pattern:

> Susan is *politer* than Alice. Susan is the *politest* person in her class.
> Susan is *more polite* than Alice. Susan is the *most polite* person I know.

Here are two generalizations that can help in deciding which type of comparative and superlative to use:

1. Two-syllable adjectives that end in an unstressed vowel sound tend to use the *-er/-est* pattern. Two-syllable adjectives ending in *-le* or *-y* are especially common. For example:

-LE

Base	Comparative	Superlative
able	abler	ablest
feeble	feebler	feeblest
gentle	gentler	gentlest
noble	nobler	noblest
simple	simpler	simplest

-Y

Base	Comparative	Superlative
tacky	tackier	tackiest
early	earlier	earliest
happy	happier	happiest
noisy	noisier	noisiest
pretty	prettier	prettiest

Notice that when the base form ends in -*y*, the comparative and superlative forms change the -*y* to -*i*. This change is a general spelling rule that we also saw in forming the plural of nouns that end in -*y*—for example, *lady-ladies, history-histories, story-stories.*

2. Adjectives that are derived from verbs ending in -*ing* or -*ed* form their comparative and superlative with *more* and *most*. For example:

-ING

Base	Comparative	Superlative
amusing	more amusing	most amusing
charming	more charming	most charming
discouraging	more discouraging	most discouraging
tempting	more tempting	most tempting
trusting	more trusting	most trusting

-ED

Base	Comparative	Superlative
exploited	more exploited	most exploited
recorded	more recorded	most recorded
respected	more respected	most respected
strained	more strained	most strained
startled	more startled	most startled

A few irregular comparatives and superlatives survive from older forms of English:

Adjective	Comparative	Superlative
bad	worse	worst
good	better	best

The adjective *far* is peculiar in that it has two sets of comparative and superlative forms with slightly different meanings:

Adjective	Comparative	Superlative
far	farther	farthest
far	further	furthest

We use *farther* and *farthest* for distance in space. For example:

Please take the *farthest* seat.

We use *further* and *furthest* for all other kinds of sequences or progressions. For example:

Are there any *further* questions?

Exercise 2.2

Give the comparative and superlative forms of the following adjectives.

Base	Comparative	Superlative
worried	*more worried*	*most worried*
1. sad	_____	_____
2. costly	_____	_____
3. sound	_____	_____
4. valuable	_____	_____
5. likely	_____	_____
6. sunny	_____	_____
7. patient	_____	_____
8. improved	_____	_____
9. normal	_____	_____
10. blue	_____	_____
11. bad	_____	_____
12. tiring	_____	_____

13. physical   _____   _____

14. strange   _____   _____

15. probable   _____   _____

16. recent   _____   _____

17. available   _____   _____

18. developed   _____   _____

19. shady   _____   _____

20. fulfilling   _____   _____

Sequence of multiple true adjectives

We often use two or three true adjectives to modify a single noun. For example, consider the following phrase:

> huge old white house

Here the adjectives *huge*, *old*, and *white* all modify the noun *house*.

When multiple true adjectives modify the same noun, there is a fixed left-to-right order to the adjectives based on their meaning. For example, we cannot change the order of the adjectives in the above example without being ungrammatical:

> **X** huge white old house
> **X** white huge old house
> **X** white old huge house
> **X** old huge white house
> **X** old white huge house

Generalizing these examples to whole categories of adjectives, we can make the following rule about order of true adjectives based on meaning:

Size	Age	Color	Noun
large	old	dingy	apartment building
small	new	paisley	shirt
tiny	ancient	grey	car

Exercise 2.3

Rearrange the adjectives in the following phrases to put them into the correct sequence based on their meaning.

| | shiny | brand-new | huge | refrigerator |
	huge	*brand-new*	*shiny*	*refrigerator*
1.	brown	capacious	worn	overcoat
2.	antique	gold	miniature	locket
3.	overripe	yellow	great	pear
4.	early	sizeable	black and white	photographs
5.	modern	black	long	desk
6.	large	grey	aged	cat
7.	young	petite	green	peas
8.	bulky	pink	old	sweater
9.	off-white	new	immense	mansion
10.	white	up-to-date	slim	drapes

3

Articles

Articles are by far the most common and the most complex type of pre-adjective noun modifier. They also account for the great majority of nonnative speaker errors in noun modification. There are two types of articles: the **definite article** *the* and the **indefinite articles** *a/an* and *some*.

Definite articles

The definite article *the* is normally unstressed. It is pronounced /ðə/ (rhymes with *duh*) before words beginning with a consonant sound. For example:

> the (/ðə/) team
> the (/ðə/) bridge
> the (/ðə/) song

The is pronounced /ðiy/ (rhymes with *see*) before words beginning with a vowel sound. For example:

> the (/ðiy/) accident
> the (/ðiy/) example
> the (/ðiy/) orange

Note: If *the* before a consonant sound is given extra emphasis, it also is pronounced /ðiy/ instead of the expected /ðə /. For example, in the following sentence:

> The New York Yankees are not just any baseball team, they are *the* (/ðiy/) baseball team.

In all of our discussion about the pronunciation of *the*, we assume (unless stated otherwise) that we are talking about the normal, unstressed pronunciation of *the*.

Exercise 3.1

Place an "X" in the appropriate column to show the correct pronunciation of unstressed *the* with the following nouns.

Noun	/ðə/	/ðiy/
the answer		X
1. the test	_____	_____
2. the road	_____	_____
3. the action	_____	_____
4. the building	_____	_____
5. the organization	_____	_____
6. the umbrella	_____	_____
7. the desk	_____	_____
8. the name	_____	_____
9. the insurance	_____	_____
10. the eraser	_____	_____

From now on, unless it is relevant to the discussion, we will not make a distinction between writing and speaking. For the sake of simplicity, we will use the term *speaker* to mean both speaker and writer; likewise the terms *listener* and *hearer* will mean both *listener* and *reader*.

The definite article is used with both singular and plural nouns. For example:

Singular noun	Plural noun
the cause	the causes
the design	the designs
the hill	the hills
the store	the stores

Because the definite article has only a single form, *the*, and *the* can be used with both singular and plural common nouns, it would seem that the definite article is simple to use. Nothing could be further from the truth. The definite article is used when the speaker expects the listener to know which specific noun the speaker means. For example, consider the following sentence:

I am looking for *the* map.

The use of the definite article with the noun *map* tells us that the listener is expected know which particular map the speaker is talking about.

Following are helpful guidelines that will help you in deciding whether to use the definite article.

The definite article should be used if both of the following statements about the noun being modified are true:

- The speaker has a specific person, place, thing, or idea in mind.

- The speaker can reasonably assume that the listener will know which specific person, place, thing, or idea the speaker means.

Let us call a noun that meets both the above criteria a **defined noun**. Nouns can be defined in four main ways:

1. By previous mention

2. By modifiers

3. By unique reference

4. By normal expectations

We will discuss each of these ways of defining a noun.

1. Nouns defined by previous mention

Nouns are most commonly defined by previous mention. Use the definite article if you have already introduced the noun in the current context of discussion. For example:

> He sent me *a* check for the items he purchased last week. I deposited *the* check yesterday.

In the first sentence, the noun *check* is mentioned for the first time. The use of the indefinite article *a* signals that the speaker is treating the noun *check* as new information that the listener is not expected to have any previous knowledge of. However, once the noun *check* has been introduced, the next use of the same noun is now a defined noun, which must be used with a definite article. That is, from the second mention onward, the speaker expects the listener to know which specific check is being referred to, and thus all future mentions of the noun *check* in this context must use *the*. (Notice that we need to constantly qualify the discussion with "in this context." If the speaker were to shift topics, then the noun *check* would no longer be a defined noun. Any mention of the noun *check* in this new context would require an indefinite article the first time it is used.)

Exercise 3.2

In the following paragraphs, many nouns are preceded by a blank space. If the noun has been mentioned previously, fill in the blank with the definite article. Otherwise, fill in the blank with the indefinite article *a*.

On my first trip to Manhattan, I bought __*a*__ city map and tried to get _____ sense of its geography. I quickly discovered what every person there knows: to find out where you are, you need to know two things: whether you are facing "uptown" (north) or "downtown" (south), and whether you are facing east or west.

To find out, you have to go to _____ street sign. _____ street sign will tell you both street and avenue numbers. _____ numbers by themselves tell you nothing. They just define one point on _____ grid. They tell you where you are on _____ grid, but you still do not know which way you are facing on _____ grid. To know that, you have to go to _____ next street sign and compare _____ street and avenue numbers there. If _____ new street number has gotten larger, you are going north. If _____ new street number has gotten smaller, you are going south. If _____ new avenue number has gotten larger, you are going west. If _____ the avenue number has gotten smaller, you are going east. If _____ avenue has _____ name rather than _____ number, then you have to take out _____ map again and compare _____ numbers and/or names of _____ two avenues. Everybody has to memorize _____ names and numbers of _____ avenues.

2. Nouns defined by modifiers

Even if a noun has not been previously mentioned, the noun can be uniquely defined by its modifiers. To see how modifiers can define a noun, compare the following two sentences:

Not defined:	Take *a* bus to 92nd Street.
Defined:	Take *the* first bus that comes to 92nd Street.

In the first example, the noun *bus* is undefined because it is the first time it has been mentioned and there is no further identification; therefore, we have to use the indefinite article *a*. In the second example, the noun *bus* is uniquely defined by its modifiers. The pre-noun modifier *first* and the post-noun modifier *that comes* define for the hearer which bus the speaker is talking about. In other words, even though this is the first time the noun *bus* has been mentioned, the speaker has restricted the meaning of the noun *bus* to just one specific bus—namely, the one that comes first. *Bus* is now a defined noun that must be used with the definite article *the*. Here is another example:

Not defined:	Do you have *a* pencil?
Defined:	Do you have *the* pencil that Bob gave you?

In the first example, we use the indefinite article *a* because this is the first mention of the noun *pencil* and it is otherwise undefined. In the second example, however, we use the definite article *the* because the post-noun modifier *that Bob gave you* uniquely defines the noun *pencil*, even though the pencil has not been previously mentioned. The use of *the* signals two things: (1) that the speaker has a specific pencil in mind, and (2) the speaker can reasonably assume that the hearer knows about Bob's giving the hearer a pencil. For the use of *the* to be valid, both of these assumptions must be true.

The most difficult part of defining nouns by modifiers is that for a noun to be defined, we must be sure that the hearer knows which specific noun the speaker is talking about. It is not enough that the speaker has in mind a specific noun; the speaker has to be sure that hearer also knows what it is.

The following sentence illustrates how difficult this can be:

Not defined:	I bought her *a* present that will really surprise her.
Defined:	I bought her *the* present that we talked about.

In both sentences the noun *present* is modified by an adjective clause beginning with *that*. In the first example, the modifying clause does not define for the hearer which actual present the speaker bought. The hearer has been told that it will surprise the receiver, but that fact does not define what the present is for the hearer. Since the hearer does not know which present the speaker is talking about, the speaker must use the indefinite article *a*. In the second sentence, however, the speaker has defined the present in such a way that the hearer knows which present is being talked about. Now the speaker must use the definite article *the*.

Exercise 3.3

In each blank space, use an indefinite article (*a* or *some*) if the noun is not defined or the definite article *the* if the noun is defined by modifiers.

There is __*a*__ cat on top of your car.

1. Did you hear _____ cat that was making all that noise last night?

2. We need to buy _____ baseballs for the game tonight.

3. _____ baseballs you got for the game are in Rob's car.

4. _____ question about compound interest rates seemed really difficult, didn't it?

5. They wanted to establish _____ new network for the office.

6. We need to pick _____ topic that everyone will identify with.

7. _____ engineer employed by a subcontractor filed a complaint.

8. _____ suggestions we gave them were mostly accepted.

9. Did you see _____ magazine in the backseat of the car?

10. I made _____ resolution to cut back on coffee.

11. There was _____ big fight about the budget.

12. It was _____ occasion that all of us had hoped it would be.

13. I contacted _____ agency that I had seen advertised in a trade journal.

14. It was _____ expense that we had never even thought about.

15. Did you get _____ newspaper I asked you for?

16. We all felt that it was _____ injustice to treat the employees like that.

17. It made _____ real impact on all of us.

18. We consulted one of _____ experts you had previously identified.

19. Do you know _____ restaurant in Sacramento where we can all eat?

20. Do you remember _____ restaurant in Sacramento where we all ate?

3. Nouns defined by unique reference

A certain number of nouns are always used with the definite article because the things they represent are unique. There is, for example, only one horizon, so there can be no question which horizon is meant. Here are some examples of these one-of-a-kind nouns: _sun, atmosphere, ocean, moon, horizon, earth_ (the planet), _ground,_ and _dirt_. Note that all of these nouns are ordinarily singular. Here are some examples used in sentences:

> _The_ moon was just rising above _the_ horizon.
> I stuck a shovel into _the_ ground.
> Everyone is concerned about increasing pollution in _the_ atmosphere.

4. Nouns defined by normal expectations

Often we use a definite article with a previously unmentioned, unmodified noun because there is a normal expectation of what the noun represents in the context of what the sentence is talking about. It is easier to give some examples of this concept than it is to explain it in the abstract:

> My computer is only a month old, but already _the_ software needs updating.

This is the first time software has been mentioned. Why, then, would we use *the*? The answer is normal expectation. We expect that computers will come with software. So in the context of talking about my computer, the hearer knows I am talking about the software that came with my computer. Accordingly, since this makes *software* a defined noun, we would use the definite article *the* with it. Here is another example:

Tom searched through a number of books, opening each and scanning *the* indexes.

We expect that books come with indexes. Thus the hearer knows which indexes we are talking about—the indexes in all the books Tom searched through. *Indexes* is thus a defined noun, and accordingly we use *the* with it. Here is a third example:

We went to Sunset Beach and watched *the* waves.

We expect there to be waves at a beach, so the hearer knows which waves we are talking about—the waves at Sunset Beach. *Waves* is therefore a defined noun and used with *the*. Here is our final example:

I went into an office building and took *the* elevator to *the* top floor.

We expect there to be elevators and top floors in office buildings, so both nouns are defined—the elevator and the top floor in the building the speaker went into. Accordingly, both *elevator* and *top floor* are used with *the*.

Sometimes it is surprising what counts in English as normal expectations. Perhaps the oddest examples are the names of places and things that are expected in particular environments. For example, in a house all the rooms and the things that are usually found in those rooms are considered defined nouns:

We went to Ralph's house and replaced *the* chairs
the kitchen table
the living room rugs
the couch
the draperies
the pots and pans

In a person's office we would expect things like the following:

I need to replace *the* desk
the armchair
the computer
the wastebasket

the telephone

the answering machine

In a city we would expect a whole range of buildings and places. For example:

I have to go to *the* post office

the bank

the train station

the airport

the drugstore

the grocery store

Some of the places listed above are unique. For example, in any particular city there is usually only one airport and one train station. Since these are unique places, the use of the definite article makes sense. However, there are many banks, drugstores, and grocery stores in a city, so it seems odd that we would use *the* with these nouns when the listener has no way of knowing which particular bank, drugstore, or grocery store the speaker is talking about. Even though it doesn't really make any sense, it is absolutely correct to use *the* with these place names.

There is a similar odd use of *the* with the names of places of recreation. For example:

Let's go to *the* beach

the movies

the mountains

the park

Even though the listener has no way of knowing which movie or park the speaker has in mind (if, in fact, the speaker has any particular one in mind), it is still conventional to use the definite article with these nouns.

Exercise 3.4

In each blank space, use an indefinite article (*a* or *some*) if the noun is not defined or the definite article *the* if the noun is defined by normal expectations.

I had to replace __*the*__ windshield wipers on my car.

1. My parents always have _____ TV on too loud.

2. I need to buy _____ new suitcase.

3. We all went outside to look at _____ sunset.

4. Go down Elm Street and turn left at _____ corner.

5. _____ trees in _____ park are beginning to turn color.

6. We are planning _____ trip to visit _____ college friends.

7. _____ water pipes in old houses often need to be replaced.

8. _____ owl has made _____ nest behind our house.

9. There is _____ storm warning. Turn on _____ radio.

10. _____ climate does seem to be getting warmer.

11. What is _____ capital of North Dakota?

12. Could we get _____ table that is less noisy than this one?

13. Excuse me, but I need to answer _____ phone.

14. I need to return _____ books to _____ library.

15. Did you see _____ newspaper this morning?

16. The Smiths were in _____ accident last night.

17. They were driving in _____ right lane and _____ truck in _____ left lane hit them.

18. Fortunately, nobody was hurt, but they did have to call _____ police.

19. _____ heavy smell of decay was hanging in _____ air.

20. They are going to replace _____ windows on _____ south side of their house.

21. She found _____ mistakes in the most recent revision.

22. I have _____ question for you.

23. We are planning _____ picnic in _____ park.

24. Are you connected to _____ Internet?

25. We had to shade our eyes from _____ bright sunshine.

As we have seen, we use *the* with common nouns when the noun being modified is a **defined noun**. A defined noun meets two criteria:

1. The noun is known to the speaker.

2. The speaker can reasonably assume that the listener will also know which specific noun the speaker has in mind.

Nouns are defined in four ways:

1. The noun has been previously mentioned.

2. The noun is uniquely defined by its modifiers.

3. The noun has a unique reference.

4. The noun is defined by normal expectations.

Exercise 3.5

In the following paragraphs, fill in the blank spaces with the appropriate article. If the noun is defined in one or more of the four ways mentioned above, use the definite article *the*. Otherwise, fill in the blank with the indefinite article *a* (singular noun) or *some* (plural nouns).

During __*the*__ Christmas holidays, I flew to Los Angeles to visit with _____ friends. They picked me up at _____ airport in _____ old car one of them was leasing. Since _____ company my friend was working for required him to have _____ car, he got reimbursed for most of his driving expenses. It was _____ first car any of them had ever had. Not having _____ car in Los Angeles is not really _____ option since there is no public transportation system to speak of. As _____ result, _____ traffic is just awful.

They were renting _____ apartment in Santa Monica, _____ really nice town on _____ beach about twenty miles from _____ center of _____ city. _____ apartment building they lived in even had _____ swimming pool. We went in _____ pool every day. It was fine as long as _____ pool was in _____ sun. From _____ apartment we could walk to most of _____ stores we needed. The only thing that we had to take _____ car for was going to _____ grocery store. There was simply no place to buy groceries in _____ neighborhood.

I had hoped to go swimming in _____ ocean, but I quickly discovered that _____ water was too cold. My friends said that if I wanted to go swimming, I would have to get _____ wet suit. There is _____ current of icy-cold water that comes down _____ coast from Alaska. Even in _____ summer, _____ water is pretty cold.

Indefinite articles

English has two indefinite articles, *a/an*, which is used with singular nouns, and *some*, which is used with plural nouns and with noncount nouns.

The indefinite articles *a/an* and *some* are used in two situations:

1. When the speaker does not have a specific noun in mind

2. When the speaker does have a specific noun in mind, but knows that the listener does not know which noun it is

Here are some examples of the first situation:

> Do you have *a* minute?

In this example, the speaker does not have any exact minute in mind.

> When you travel a lot by air, you have to expect *some* delayed flights.

In this example, the speaker is talking hypothetically. The speaker has no specific delays in mind.

More often, however, the speaker has something or someone in mind, but knows that the listener does not share the speaker's knowledge. The use of the indefinite article indicates that the speaker does not expect the listener to know which particular thing the speaker is thinking of. Here are some examples:

> I would like you to come over this evening and meet *a* friend of mine.

The use of the indefinite article *a* signals the listener that the speaker knows that the friend of the speaker is a stranger to the listener. Compare the above sentence with the following:

> I would like you to come over and meet *the* friend I was telling you about.

The use of the definite article establishes that the listener already knows which friend the speaker is talking about.

Here is a second example, this time with *some* used with a plural count noun:

> I have *some* questions for you.

The use of *some* signals that the listener is not expected to know in advance what the questions are.

Here is a third example, this time with *some* used with a singular, noncount noun:

> I think that there will be *some* opposition to the new offer.

The use of *some* with the noncount noun *opposition* signals that the speaker anticipates opposition. The exact nature of that opposition, however, is not shared knowledge between the speaker and hearer.

The indefinite articles *a* has a second form, *an*, that is used before vowel sounds. For example, we say *a banana* but *an apple*. The rule governing the use of *an* pertains to vowel pronunciation, not vowel spelling. For example, the following words use *a* where the spelling would seem to require *an* because the pronunciation of the nouns actually begins with a /y/ consonant sound:

> *a* unicorn
> *a* uniform
> *a* unit
> *a* usage

Both *a* and *an* are normally unstressed. Unstressed *a* is pronounced /E/, rhyming with *duh*. Unstressed *an* is pronounced /En/, rhyming with *bun*. (When we talk about *a* and *an* in isolation, we stress them so that they have quite different pronunciations. Stressed *a* is pronounced /ey/, rhyming with *day*, and stressed *an* is pronounced /An/, rhyming with *can*. Don't confuse these stressed pronunciations with the normal unstressed pronunciations in sentences.)

The reason for the two forms *a* and *an* is historical. Both *a* and *an* come from the word *one*. Over the years, the pronunciation of *one* used as a noun modifier (as opposed to the use of *one* as a number) became contracted: the *n* in *one* was preserved before words beginning with vowels and lost before words beginning with a consonant sound. As a result, today we have the two forms of the indefinite article: *a* before consonant sounds and *an* before vowel sounds.

The origin of the indefinite article from the number *one* also deeply affects the way it is used in modern English. Since *a* and *an* both come from the word *one*, like the number *one*, *a/an* is inherently singular. Thus we cannot use *a/an* to modify plural nouns: **X** *a books*, **X** *an oranges*.

Since the indefinite article *a/an* is restricted to modifying singular count nouns, what do we use for plural nouns and noncount nouns? The answer, of course, is *some*. Here are some examples first with plural count nouns and then with noncount nouns, which are inherently singular:

Plural count nouns
I would like *some* apples, please.
There are *some* umbrellas in the stand over there.
I've made *some* sandwiches for you to take.
I need to buy *some* stamps.
I need to write up *some* notes after today's meeting.

Noncount nouns (always singular)
I'm afraid that there has been *some* confusion about your order.
Please bring me *some* water.
There is *some* question about his visa.
We will get *some* information to you about that as soon as we can.
Would you like *some* soup?

Exercise 3.6

Fill in the blanks with the indefinite articles *a, an,* or *some* as appropriate.

Would you turn __*a*__ light on?

1. We need to order _____ more supplies.

2. My mother is going to the hospital tomorrow for _____ operation.

3. Darn, I have _____ rock in my shoe.

4. There is still _____ coffee left if you want it.

5. I'll get _____ cup for you.

6. Somebody left _____ trash on our front lawn.

7. Please pick up _____ bananas on your way home.

8. It is _____ unexpected answer.

9. I spilled _____ milk on the counter.

10. It began as _____ day like any other day.

11. It was _____ unusual request.

12. Apparently her proposal came as _____ complete surprise to the board.

13. It was _____ offer he couldn't refuse.

14. We found the apartment through _____ ad in the newspaper.

15. I've got to get _____ envelopes before I can mail these letters.

Making generalizations without any articles

We expect common nouns to be modified by some kind of article or other pre-adjective modifier. There is one important exception: using plural nouns or noncount nouns without any article or other pre-adjective modifier to signal that we are making a generalization or general statement about the noun. For example, compare the difference in meaning between the two following sentences:

Birds start migrating north early in the spring.
Some birds have nested in our oak trees.

The absence of any pre-noun modifier with the plural noun *birds* in the first sentence signals that the speaker is making a general statement about all birds, not any particular group of birds. The presence of the indefinite article *some* in the second sentence signals that the speaker is talking only about one particular group of birds, namely the birds that have nested in the speaker's oak trees.

Here is a second pair of examples, this time using the noun *airplanes*:

> Airplanes have totally changed the way we travel.
> The airplanes that you see were all made by Boeing.

The absence of any article in the first sentence tells us that the noun is being used to make a generalization about the nature of airplanes. The use of the article in the second sentence tells us that we are talking about specific airplanes and not making a generalization about all airplanes.

Sometimes it is difficult to tell whether plural count nouns or noncount nouns are being used to make a generalization. There are two clues in the nature of the sentence that help identify when a sentence is making a generalization: the use of present tense forms and adverbs of frequency.

1. Generalities use present tense forms. Sentences that make generalizations are usually in a present tense form, either the simple present, the present progressive, or the present perfect. In the following examples, the noun being used to make a generalization is underlined and the present tense verb is in italics:

Present:	Airports *seem* impossibly crowded these days.
Present progressive:	Airports *are getting* more crowded every day.
Present perfect:	Airports *have become* way too crowded.

Here is an example with a noncount noun:

Present:	Flying *is* more difficult every day.
Present progressive:	Flying *is getting* more difficult every day.
Present perfect:	Flying *has become* more difficult every day.

2. Generalizations use adverbs of frequency. Sentences that make generalizations often contain adverbs of frequency such as *always, often, generally, frequently,* and *usually* or the negative adverb *never*. In the following sentences, the count noun being used to make a generalization is underlined and the adverb of frequency is in italics:

> Rain storms *always* come in from the south.

> Sweet apples *never* make very good pies.

Dogs are *usually* protective of their territory.

American television programs *often* use laugh tracks.

Here are some examples with noncount nouns:

Conflict *always* has the potential to get out of hand.

Wood is *usually* more expensive than plastic.

Miscommunication *frequently* results in misunderstanding.

Sunshine *generally* gets rid of moldy patches.

Exercise 3.7

Use the appropriate article in the blank spaces in the following sentences. If the sentence is making a generalization, put ∅ in the blank space to show that no article is used.

___∅___ olives are usually too salty for me.

1. _____ Western movies have horse chases rather than car chases.

2. All too often, _____ politicians just tell people what they want to hear.

3. We are waiting until we get back all _____ replies to our request.

4. We only order _____ supplies when we run out.

5. _____ trucks are never allowed in the left lane.

6. We are required to have 1,000 units of _____ blood on hand at all times.

7. _____ highways are free of ice, but I am worried about _____ bridges being slippery.

8. _____ bridges are inspected by _____ independent state agency.

9. In _____ park, _____ trees are beginning to turn green.

10. _____ trees play _____ major role in controlling _____ excess carbon dioxide.

11. We must get _____ permission slips before every school outing.

12. At this time of year, _____ snow can cause delays.

13. I can't stand wearing _____ shoes without _____ socks.

14. In _____ hotel's formal dining room, _____ jackets and _____ ties are required.

15. When I travel overseas, _____ sleep becomes _____ big problem for me.

Exercise 3.8

Fill in the blanks in the following paragraph with the appropriate article. Use ∅ if no article is used because a plural count noun or noncount noun is being used to make a generalization.

_____∅____ travel by _____ air has become everyone's favorite topic to complain about. We all have heard _____ stories about _____ passengers being stuck for hours on _____ runways and _____ stories about _____ endless lines at _____ ticket counters. These are all true. _____ problem is that none of us is willing to pay what it would cost to fix _____ problems. None of us wants to pay _____ penny more than we have to. When _____ airlines try to raise _____ prices to improve their services, we all go to _____ airlines that have not raised their prices. When _____ airports try to get approval to raise _____ taxes to pay for _____ airport improvements, we vote _____ bond issues down.

We have now covered the major uses of articles with common nouns. We can summarize the use of the indefinite articles in the following table:

INDEFINITE ARTICLES

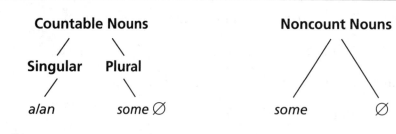

∅ = no article

Remember that the choice of not using an article to signal that a plural count noun or a noncount noun is being using to make a generalization is just as much a choice as using *a* or *the*.

Exercise 3.9

Use the appropriate article in the blank spaces in the following sentences. If the sentence makes a generalization, put ∅ in the blank space to show that no article is used.

Could you answer __*the*__ phone?

1. There's _____ program on TV tonight that I would like to watch.

2. Did we ever get _____ answer from the Smiths?

3. _____ train from Chicago is just pulling into _____ station.

4. Can you get _____ bread and milk when you go shopping?

5. _____ reception on my cell phone is not very good.

6. _____ weather forecast is for _____ big storm over _____ weekend.

7. _____ storm that hit us caused _____ huge power failure all along _____ East Coast.

8. I always enjoy reading _____ comics in _____ Sunday paper.

9. In Italy, _____ wine is taxed as _____ food.

10. Robert is _____ last person to know what's going on.

11. We are planning to go on _____ hike this weekend.

12. She raised _____ really good issues in class today.

13. I have _____ problem that I need to discuss with you.

14. _____ restrooms at _____ train station are always dirty.

15. Whenever we go to _____ movies, we always get _____ big bag of popcorn.

16. Everyone has to have _____ insurance.

17. I've just had _____ idea.

18. There was _____ fire at _____ old Brown place last night.

19. Can I get _____ information from you?

20. Bad news travels around _____ world before good news gets its shoes on.

21. Susan lost _____ baby tooth today.

22. I have _____ information that _____ group will be interested in.

23. _____ newspapers all across _____ country are losing _____ readers.

24. I never get _____ clear answer from _____ personnel department.

25. We got _____ real shock when _____ contractor gave us _____ final bill.

Post-Noun Modifiers

In this chapter we will examine two of the most important types of noun modifiers that follow the nouns that they modify: **adjectival prepositional phrases** and **adjective clauses** (also known as **relative clauses**). Here is an example of each of the types. The noun being modified is under-lined, and the modifier is in italics:

Adjective prepositional phrase:	The <u>house</u> *on the corner* belongs to the Smiths.
Adjective clause (relative clause):	The <u>house</u> *that is on the corner* belongs to the Smiths.

Before we can talk about these modifiers, we need to introduce a new term: noun phrase. A **noun phrase** is a noun together with all of its modifiers, both pre-noun and post-noun. For example, look at the following sentence:

The tall young man in the yellow jacket is my cousin.

The noun *man* is modified by three pre-noun adjectives, *the tall young*, and the post-noun adjectival prepositional phrase *in the yellow jacket*. Together they all make up the noun phrase *the tall young man in the yellow jacket*. We can also represent the noun phrase this way:

```
pre-noun
modifiers      noun    post-noun modifiers
The tall young man in the yellow jacket
```

There is one remarkable fact about noun phrases. They can always be identified by third-person pronoun replacement. In other words, a noun phrase is a group of words that can be replaced by a third-person pronoun. For example, we can replace our noun phrase with the third-person pronoun *he*:

The tall young man in the yellow jacket is my cousin.

He is my cousin.

There are four third-person pronouns. Here is the complete list in both subject and object form:

Subject form	Object form
he	him
she	her
it	it
they	them

All noun phrases, no matter what role they play in a sentence and no matter what their internal structure is, can be replaced by one of the eight third-person pronouns listed above. Here is an example using each third-person pronoun:

He:	A small boy who looked about five years old came into the room.
	He came into the room.
She:	My sister who goes to school here is getting her driver's license.
	She is getting her driver's license.
It:	The TV mounted in the back of the room suddenly went blank.
	It suddenly went blank.
They:	All of the employees at my company belong to unions.
	They belong to unions.
Him:	Did you see a tall man dressed in a black jacket?
	Did you see *him*?
Her:	Bring a menu for the young lady seated over there.
	Bring a menu for *her*.
It:	I didn't get the last question on the exam.
	I didn't get *it*.
Them:	Please ask all the people who are waiting in the hall to come in.
	Please ask *them* to come in.

Exercise 4.1

Underline all the noun phrases (except ones that are just pronouns by themselves) in the following sentences. Show that your answer is correct by writing the appropriate third-person pronoun above the noun phrase that you have underlined.

                        It
The book you asked for finally came in.

1. They have commissioned a new statue of him.

2. You should send it to all the people who might be interested.

3. All of the presenters who have registered should arrive early.

4. I am trying to eat a lot more vegetables that are grown locally.

5. It is not easy to get ripe, locally produced organic apples.

6. The people who live there often have to commute long distances.

7. Did you ever get the documents that you requested?

8. Everyone is curious about the new employees who were just hired.

9. The building where I work is being remodeled.

10. The last telephone number that you gave me doesn't work.

11. The new engine will burn any fuel that can be made into a liquid at room temperature.

12. The Harry Potter books, which have sold in the millions, have encouraged reading.

13. People who drive to work every day need to get parking permits from the office.

14. The new regulation has improved hospitals' safety records.

15. He is a director whose movies have been very successful.

Adjectival prepositional phrases

Prepositional phrases always consist of a preposition plus its object. Objects of prepositions are nouns or pronouns (plus other more complex structures like gerunds and noun clauses that we will address later). For example:

Preposition	Noun phrase object
to	the office
under	a big oak tree nearby
by	Shakespeare
from	all my friends
before	next weekend

Preposition	Pronoun object
with	them
after	it
over	me

beyond	her
between	us

Adjectival prepositional phrases often give information about space or time. Here are some examples with the preposition in italics and the entire prepositional phrase underlined:

Space information
the house *on* the corner
the chair *by* the window
the window *behind* the desk
the floor *above* this one
the freeway *to* Seattle

Time information
the day *after* tomorrow
a week *from* Wednesday
some time *during* the week
the period *between* semesters
an hour *from* now

However, many other adjectival prepositional phrases express a wide range of meanings that fall outside of space and time. It is very difficult to classify these in any simple way. Here are some examples:

a book *by* Dickens
a book *about* Dickens
a man *with* a baseball cap
the causes *of* depression
everybody *except* me

Exercise 4.2

Underline the adjectival prepositional phrases in the following sentences. Above each prepositional phrase write *space*, *time*, or *other* as appropriate to the meaning.

          place   other
Somebody <u>at work</u> gave a good analysis <u>of the problem</u>.

1. The mood at work has not been very good during this difficult period.

2. The severe flooding over the weekend has increased the risk of infection.

3. The senator from California expressed her concern about the problem.

4. A reporter in China broke the story about the peace talks.

5. The door in the dining room really needs a new coat of paint.

6. They had a big victory despite all the odds.

7. A new painting by the English painter Turner has just been discovered.

8. I had no illusions about my chances.

9. The witness to the crime refused to testify.

10. We couldn't understand his motive for lying.

11. The rim of the cup was chipped.

12. It was no time for indecision.

13. The waiting period in the clinic is nearly an hour.

14. It seemed like we visited every old church in the city.

15. The period just after sunset is the most dangerous time to drive.

It is not very difficult to recognize prepositional phrases. It is more difficult to figure out whether they are adjectival (noun modifiers) or adverbial (modifiers of verbs and other adverbs). Adjectival and adverbial prepositional phrases look exactly alike. For example, compare the prepositional phrase *with friends* in the following sentences:

> We had a nice dinner last night *with friends*.
> A nice dinner *with friends* is always a great pleasure.

In the first sentence, *with friends* is adverbial, but in the second sentence, *with friends* is adjectival, modifying the noun *dinner*. The only way to reliably identify adjectival prepositional phrases is by testing the prepositional phrase by third-person pronoun substitution. When a prepositional phrase (along with the noun) can be replaced by a third-person pronoun, that phrase must be a noun modifier. Likewise, when a prepositional phrase *cannot* be replaced by a third-person pronoun, that prepositional phrase is adverbial. Here is the third-person pronoun replacement test applied to the two example sentences given above:

it

We had <u>a nice dinner</u> last night <u>*with friends*</u>.

It

<u>A nice dinner *with friends*</u> is always a great pleasure.

As you can see, the third-person pronoun substitution test shows that the prepositional phrase is not adjectival in the first sentence because it is outside the boundaries of the third-person pronoun substitution. In the second sentence, however, the the third-person pronoun *it* can be substituted for the noun and prepositional phrase, proving the prepositional phrase is part of the noun phrase and thus a noun modifier.

Exercise 4.3

Underline all the prepositional phrases in the following sentences. Above each prepositional phrase write *Adj* if it is adjectival or *Adv* if it is adverbial. If it is adjectival, confirm your answer by using the third-person pronoun substitution test.

>   Adv   Adj
> In the last quarter, we expect to see *an improvement in our earnings*.
> In the last quarter, we expect to see *it*.

1. The road by our house is being paved.

2. The frozen chickens in the supermarket are not very good.

3. Breakfast will be served in the main dining room.

4. Their discovery of an error has caused the company to restate its earnings.

5. A restaurant in our neighborhood serves really good Chinese food.

6. After much debate, we decided to consult a specialist in toxic waste removal.

7. We finally found the book we wanted online.

8. The star of the show was a young singer from Australia.

9. Ignorance of the law is not a valid defense in court.

10. Visitors from China are always welcome in our company.

11. The floor in the cabin was rough, unfinished wood.

12. The popularity of his book was a big factor.

13. During the night, there was a fire that caused some damage.

14. He has the heart of a lion and the brain of a jellyfish.

15. At lunchtime, I bought a new coat at the mall.

Adjective (relative) clauses

Adjective clauses (also known as relative clauses) have their own internal subject-verb agreement structure (like independent clauses), but unlike independent clauses, adjectives clauses can never stand alone as independent sentences. Adjective clauses are thus a type of **dependent clause**. Adjective clauses are always attached to the nouns that they modify. Here are some examples with the noun being modified underlined and the adjective clause in italics:

> The <u>book</u> *that I need* is not in the library.
> I answered all of the <u>questions</u> *that I could.*
> The <u>editorial</u>, *which had appeared in the Times*, was the talk of the town.
> The <u>man</u> *who introduced the speaker* is the vice-president of the society.
> <u>Alice Johnson</u>, *who is the head of personnel*, will be at the interview.
> The <u>students</u> *whom I was talking about earlier* are all in their first year here.
> We interviewed the <u>parents</u> *whose children participated in the study.*
> Did you find a <u>place</u> *where we can park overnight*?
> We need to pick a <u>time</u> *when we can all meet.*

We can always identify adjective clauses by the third-person pronoun replacement test. Adjective clauses are the only type of dependent clause that will be inside the boundaries of the third-person pronoun substitution. Here is the third-person pronoun test applied to all of the above examples of adjective clauses:

> The **book** *that I need* is not in the library.
> *It* is not in the library.
>
> I answered all of the **questions** *that I could.*
> I answered all of *them.*
>
> The **editorial**, *which had appeared in the Times*, was the talk of the town.
> *It* was the talk of the town.
>
> The **man** *who introduced the speaker* is the vice-president of the society.
> *He* is the vice-president of the society.
>
> **Alice Johnson**, *who is the head of personnel*, will be at the interview.
> *She* will be at the interview.
>
> The **students** *whom I was talking about earlier* are all in their first year here.
> *They* are all in their first year here.

We interviewed the **parents** *whose children participated in the study.*
We interviewed *them.*

Did you find a **place** *where we can park overnight?*
Did you find *it?*

We need to pick a **time** *when we can all meet.*
We need to pick *it.*

Exercise 4.4

Underline the adjective clauses in the following sentences. Confirm your answer by using the third-person pronoun replacement test.

The opera that we saw was sung in Russian.
It was sung in Russian.

1. We are going to refinance the mortgage that we have on our house.

2. Most of the staff who work at my office will be attending the office party.

3. The place where the pipe connects to the water line is badly corroded.

4. We talked to the subjects whom we had previously identified.

5. Ralph, whom you met on your last trip here, will take you around.

6. They examined the building where the meetings would be held.

7. That week was a period when everything seemed to go wrong.

8. They asked us to redo the tests that we had done earlier.

9. It was a memorial to the pioneers who first settled this area.

10. We took them to the laboratory, which is in the basement.

11. They took pictures of the river where the bridge had washed out.

12. I didn't know the person whom they were discussing.

13. We had an adventure that we certainly had not planned on.

14. My parents, who live in a small town, always enjoy visiting the city.

15. The manager, whom we had contacted earlier, approved our check.

16. Some fans whose enthusiasm knew no limits climbed up on stage.

17. Berlin, which had been a divided city, is now open to everyone.

18. Our friends went to a museum where there was free admission on Mondays.

19. That was the moment when I knew we were in big trouble.

20. The yogurt, which had been in our refrigerator for months, had to be thrown out.

The internal structure of adjective clauses

Virtually all languages have adjective clauses. The internal structure of adjective clauses in English, however, is unusually complicated. All adjective clauses must begin with a special pronoun called a **relative pronoun.** (The term *relative pronoun* refers to the fact that these pronouns are used only in forming relative clauses.) The choice of which relative pronoun to use is governed by two factors: (1) the role of the relative pronoun inside its own adjective clause (i.e., whether the relative pronoun is a subject, object, possessive, adverb of space, or adverb of time), and (2) the nature of the noun that the adjective clause modifies. This noun is known as the **antecedent** of the relative pronoun. We will examine both of these factors in more detail.

Role of the relative pronoun inside its own clause. We choose between *who, whom,* and *whose* depending on the role the relative pronoun plays. If the relative pronoun plays the role of subject, we must use *who.* If the relative pronoun plays the role of object, we must use *whom.* (The *m* in *whom* is historically the same object marker as in *him* and *them.*) If the relative pronoun is possessive, we must use *whose.* In the following examples the relative pronoun is in italics and the entire adjective clause is underlined.

Relative pronoun plays the role of subject
He is a person *who* will always do the right thing.

In this sentence, *who* is the subject of the verb *do.*

Please give your dues to Ms. Walker, *who* is the treasurer of the organization.

Here *who* is the subject of the verb *is.*

The musicians *who* played for us today are all from local schools.

In this sentence, *who* is the subject of the verb *played.*

Relative pronoun plays the role of object
He is a person *whom* I have always admired.

In this sentence, *whom* is the object of the verb *admired*—as in "I have always admired *him*."

Please give your dues to Ms. Walker, <u>*whom* you all met earlier</u>.

Here *whom* is the object of the verb *met*—as in "We all met *Ms. Walker* earlier."

The musicians, <u>*whom* we selected from local schools</u>, will play for us today.

Whom is the object of the verb *selected*—as in "We selected *the musicians* earlier."

Relative pronoun as possessive
Mr. Smith, <u>*whose* father founded the company</u>, has worked here many years.

In this sentence, *whose = Mr. Smith's*.

The companies <u>*whose* employees are full time</u> have done better.

Here *whose = the companies' employees*.

Those bridges <u>*whose* supports were damaged in the flood</u> have been closed.

Here *whose = those bridges'*.

Exercise 4.5

The adjective clauses in the following sentences have been underlined. Replace the word(s) in parentheses with the appropriate relative pronoun.

whom
The actor (~~the actor~~) <u>I met last year</u> is now starring in a new movie.

1. Anybody (anybody) <u>wants to leave now</u> may do so.

2. The person (the person) <u>you met at the reception</u> is Paul Kennedy.

3. Jason Grant, (Jason Grant's) <u>daughter is a friend of Susan's</u>, teaches at MIT.

4. Did you ever hear from the client (the client) <u>left a message for you yesterday</u>?

5. The flower (the flower's) <u>name I couldn't recall</u> is a hydrangea.

6. This is my husband (my husband) <u>I don't think you have met before</u>.

7. We need to replace the window (the window's) <u>glass was broken in the storm</u>.

8. The club's new president, (the president) has been here forever, is very popular.

9. All the employees (the employees) were hoping for a raise will be disappointed.

10. The new secretary (the secretary's) name I can never remember left a message.

11. The drivers (the drivers) the company had hired were all new to the area.

12. We went back to the waiter (the waiter) had waited on us earlier.

13. I looked up the lawyer (the lawyer) you recommended.

14. I looked up the lawyer (the lawyer) wrote the contract.

15. I looked up the lawyer (the lawyer's) presentation we all liked.

The nature of the noun that the relative clause modifies. The relative pronoun always immediately follows the noun that relative pronoun refers to. This noun is called the **antecedent** of the relative pronoun. For example, look at the following sentence:

> We need to talk about the **courses** *that* you are going to take next term.

The antecedent of the relative pronoun *that* is the noun *courses*. Even when the relative pronoun is a possessive, the possessive must refer to the possessive form of the antecedent noun. For example, in the following sentence

> The **organization** *whose* offices you visited was written up in a magazine.

Whose refers to the possessive form of the antecedent noun *organization*, that is, you visited the *organization's* offices.

The nature of the antecedent also exerts control over which relative pronoun we use.

• If the antecedent is human, we must use *who, whom,* or *whose* as the relative pronoun. (The choice among *who, whom,* and *whose* is governed by the role of the relative pronoun inside the adjective clause.)

• If the antecedent is not human, we must use *that* or *which* as the relative pronoun. (We will discuss the distinction between *that* and *which* in great detail later in this chapter. For now, we will use *that* in all of our examples because the distinction between *that* and *which* is irrelevant to our discussion of how relative clauses are formed.)

• If the antecedent is a noun that refers to space (a spatial noun), we use *where* as the relative pronoun.

• If the antecedent is a noun that refers to time (a temporal noun), we use *when* as the relative pronoun. (We can also use *that*.)

In the following examples, the antecedent noun is in bold:

Human:	This is the young **man** *whom* <u>I was telling you about.</u>
Nonhuman:	This is the **computer** *that* <u>I was telling you about.</u>
Spatial noun:	This is the **place** *where* <u>we agreed to meet.</u>
Temporal noun:	This is the **time** *when/that* <u>we agreed to meet.</u>

Exercise 4.6

Fill in the blank with an appropriate relative pronoun. The antecedent noun is in bold and the adjective clause is underlined.

I know a **Chinese restaurant** (*where*) <u>we can get really good dim sum.</u>

1. It is a **book** _____ <u>has influenced us all.</u>

2. It is a **book** _____ <u>message really influenced me.</u>

3. He is staying with a **cousin** _____ <u>name is Williams.</u>

4. He is staying with a **cousin** _____ <u>lives somewhere in Brookline.</u>

5. We picked a **date** _____ <u>we could all get together.</u>

6. Let me introduce you to my **Uncle Jackson** _____ <u>lives in Florida.</u>

7. Let me introduce you to my **Uncle Jackson** _____ <u>I believe you have met before.</u>

8. Let me introduce you to my **Uncle Jackson** _____ <u>company you may know about.</u>

9. Hollywood is a **city** _____ <u>dreams seldom come true.</u>

10. Do you remember the **year** _____ <u>Donna graduated from college?</u>

11. The **meals** _____ <u>you get at camp</u> leave a lot to be desired.

12. English is especially difficult for **nonnative speakers** _____ <u>school systems never used English as a language of instruction.</u>

13. The **stove** _____ <u>they just bought</u> takes up most of their kitchen.

14. Please ask the **operator** _____ <u>is on duty.</u>

15. Please ask the **operator** _____ <u>you already talked to.</u>

16. The union called off the **strike** _____ <u>was scheduled to take place tomorrow.</u>

17. **Residents** of the city _____ <u>have not registered</u> will not be able to vote.

18. The **neighborhood** _____ I live is getting more expensive all the time.

19. A **professor** _____ I had in college advocated pricing oil in Euros.

20. A **professor** _____ you all know advocates pricing oil in Euros.

The following chart summarizes the basic rules about how the external and internal considerations jointly determine the form of the relative pronouns:

RELATIVE PRONOUN'S ROLE INSIDE ADJECTIVE CLAUSE

External antecedent	Subject	Object	Possessive Adverb
Human	who	whom	whose
Nonhuman	that, which	that, which	whose
Spatial noun	where		
Temporal noun	when		

Exercise 4.7

Underline all the adjective clauses in the following sentences.

The seeds <u>that you gave me</u> have not sprouted.

1. My wife, whose enthusiasm knows no limits, has invited all of our friends over.

2. I couldn't keep up with the pace that they were setting.

3. The track where we were running is in excellent shape.

4. The soloist was a pianist whom I had never even heard of before.

5. They damaged the gear that raises the front ramp.

6. He was a rare builder who never cut corners on anything.

7. We need to fly to Dallas where the meeting will be held.

8. The accident caused a concussion that has temporarily affected his short-term memory.

9. We proposed a site where there would be little impact on the environment.

10. They will identify the company whose bid won the contract.

11. Never pick a fight that you can't win.

12. Everybody appreciated the breakfast that was given by the hosting organization.

13. The key that the desk clerk gave us would not unlock the door.

14. All of the scientists whose work we consulted were in substantial agreement.

15. All the difficulties that we went through were worth it.

16. The questions were answered by an official who asked not to be identified.

17. John Marshall, whose foundation sponsored the conference, gave the opening address.

18. Any extras that you have should be returned to the office.

19. We ended up watching a boring game whose outcome was never in doubt.

20. The commercials that we reviewed were all pretty bad.

Adjective clauses in casual conversation

The description of adjective clauses that we have given to this point is an accurate picture of formal, written English. In casual conversation, however, adjective clauses are simplified in two different ways: *who* and *whom* may be replaced by *that*, and relative pronouns that play the role of objects may be deleted.

Who and whom replaced by that

The relative pronouns *who* and *whom* are often replaced by *that*. For example, in written English, you might see this more formal sentence:

The reporter *who* covered the story has received numerous journalism awards.

In conversation, you would be more likely to hear this:

The reporter *that* covered the story has received numerous journalism awards.

The relative pronoun *whom* is nearly always replaced by *that* in conversation. For example:

| **Written:** | The people *whom* we met with were all pretty upset. |
| **Conversation:** | The people *that* we met with were all pretty upset. |

| **Written:** | All the players *whom* the team nominated were selected for the all-star team. |
| **Conversation:** | All the players *that* the team nominated were selected for the all-star team. |

| Written: | Someone *whom* you know told me all about what happened. |
| Conversation: | Someone *that* you know told me all about what happened. |

However, we do not use *that* instead of *who* or *whom* if the antecedent is a proper noun. For example, we would say this:

My Aunt Mary, *whom* you saw at the reception, asked about you.

rather than this:

X My Aunt Mary, *that* you saw at the reception, asked about you.

However, if we used the common noun *aunt*, then we would be likely to use *that* in conversation:

The aunt *that* you saw at the reception asked about you.

Exercise 4.8

All of the following sentences are written in an informal, conversational style. Rewrite the sentences in a more formal style by changing *that* to *who* and *whom* where appropriate. If no change is necessary, write OK above *that*.

who
The person ~~that~~ normally schedules the deliveries is not here today.

1. We certainly owe the staff *that* worked on the project a big thanks.

2. It was all the proof *that* we needed.

3. We deserve the politicians *that* we elect to office.

4. Most Americans think the people *that* live in Texas are a little strange.

5. The few pedestrians *that* we saw out were all dressed in heavy jackets.

6. We have no accurate record of all the sales *that* we made in July.

7. The crowds *that* had filled the streets earlier had all disappeared.

8. We almost never heard the children *that* she was taking care of.

9. The committee arranged meetings with all the candidates *that* they wanted to interview.

10. I phoned all the people *that* were on my list.

11. The members *that* wanted to renew had to fill out a registration form.

12. They identified all the voters *that* we thought were most likely to actually turn out.

13. The academics *that* had studied the issue were in near unanimous agreement.

14. None of us like the alternatives *that* we were given.

15. Even the few treasury officers *that* would speak on the record were noncommittal.

Relative pronouns deleted

Relative pronouns that play the role of objects are often deleted. Here are some examples of deleted relative pronouns playing the role of objects:

> The project ~~that~~ <u>I am in charge of</u> has been reasonably successful.
> The subjects ~~whom~~ <u>we surveyed</u> had all completed the questionnaire.
> I am still close to the friends ~~whom~~ <u>I went to school with.</u>
> I bought it at the store ~~that~~ <u>you had recommended.</u>
> The injuries ~~that~~ <u>she received in the accident</u> are not serious.

You will notice that Americans in casual conversation almost always prefer to avoid the relative pronoun *whom*. They will either replace it with *that* or delete it entirely. For example, you are much more likely to hear this:

> The people *that* I met in Spain were very friendly.

or this (where $\varnothing$ = a deleted relative pronoun):

> The people $\varnothing$ I met in Spain were very friendly.

rather than this:

> The people *whom* I met in Spain were very friendly.

Another reason Americans avoid both *who* and *whom* is that it is hard to determine which of these words to use. Using *that* or no relative pronoun at all nicely avoids having to make the tricky grammatical choice between *who* and *whom* in the quick give-and-take of conversation.

Exercise 4.9

All of the following sentences contain at least one adjective clause. Underline all the adjective clauses. Cross out the relative pronouns that can be deleted (including *that*). If the relative pronoun cannot be deleted, write OK above it.

The Japanese ~~whom~~ we met at the trade conference were interested in our products.

1. I like authors who create a strong sense of place in their books.

2. The movie stars that we have today are not the role models that movie stars used to be.

3. "Yellow Dog" is a political term used to describe a Democrat who would vote for a yellow dog before he would vote for a Republican.

4. You should take a jacket that you can wear if it gets cold.

5. They were the players whom the press identified as taking payoffs.

6. I didn't know any of the girls who were at the party.

7. They listed the names of those students that had passed their final exams.

8. The reporters interviewed the policemen who had arrived at the scene first.

9. Could we talk to the boys that we saw fishing off the pier?

10. The players whom we interviewed were very unhappy with the officials who refereed the game.

11. He asked the buyers who had already made a payment if they would accept a refund.

12. The receptionist that we talked to told us to take a seat.

13. Next, we had to clean all the fish that we had caught.

14. The people who lived nearby all began to drift away.

15. The people that the speaker had named all stood up and received a round of applause.

   The deletion of relative pronouns that play the role of object in their own clauses makes relative clauses much more difficult for nonnative speakers to recognize because the relative pronoun, the flag word that marks the beginning of an adjective clause, is no longer there. The following exercise will give you practice in identifying adjective clauses when the relative pronoun has been deleted.

Exercise 4.10

All of the following sentences contain at least one adjective clause with the relative pronoun deleted. Underline the adjective clause and restore an appropriate relative pronoun.

   The equipment you ordered last week has just arrived.
   The equipment *that* you ordered last week has just arrived.

1. The Shakespearean characters we all know are either villains or lovers.

2. The police arrested the demonstrators they had photographed the day before.

3. He defeated every opponent at chess he had faced.

4. All the tourists we saw at the beach were badly sunburned.

5. The planets they discussed during the lecture all orbited distant suns.

6. We had to return because the horse I was riding pulled up lame after half an hour.

7. We all had to approve the music they had picked for the wedding ceremony.

8. The performers we saw at the Chinese opera were as much acrobats as they were singers.

9. The tune they played during intermission kept running through my mind all night.

10. Lee is a person everyone likes at first meeting.

11. An associate I had never met before took me into the conference room.

12. The meeting was a total disaster we should have seen coming.

13. The flight to Baltimore I had reservations for was cancelled, so I was out of luck.

14. The Christmas I remember best was when I was eight years old.

15. The artists we admire the most now are the French Impressionists.

16. The babysitter we had hired just called to say she couldn't make it.

17. The defeat Thomas Dewey suffered at the hand of Truman in 1948 is the most famous upset in American political history.

18. It was not the retirement we had planned for ourselves.

19. The type of cowboys we saw in the old movies never existed in reality.

20. The jury was not persuaded by the hypothetical arguments the defense put forward.

Restrictive and nonrestrictive adjective clauses

All adjective clauses modify the nouns that they follow (their antecedents). However, not all adjective clauses are equal. Some adjective clauses significantly restrict or limit the meaning of the nouns they modify. Accordingly, these are called **restrictive adjective clauses**. Other adjective clauses, called **nonrestrictive adjective clauses**, do not affect the meaning of the nouns they modify at all. They merely offer additional information about an already defined noun. Put in other terms, the difference between restrictive and nonrestrictive clauses is the difference between essential, defining information (restrictive) and nonessential, supplementary information (nonrestrictive).

Here are examples of restrictive and nonrestrictive adjective clauses. Carefully compare how the adjective clause relates to the noun it modifies. The adjective clauses are underlined, and the relative pronouns are in italics:

> **Restrictive:**   The house *that* is on the corner of Elm and 17th Street is for sale.
> **Nonrestrictive:**   Our house, *which* is on the corner of Elm and 17th Street, is for sale.

If we delete the restrictive adjective clause from the first sentence, we get a new sentence:

> The house is for sale.

In this new sentence, we have no way of knowing which house is for sale. In that sense, the revised sentence no longer means the same thing at all as the original sentence.

However, when we delete the nonrestrictive adjective from the second example, the basic meaning of the original sentence remains unchanged:

> Our house is for sale.

Obviously, when we delete the nonrestrictive adjective clause, we lose the information that the clause contained, namely the exact location of our house. Nevertheless, the basic meaning of the main sentence is unchanged: we are selling our house. Our house is still our house no matter where it is located, and we are still selling it.

Here are some more examples of pairs of restrictive and nonrestrictive adjective clauses:

> **Restrictive:**   The doctor *who* operated on my knee is an orthopedic specialist.
> **Nonrestrictive:**   Dr. Johnson, *who* operated on my knee, is an orthopedic specialist.

> **Restrictive:**   The plumber *whom* we had before has moved away.
> **Nonrestrictive:**   Artie Brown, *whom* we had hired before, has moved away.

> **Restrictive:**   The key *that* unlocks the supply cabinet is in my desk.
> **Nonrestrictive:**   The key to the supply cabinet, *which* I gave you yesterday, should have been returned to me when you were finished.

From these three pairs of examples we can see two important characteristics of restrictive and nonrestrictive adjective clauses:

1. By far the most important difference between them is the use of commas. Restrictive adjective clauses are never set off with commas. Nonrestrictive adjective clauses are always set off with commas. The difference in comma use is the only thing that absolutely defines which adjective clauses are restrictive and which are nonrestrictive. This difference in comma use cannot be overemphasized.

It is helpful to think of the restrictive modifier as part of the meaning of the antecedent noun. Since the restrictive modifier is part of the meaning of the noun, the restrictive modifier can never be separated from that noun by commas. Conversely, the pair of commas around a nonrestrictive clause signal that the adjective clause is only loosely attached to the noun it modifies. Nonrestrictive clauses are optional modifiers—they can be deleted without changing the basic meaning of the nouns they modify.

2. The internal grammatical structures of restrictive and nonrestrictive clauses are identical except (according to some writers) for the choice of whether to use *that* or *which* as the relative pronoun. Some authorities (mostly authors of technical writing books) strongly advise that we use *that* in restrictive clauses and *which* in nonrestrictive clauses. Notice that the two examples above have followed this convention: the restrictive clause uses *that* and the nonrestrictive clause uses *which*.

In actual fact, the behavior of native speakers is more complicated. It is indeed true that native speakers use *which* in nonrestrictive clauses. Using *that* in nonrestrictive clauses is ungrammatical. For example:

Nonrestrictive:	**X** Our house, *that* is on the corner of Elm and 17th Street, is for sale.

The problem is that native speakers freely interchange *that* and *which* in restrictive clauses in all but the most formal situations. For example:

Restrictive:	The shirt *that* you bought for me has lost a button
Restrictive:	The shirt *which* you bought for me has lost a button.
Restrictive:	We gave the tickets to the people *that* were already in line.
Restrictive:	We gave the tickets to the people *which* were already in line.
Restrictive:	They reviewed the instructions *that* they had been given.
Restrictive:	They reviewed the instructions *which* they had been given.
Restrictive:	The car *that* had just passed us suddenly spun on the ice.
Restrictive:	The car *which* had just passed us suddenly spun on the ice.

You can never go wrong following the conservative recommendation to use *that* in restrictive clauses and *which* in nonrestrictive. Do not expect, however, that native speakers will also follow this advice.

Choosing between restrictive and nonrestrictive clauses

Here are two tips that will make the choice between restrictive and nonrestrictive clauses somewhat easier:

1. It follows from the definitions given earlier that proper nouns can only be modified by nonrestrictive adjective clauses. The reason is simple: a proper noun always refers to one specific person, place, or thing. Since adding an adjective clause can never change who or what that person, place, or thing is, all adjective modifiers of proper nouns must be nonrestrictive. Here are some examples using various relative pronouns (except, of course, for *that*, which is best avoided in nonrestrictive adjective clauses):

Nonrestrictive adjective clauses
Mr. Thompson, *who* teaches English at my school, used to live in Peru.
Mr. Thompson, *whom* we all adored, finally retired this year.
The Empire State Building, *which* is now the tallest building in New York, was completed during the Depression.
The Shadow Café, *where* we had lunch recently, is just off Main Street.
The year 1776, *when* the Declaration of Independence was signed, is probably the most important year in American history.

2. Common nouns that are used with an indefinite article (*a/an* or *some*) will normally take **restrictive** adjective clauses. We use indefinite articles to signal that the hearer is not expected to know in advance which particular noun we are talking about. In this sense, common nouns with indefinite articles are the opposite of proper nouns. The function of the adjective clause is to narrow and define the broad generic meaning of the common noun. Here are some examples:

Restrictive adjective clauses
Every morning at seven, a church *that* is in the neighborhood rings a bell.
He takes a pill *that* reduces his blood pressure.
Do you know a store *that* would carry computer accessories?
We are looking for a programmer *who* is an expert in C++.
Some glasses *that* we got on sale have chips on their rims.
I can't stand some commercials *that* are aired on late-night TV.
Some employees *who* work in accounting first noticed the problem last week.

Since we typically use restrictive adjective clauses with nouns modified by indefinite articles, it is tempting to leap to the generalization that we must use nonrestrictive adjective clauses with nouns modified by definite articles. This is definitely not the case. Nouns modified by definite articles can use either type of adjective clause, as in the following example:

> Restrictive: The contracts *that* are approved by the Board are binding.
> Nonrestrictive: The contracts, *which* are approved by the Board, are binding.

Needless to say, these two adjective clauses have substantially different meanings. The first sentence with the restrictive clause means that *only* those contracts that are approved by the Board are binding (contracts not approved by the Board are not binding). The second sentence with the nonrestrictive clause means that all the contracts are binding. The fact that all contracts are approved by the Board is only incidental information. Disputes about whether an adjective clause is restrictive or nonrestrictive are the single most common source of lawsuits related to grammatical issues in legal documents.

Exercise 4.11

Underline all the adjective clauses in the following sentences. Write *restrictive* or *nonrestrictive* above each clause as appropriate, and then add commas if the clause is nonrestrictive.

> Queen Latifah who is best known as a rap artist is now a successful actress.
>
> nonrestrictive
> Queen Latifah, who is best known as a rap artist, is now a successful actress.

1. Let's meet at the restaurant where we had dinner last night.

2. Strangely enough, houses that are made of wood often survive earthquakes better than houses made of concrete.

3. My roommate whom I knew in high school is from Yemen.

4. The forests that grow in the Pacific Northwest are mostly conifers.

5. The economics test that we just took was harder than I expected it to be.

6. I live in a small town that is on the Mississippi River.

7. My boss who commutes an hour each way likes to work from home when she can.

8. The computer that I use at work is not capable of running the program that I need.

9. Mr. Brown who works for our parent company will be visiting us next week.

10. The euro-dollar exchange rate which has fluctuated wildly lately is the topic of today's presentation.

11. There is an accident that has completely blocked the tri-city bridge.

12. The tri-city bridge which crosses the James River is far too small for today's traffic.

13. An attorney who represents our company will give you a call this afternoon.

14. The chief engineer who reports directly to the CEO has issued a new warning.

15. My brother bought a new truck which he promptly wrecked the first time he drove it.

16. It was a request that I could hardly refuse under the circumstances.

17. Last winter which was the coldest in twenty years damaged a lot of our trees.

18. Some banks that were engaged in overly aggressive loans are now in trouble.

19. I got concerned by the sounds that were coming from my printer.

20. The statue commemorates the soldiers who were killed in World War I.

21. My parking permit which cost me over a hundred dollars does not allow me to park next to my building.

22. We should throw away all the food that was not refrigerated right after the party.

23. The building where my dentist has her office is going to be closed for repairs.

24. The state of Washington produces most of the apples that are consumed in the United States.

25. My manager who is not noted for his sense of humor threw the magazine in the trash.

Pronouns

In this chapter we will discuss two types of pronouns: **personal** and **reflexive.**

Personal pronouns

You are probably familiar with the traditional definition of **pronoun**: "a pronoun is a word that replaces one or more than one noun." The "one or more than one noun" part of the definition deals with **compound nouns** (two nouns joined by *and* or *or*). For example, consider the following sentence:

> *Tom and Harry* are good friends of mine.

We can replace the compound noun *Tom and Harry* with the single third-person pronoun *they*:

> *They* are good friends of mine.

However, if we were to take the definition literally, we would have a problem. For example, consider the following sentence:

> A tall young *woman* in the front row raised her hand.

If we were to replace the noun *woman* in the above sentence with *she*, we would get the following nonsensical result:

> **X** A tall young *she* in the front row raised her hand.

Clearly, what the pronoun *she* really replaces is the entire noun phrase *a tall young woman in the front row*:

> A tall young *woman* in the front row raised her hand.
> *She* raised her hand.

Here is how we should rephrase the traditional definition of pronoun: a third-person pronoun is a word that replaces one or more than one noun *and all the modifiers of those nouns*.

In grammatical terms, what the revised definition says is that third-person pronouns replace entire noun phrases. A **noun phrase** is a noun together with all of that noun's modifiers. In the example, *she* replaces the noun *woman* along with all of the words that modify *woman*: the pre-noun modifiers *a tall young* and the post-noun adjectival preposition phrase *in the front row*.

The noun in the noun phrase determines which third-person pronoun to use, as we can see in the following examples:

> A tall young *man* in the front row raised his hand.
> *He* raised his hand.

> Two *men* in the back row both raised their hands at the same time.
> *They* both raised their hands at the same time.

Here is the complete list of third-person pronouns that can replace noun phrases:

	Singular	**Plural**
Subject	he, she, it	they
Object	him, her, it	them

Here are examples of all of the third-person pronouns replacing noun phrases. In these examples, the noun is in italics and the entire noun phrase is underlined:

Subject

He:	My *grandfather* on my mother's side was a prospector in Alaska.
	He was a prospector in Alaska.
She:	The *woman* who was ahead of me in the line dropped all of her packages.
	She dropped all of her packages.
It:	A *truck* pulling a long trailer suddenly pulled out in front of me.
	It suddenly pulled out in front of me.
They:	All of the *employees* in the department went to Larry's retirement party.
	They went to Larry's retirement party.

Object

Him:	I signaled to the *waiter* who had taken our order.
	I signaled to *him*.
Her:	I signaled to the *waitress* who had taken our order.
	I signaled to *her*.
It:	Did you see the new *car* parked outside the restaurant?
	Did you see *it*?
Them:	The new telescope can detect *planets* that are circling distant suns.
	The new telescope can detect *them*.

Exercise 5.1

Write the appropriate third-person pronoun above the underlined noun phrase. Use *he/she* or *him/her* for persons whose gender is not specified.

He/She
The taxi cab driver had a GPS system in the cab.

1. The Mississippi river system drains the central United States.

2. She really enjoyed photographing wild animals in their natural habitat.

3. All the senior executives of the company were called to a special meeting.

4. My brother intends to continue to run the farm that we inherited from our parents.

5. The screenwriter for that movie has been nominated for an Academy Award.

6. The whole family plans to celebrate our parents' fiftieth wedding anniversary in July.

7. Both of my roommates at school come from Alabama.

8. The class interviewed the reporter who wrote the series on judicial misconduct.

9. The population of North Dakota is one of the few in the United States that is actually falling.

10. It is hospital policy to get blood samples from all patients with unexplained fevers.

11. The Southern Cross is the best-known constellation in the Southern Hemisphere.

12. I will vote for the candidate that has expressed the greatest concern for health costs.

13. My husband and his friends have taken the kids camping this weekend.

14. A good portfolio requires a mixture of both stocks and bonds.

15. The weather reporter on the 10 o'clock news is predicting more snow this weekend.

Third-person pronouns are unique among pronouns. The ability of third-person pronouns to substitute for noun phrases is not shared with first- and second-person pronouns, which do not replace anything.

The first-person pronouns (*I, me, we, us*) refer only to the speaker or writer of a sentence, and the second-person pronoun (*you*) refers only to the real or imagined audience of the sentence. For example, consider the following sentence:

> *I* see *you*.

Here the first-person pronoun *I* and the second-person pronoun *you* do not substitute for other noun phrases. They are just themselves—speaker and audience respectively.

Personal pronouns have different forms depending on their **person** (first, second, or third), **number** (singular or plural), and **form** or **case** (subject, object, or possessive). The following chart represents all the personal pronouns, with form and person along the left axis of the chart and number across the top:

PERSONAL PRONOUNS

Form (Case)	Singular	Plural
First-Person Pronouns		
Subject	I	we
Object	me	us
Possessive pronominal	mine	ours
Possessive adjectival	my	our
Second-Person Pronouns		
Subject	you	you
Object	you	you
Possessive pronominal	yours	yours
Possessive adjectival	your	your
Third-Person Pronouns		
Subject	he, she, it	they
Object	him, her, it	them
Possessive pronominal	his, hers, its	theirs
Possessive adjectival	his, her, its	their

Notice that the possessive pronouns have two different sets of forms. The pronominal forms (*mine, ours, yours, his, hers, its, theirs*) act as true pronouns in the sense that they can play the standard noun roles of subject, object, and complement of linking verbs. For example:

Subject:	*Mine* was the only correct answer.
	Ours didn't stand a chance.
Object:	Bob couldn't find his program, so I gave him *yours*.
	The children lost *theirs* again.
Complement:	The decision is *yours*.
	The missing purse was *hers*.

Adjectival forms (*my, our, your, his, her, its, their*) act as adjectives modifying nouns. Here are some examples of this use:

My answer was the only correct one.
I gave him *your* program.
It was *your* decision to make.

Of particular importance are the possessive pronoun forms that are different from each other:

	First-person singular & plural	Third-person singular	Third-person plural
Adjectival	your	her	their
Pronominal	yours	hers	theirs

The adjectival and pronominal forms of *his* and *its* are the same. Here are some sentences that illustrate the difference between pronominal and adjectival forms:

Your/yours
Adjectival:	I didn't understand *your* answer.
Pronominal:	I didn't understand *yours*.

Her/hers
Adjectival:	It is *her* decision to make.
Pronominal:	It is *hers* to make.

Their/theirs
Adjectival:	*Their* task is a dangerous job.
Pronominal:	*Theirs* is a dangerous job.

Exercise 5.2

Select the proper form of the two italicized possessive pronouns by underlining the correct form.

Mary needs to see *her/hers* accountant about a tax matter.

1. I couldn't make out what they were saying about *their/theirs*.

2. We were naturally very sad to hear about *your/yours* loss.

3. Nobody had anything to say about his or *her/hers* decision.

4. My team's performance was even worse than *your/yours*.

5. My candidate has not been able to gather much support. How about *your/yours*?

6. In light of all the difficulties, you really have to admire *their/theirs* attitude.

7. I got mine. Did you get *your/yours*?

8. The poor quality of produce in the marketplace really made me want to get *her/hers*.

9. When the lights went out, nobody could find *their/theirs* way back.

10. Miss Jones was concerned about where she had left *her/hers* in the classroom.

We need to be careful when we use the masculine and feminine singular pronouns *he* and *she*. There is no problem using *he* to refer to males and *she* to females. The problem arises when we use them in a sexist or stereotyped way. One problem is using *he* to refer to people in general. Here is an example:

Whenever a person makes an investment, *he* should minimize sales commissions.

Many people would find this sentence to be objectionable because it sends a message that males are the only kind of people who make investments.

There are two ways of rewriting this type of sentence to eliminate the generic *he*. One way is to replace *he* with the compound *he or she*:

Whenever a person makes an investment, *he or she* should minimize sales commissions.

The other way is to replace *he* with the plural pronoun *they*. This solution will require the subject of the sentence to be rewritten as a plural (*people* rather than *a person*) so that *they* will have an appropriate plural antecedent:

When **people** first use computers, *they* tend to be completely overwhelmed.

Of the two solutions, the second alternative is usually better even though it requires more sentence revision. The option with *he or she* often seems clumsy.

A second problem is using *he* and *she* in a way that stereotypes occupations or tasks. For example:

> Let's find a pilot and see what *he* says.
> Let's find a nurse and see what *she* says.

The use of *he* in the first example and *she* in the second implies that all pilots are males and all nurses are females. Some people have become very sensitive to this kind of gender stereotyping. You should be careful to avoid it.

Again, we can solve the problem by using the compound *he or she*:

> Let's find a pilot and see what *he or she* says.
> Let's find a nurse and see what *he or she* says.

However, since the *he or she* compound is so awkward, a better solution would be to rewrite the sentences to avoid the pronoun altogether. For example:

> Let's see what a pilot would say.
> Let's see what a nurse would say.

Exercise 5.3

Rewrite the following sentences to avoid the inappropriate use of *he* and *she*. Do not use the compound *he or she* in your answers.

> Every employee must wash his hands before returning to work.
> All employees must wash their hands before returning to work.

1. A good writer chooses his words carefully.

_____

2. A geologist spends most of his research time in the field.

_____

3. A teacher should allow her students time to finish their work.

_____

4. When a parent arrives, ask her to take a seat.

_____

5. We need someone who will try his best.

_____

6. Each farmer in the neighborhood has already harvested his crops by now.

_____

7. Every painter has to learn how to keep his brushes in good condition.

_____

8. Find an officer and tell him what happened.

_____

9. Any secretary we hire must have Excel in her resume.

_____

10. Any child who is invited here must mind his manners.

_____

11. Call a doctor and tell him we have an emergency here.

_____

12. No CEO would pass up an opportunity to improve his company.

_____

13. We cannot hire any foreign citizen unless we see his green card.

_____

14. If a visitor stops by, ask him to wait in the library.

_____

15. No member of the Republican Party would lend his name to a cause like that.

_____

Reflexive pronouns

Reflexive pronouns are a unique group of pronouns that always end in either *-self* or *-selves*. Here is the complete list:

Person	Singular	Plural
First person	myself	ourselves
Second person	yourself	yourselves
Third person	himself	themselves
	herself	themselves
	itself	themselves

Reflexive pronouns have no independent meaning; they must refer back to some noun (or pronoun) mentioned earlier in the same sentence. This previously mentioned noun is called the **antecedent** of the reflexive pronoun. The word *reflexive* comes from a Latin word meaning "to bend back." Reflexive pronouns must "bend back" to their antecedent, the nearest appropriate noun—usually but not always the subject of the sentence. Here are some examples with the reflexive pronouns in italics and their antecedents in bold:

The **queen** smiled at *herself* in the mirror.
The **movie** refuses to take *itself* seriously.
The **couple** had accidentally locked *themselves* out of their car.
The **computer** shut *itself* off.
I want to do it by *myself.*

Notice that in all of these examples, the antecedent of the reflexive pronoun is the subject of the sentence. While this is generally the case, the antecedent can also be the object of the preceding verb. For example, look at the following sentence:

Mary told **John** to help *himself* to some dessert.

Here the antecedent of the reflexive pronoun *himself* is not the subject of the sentence, *Mary*, but the object, *John*. If we tried to make the subject the antecedent, the result would be ungrammatical:

X Mary told John to help *herself* to some dessert.

The general rule is that the antecedent of a reflexive pronoun is the nearest preceding noun that plays the role of subject or object of a verb. Here are some more examples of objects being the antecedent:

> Mary wanted **Ralph** to dress *himself* as a pirate for the costume party.
> I wish **you** would behave *yourself*.
> We will give **them** a chance to redeem *themselves*.
> She told the **kids** to behave *themselves*.

Very often in conversation you will hear a reflective pronoun that seems to have no antecedent. For example:

> Take care of *yourself*!
> Behave *yourselves*, now!
> Do *yourselves* a favor.
> Don't hurt *yourself*!
> Just be *yourself* and you will be fine.

All of these sentences are commands with an understood *you* (which can be either singular or plural) as subject. The understood *you* is the antecedent to the reflexive pronouns *yourself* or *yourselves*.

> (**You**) take care of *yourself*!
> (**You**) behave *yourselves*, now!
> (**You**) do *yourselves* a favor.
> (**You**) don't hurt *yourself*!
> (**You**) just be *yourself* and you will be fine.

Exercise 5.4

Fill in the blank with the appropriate reflexive pronoun. Confirm your answer by underlining the pronoun's antecedent. If the antecedent is understood, insert *you*.

> He tends to repeat _____.
> <u>He</u> tends to repeat *himself*.

1. Please! I can do it by _____.

2. They refused to allow _____ to give up hope.

3. My little girl always sings _____ to sleep.

4. I told them that I would do it by _____.

5. It was so noisy that we couldn't hear _____ think.

6. The trip could almost pay for _____.

7. The workers were putting _____ out of a job.

8. It was such an interesting book that the pages seemed to turn _____.

9. The system is designed to shut _____ off in the event of an emergency.

10. Don't be so hard on _____.

11. All successful politicians believe in _____.

12. We wanted the children to be able to look after _____.

13. Jane encouraged Sam to do it _____.

14. Try doing it by _____.

15. I can't stand traveling by _____.

There is another, completely different use of reflexive pronouns as well. We can add reflexive pronouns to a sentence just for emphasis. For example, consider the following sentence:

> **I** wouldn't turn down the offer *myself.*

Here the reflexive pronoun *myself* has been added to an already complete sentence just for emphasis. Unlike a normal reflexive pronoun that plays the role of object of a verb or a pronoun, this pronoun has no grammatical role at all. We can delete it:

> **I** wouldn't turn down the offer ~~myself~~.

or move it right after its antecedent:

> **I** *myself* wouldn't turn down the offer.

Here are some more examples of reflexive pronouns added for emphasis, each with a paraphrase showing that the emphatic reflexive pronoun can be deleted or moved to a position immediately following the antecedent.

He wouldn't do that *himself.*
Deleted: **He** wouldn't do that.
Moved: **He** *himself* wouldn't do that.

They did not know the answers *themselves.*
Deleted: **They** did not know the answers.
Moved: **They** *themselves* did not know the answers.

We intended to go to Italy *ourselves.*
Deleted: **We** intended to go to Italy.
Moved: **We** *ourselves* intended to go to Italy.

She decorated the new house *herself.*
Deleted: **She** decorated the new house.
Moved: **She** *herself* decorated the new house.

Needless to say, we cannot delete or move a reflexive pronoun used in the normal way since it is the object of the verb or of a preposition.

I cut *myself.*
Deleted: **X I** cut ~~*myself*~~.
Moved: **X I** *myself* cut.

We wanted to finish it by *ourselves.*
Deleted: **X We** wanted to finish it by ~~*ourselves*~~.
Moved: **X We** *ourselves* wanted to finish it by.

Exercise 5.5

Underline the reflexive pronouns in the following sentences. Write *emphatic* or *functional* above each one as appropriate. If the pronoun is emphatic, confirm your answer by moving it to a position next to its antecedent.

                              emphatic
I gave him the assignment <u>myself</u>.
I *myself* gave him the assignment.

1. The District Attorney took the case himself.

2. The engine started running again by itself.

3. They saw the accident on the freeway themselves.

4. I couldn't help smiling myself.

5. Their mortgage takes nearly half their income itself.

6. Senator Blather declared himself the winner.

7. She proposed the idea herself.

8. You need to separate yourself from the rest of the candidates.

9. I did all the necessary paperwork myself.

10. The consultants were opposed to the new project themselves.

Gerunds and Infinitives

Gerunds and **infinitives** are verb forms used as nouns. (Infinitives can also be used as other parts of speech, but in this chapter we will deal only with infinitives used as nouns.) Here are some examples of gerunds and infinitives used as subjects (in italics).

Gerunds

Breathing is difficult when you are at high altitudes.
Eating was the last thing on my mind.
Driving is a privilege, not a right.
Swimming is my only real form of exercise.

Infinitives

To live is the goal of every creature.
To doubt is to hesitate.
To lose would be unthinkable.
To refuse would be dishonorable.

Gerunds and gerund phrases

Gerunds are the **present participle** forms of verbs. Present participles are formed by adding -*ing* to the base (or dictionary) forms of verbs. Present participles are mostly regular. The most common variation is the result of normal spelling rules for final silent *e* and doubled consonant spellings. For example, the final *e* of *hope* is dropped when we add a suffix beginning with a vowel: *hope-hoping*; and the final consonant of *hop* doubles when we add a suffix beginning with a vowel: *hop-hopping*. The double consonant rule does not apply to words that do not have the stress on the last syllable (*budget-budgeting*) or when the final consonant is preceded by two vowels (*sleep-sleeping*).

Exercise 6.1

The base or dictionary forms of some verbs are listed in the first column. In the second column, write the gerund (present participle) form of each verb. All of the words follow normal spelling rules.

Base form	**Gerund (present participle)**
advertise	*advertising*
1. amuse	amusing
2. become	becoming
3. choose	choosing
4. clap	clapping
5. date	dating
6. fit	fitting
7. focus	focusing
8. give	giving
9. group	grouping
10. judge	judging
11. loop	looping
12. manage	managing
13. mine	mining
14. model	modeling
15. profit	profiting
16. research	researching
17. service	servicing
18. stay	staying
19. travel	travelling
20. veto	

A gerund phrase is a gerund together with all of its modifiers and/or complements. The difference between a gerund and a gerund phrase is exactly the same as the difference between a noun and a noun phrase. For example, compare the following pairs of gerunds and gerund phrases. The gerunds are in italics, and the entire gerund phrase is underlined.

Working takes all my waking hours.
Working on this project takes all my waking hours.

Complaining won't do you any good.
Complaining about the poor service won't do you any good.

Running really helps me lose weight.
My *running* twenty miles a week really helps me lose weight.

Working out takes a lot of self-discipline.
Working out every day at the gym takes a lot of self-discipline.

Since gerund phrases are noun phrases, they can always be identified by the third-person pronoun replacement test (see Chapter 4). Gerund phrases (as well as infinitive phrases) are always singular, and since they are inanimate, gerund (and infinitive) phrases can always be replaced by *it*. For example:

        It
Working on this project takes all my waking hours.

          It
Complaining about the poor service won't do you any good.

         It
My *running* twenty miles a week really helps me lose weight.

         It
Working out every day at the gym takes a lot of self-discipline.
It takes a lot of self-discipline.

To this point, we have only looked at gerund phrases that function as subjects. Gerunds can play all noun roles: subject, object of a verb, object of a preposition, and predicate nominative (the complement of a linking verb). Here are some examples of gerund phrases playing the other roles:

Object of a verb

         it
I hate *spending* so much money on gasoline.

it
Don't you just love *taking* a couple of days off work?

it
I enjoy *working* with my hands.

Object of a preposition

it
I got my job by *working* as an intern for six months.

it
Before *doing* anything, you have to strip all the old paint off the wall.

it
We finally quit around seven after *finishing* the proposal.

it
My main concern was *getting* started so late.

it
The problem with the job is *having* to commute so far to work.

it
Right now our goal is *finishing* the job on time within the budget.

Since gerunds are derived from verbs, adverbs that originally modified the verb underlying the gerund can also modify the gerund derived from that verb. For example, consider the following sentence:

She stressed the importance of **always** *meeting* our commitments on time.

The adverb *always* modifies the gerund *meeting*.

Exercise 6.2

Underline the gerund phrases in the following sentences. Confirm your answers by replacing the gerund phrase with *it*.

it
They feared taking on such a big task.

1. Putting the schedule on the website really made it much easier to plan our meetings.

2. I vaguely recall hearing some discussion about that.

3. We need to talk about solving the quality control problems.

4. His weakness was trying to please everybody.

5. The consultants recommended cutting back on a few of our less important projects.

6. Working such long hours put a terrible strain on all of us.

7. Getting it right the first time is the best approach.

8. They are not happy about having to take such a late flight.

9. The problem is getting enough time to do everything.

10. We barely avoided sliding into the ditch.

11. Arriving at the airport a couple of hours early turned out to be a really good thing.

12. We all voted for ordering in pizza.

13. He always insists on doing the whole thing by himself.

14. Acting so quickly saved us a lot of trouble.

15. The problem was attaching such a big file to the e-mail.

16. Forget about leaving early.

17. Knowing the right thing and doing the right thing are not the same.

18. We have to focus on achieving results.

19. Getting off to such a bad start took away from our later successes.

20. Seeing is believing.

One of the hardest things about identifying gerunds is telling apart a verb in a progressive tense from a gerund that follows a linking verb. For example, compare the following sentences:

Progressive tense: The cat *was getting* ready to pounce.
Gerund: My big concern *was getting* enough sleep.

As you can see, we have exactly the same sequence of verbs, *was getting*, in both sentences. In more general terms, how can we tell when some form of *be* + a present participle is a progressive tense (*be* as a helping verb + a present participle verb) or *be* as a main verb followed by a gerund? Here are the differences between our two example sentences:

	helping verb	main verb in present participle form	
Progressive tense:	The cat *was*	*getting*	ready to pounce.

	main verb	gerund	object of verb

Gerund: My big concern *was* *getting* enough sleep.

Fortunately, there are two reliable ways of telling them apart. We can always change a progressive verb into a simple form. In the case of our example, we can change the past progressive *was getting* to the simple past tense *got*:

Progressive tense: The cat *was getting* ready to pounce.
Simple past: The cat *got* ready to pounce.

When we try to do the same thing with the gerund, the result is nonsensical:

Gerund: My big concern was *getting* enough sleep.
Simple past: **X** My big concern *got* enough sleep.

The other test is the third-person substitution test for gerund phrases. Here is the test applied to both sentences:

                                                              it
Progressive tense: The cat was *getting* ready to pounce.
Third-person pronoun test: The cat was getting ready to pounce.

Clearly, *it* does not equal *getting ready to pounce*. When we apply the same test to the gerund phrase, it makes perfect sense:

                                                              it
Gerund: My big concern was *getting* enough sleep.
Third-person pronoun test: My big concern was *getting* enough sleep.

In this case, *it* does indeed make sense as a substitute for *getting enough sleep*.

Exercise 6.3

Each of the following sentences contains a sequence of some form of the verb *be* followed by a present participle. Underline each progressive verb or gerund phrase and write *progressive* or *gerund* above it, and then confirm your answer by applying one of the tests discussed previously: paraphrasing a progressive as a simple tense or replacing a gerund phrase with *it*.

                          progressive
The discussion *was getting* out of hand.
The discussion *got* out of hand.

1. Our effort was showing a definite improvement in sales.

   _____

2. My worry is being late for an important meeting.

   _____

3. The kids were playing in the backyard.

   _____

4. The kids' favorite activity is playing in the backyard.

   _____

5. John's idea of a good time is watching football on TV.

   _____

6. Sally was studying classical Greek in Athens last summer.

   _____

7. Sally's great ambition is studying classical Greek some summer.

   _____

8. The problem was getting stuck in traffic on the way home.

   _____

9. The worst thing is losing a really close game that we could have won.

   _____

10. We are meeting them at a restaurant near the station.

   _____

Infinitives and infinitive phrases

Infinitive and infinitive phrases are generally quite similar to gerunds and gerund phrases. Most of the description of gerunds and gerund phrases will apply to infinitive and infinitive phrases.

Infinitives consist of *to* + the base or dictionary form of the verb. For example:

    to be
    to go
    to have

Infinitives can be used in many ways, but in this chapter we are only concerned with infinitives used as nouns.

An infinitive phrase is an infinitive together with all of its modifiers and/or complements. The difference between an infinitive and an infinitive phrase is exactly the same as the difference between a noun and a noun phrase. For example, compare the following pairs of infinitives and infinitive phrases used as objects. The infinitives are in italics, and the entire infinitive phrase is underlined.

We all need *to sleep*.
We all need *to sleep* for a few hours.

We want *to finish*.
We want *to finish* this job as soon as we can.

They expected *to win*.
They expected *to win* the game easily.

From now on we will use the term **infinitive phrase** for infinitives with or without modifiers and/or complements. Infinitive phrases can play three of the basic four noun roles: subjects, objects of verbs, and predicate nominatives. Unlike gerund phrases, infinitive phrases cannot be objects of prepositions. Here are some examples of infinitive phrases as subject, object of a verb, and predicate nominative:

Subject
To give up so easily would be a terrible thing to do.
To do our very best is all that anybody could ask of us.
To learn Chinese characters takes years.

Object of verb
We need *to get* some more help.
They expected *to be* in Dallas by noon today.
The office tried *to reach* him by voice mail.

Predicate nominative (complement of a linking verb)
The idea is *to arrange* a surprise party for Susan next week.
Our goal for this year was *to increase* our sales by ten percent.
The driver's responsibility is *to get* all of the guests from the airport to the hotel.

As is the case with gerund phrases, infinitive phrases are a category of noun phrases. Since infinitive phrases are nonhuman and always singular, infinitive phrases can always be replaced by *it*. Here are examples of infinitive phrases in all three noun roles, subject, object of a verb, and predicate nominative, followed by the *it* substitution.

>   It
> *To make* a decision on such an important matter was not an easy thing to do.

>   it
> The candidate refused *to answer* the reporters' questions.

>   it
> My biggest concern was *to find* a new job as soon as possible.

Exercise 6.4

Underline the infinitive phrases in the following sentences. Confirm your answers by replacing each infinitive phrase with *it*.

> To turn down such a generous offer was a hard decision to make.

>   It
> To turn down such a generous offer was a hard decision to make.

1. Our original plan was to go to the play after having dinner in town.

2. We wanted to get an apartment somewhere in easy commuting distance.

3. To operate heavy equipment requires a special license.

4. They decided to enroll in a gym or health club.

5. The lawyer's advice was to get out of the contract any way we could.

6. To teach math in middle schools requires a special kind of person.

7. Our assignment was to analyze the financial status of a small business.

8. To assume that you know what is going on may be a big mistake.

9. Our decision was to fight against the zoning change.

10. To permit such dangerous behavior is really asking for trouble.

11. I didn't want to stop for lunch because I had so much work.

12. To give up so easily would be a sure sign of weakness.

13. The plan was to make them an offer they couldn't refuse.

14. After the long flight, we really needed to stretch our legs.

15. We didn't want to think about all the awful things that could happen.

16. To receive this award from you is a great honor and privilege.

17. After much debate, the final decision was to add three new positions.

18. You will need to take a full load next semester.

19. I wanted to believe that they were telling us the truth.

20. To err is human, to forgive is divine.

Infinitive phrases differ from gerund phrases in one respect. English speakers often prefer to move longer infinitive phrases to the end of the sentence, putting an *it* in the subject position to act as a placeholder or marker. This use of *it* is called a "dummy" or "empty" *it* because *it* does not actually refer to anything outside the sentence. For example, consider the following sentence with an infinitive phrase in the subject position:

> *To turn down* such a good opportunity didn't make economic sense.

We could shift the infinitive phrase to the end of the sentence and put a dummy *it* in the position vacated by the infinitive phrase:

> **It** didn't make economic sense *to turn down* such a good opportunity.

Here are some examples of subject infinitive phrases shifted to the end of the sentence and replaced by dummy *it*.

Original:	*To drive* on the left side of the road was a strange experience.
Shifted:	**It** was a strange experience *to drive* on the left side of the road.
Original:	*To do* it the right way would cost more than we could afford.
Shifted:	**It** would cost more than we could afford *to do* it the right way.
Original:	*To insist* on a down payment seemed perfectly fair to me.
Shifted:	**It** seemed perfectly fair to me *to insist* on a down payment.

Exercise 6.5

Underline the infinitive phrases in the following sentences. Then shift the phrases to the end of the sentence, using a dummy *it* in the subject position.

> <u>To complete our research on time</u> was important for the project.
> *It* was important for the project <u>to complete our research on time</u>.

1. To get finished on time was a great feeling.

   _____

2. To unite the voters behind his candidacy was Senator Blather's goal.

   _____

3. To miss three meetings in a row was totally out of character.

   _____

4. To make the criminals pay for their crimes was of utmost importance.

   _____

5. To cut too many corners was just asking for trouble.

   _____

6. To begin eating while the hostess was in the kitchen seemed terribly rude.

   _____

7. To meet all the course prerequisites is the responsibility of every applicant.

   _____

8. To see the landscape with fresh eyes is the gift of a great painter.

   _____

9. To enforce the laws is the first obligation of a policeman.

   _____

10. To get a clear picture of what was going on seemed necessary.

    _____

7

Noun Clauses

Noun clauses are dependent clauses that function as noun phrases. (**Dependent clauses** have their own subjects and verbs, but they are not able to stand alone as complete sentences.) Noun clauses, like gerunds and infinitives used as nouns, are singular, and thus they can always be replaced by the third-person singular pronoun *it*. Here are examples of noun clauses playing the four noun roles of subject, object of verb, object of preposition, and predicate nominative (the complement of a linking verb). The noun clauses are underlined, and the examples also show how *it* can substitute for the noun clause.

	It
Subject:	What they are doing is none of our business.

                                                    it

Object of verb: I know <u>what you mean</u>.

                                                               it

Object of preposition: We worried about <u>where you had gone</u>.

                                                                           it

Predicate nominative: The decision was <u>that we will go ahead as we had planned</u>.

There are different ways of constructing noun clauses. In this book, we will cover the two main ways of forming noun clauses, which are usually referred to by the word that begins each type. The two different types are *that* clauses and *wh-* clauses (**wh- words** are so called because nearly all the initial words begin with the letters *wh-*. For example, *who, when, where,* and *why* are *wh-* words).

That clauses

That clauses are built in a very simple way. They consist of the introductory word *that* followed by a statement in its normal word order:

that clause = *that* + statement

Unlike *wh-* clauses, the other main type of noun clause, *that* clauses cannot play the role of object of preposition. For example, compare the following pair of sentences, the first with a *wh-* clause and the second with a *that* clause:

wh- clause: I am not upset at <u>*what* you did</u>.

that clause: **X** I am not upset at <u>*that* you did it</u>.

Here are some examples of *that* clauses playing the other three main roles of subject, object of a verb, and predicate nominative. In all the following examples, the introductory *that* is in italics and the entire noun clause is underlined. The examples also show how *it* can replace the noun clause.

Subject

It

<u>*That* the mistake was not caught earlier</u> was surprising.

It

<u>*That* he would say such a thing</u> upset all of us.

It

<u>*That* they succeeded against all expectations</u> is a real credit to them.

It

<u>*That* the game was so close</u> made it fun to watch.

Object of verb

it

They knew <u>*that* they would have to extend the deadline</u>.

it

We hope <u>*that* you will be able to have lunch with us</u>.

it

I pretended <u>*that* I didn't notice the embarrassing slip</u>.

it

The consultant suggested <u>*that* we were trying to expand too fast</u>.

Predicate nominative

                                 it

Her idea was *that* we would all get together tomorrow.

                          it

The trouble is *that* we are rapidly running out of time.

                             it

Our kid's hope was *that* we would be able to go to the beach that week.

                          it

The decision was *that* they would go ahead as originally planned.

Exercise 7.1

Underline the *that* clauses in the following sentences. Confirm your answer by substituting the pronoun *it* for the *that* clause.

                        it

I can't believe that they said that.

1. That the movie was in French came as something of a shock.

2. Don't you find that you get really exhausted after long flights?

3. I wish that it would stop raining.

4. That I know all the answers astonished me.

5. Our intention was that we would take a trip to New Mexico this summer.

6. I think that they should quit while they are ahead.

7. The first approximation was that we were about 10 percent under budget.

8. That we were going to be late seemed obvious at this point.

9. My friends told Barbara that she should jump at such a good opportunity.

10. Do you think that it is a good idea to go ahead?

11. After much debate, we all agreed that we would enter the competition.

12. The funny thing was that we had been right all along.

13. I said that we would be able to finish on time.

14. They just assumed that everything would be OK.

15. The conclusion was that we should stick to our original plan.

16. The kids promised that they would be home by dinner time.

17. That they loved Italian food was obvious from their empty plates.

18. Their assumption was that they could rent a car when they got there.

19. I expect that we will be hearing from them any time now.

20. The difference was that we were prepared and they were not.

While it is perfectly grammatical to use *that* clauses as subjects, most speakers prefer to move these clauses to the end of the sentence, putting an *it* in the subject position as a "dummy" placeholder or marker. (In Chapter 6, we saw exactly the same thing with infinitive phrases used as subjects.) For example, consider the subject *that* clause in the following sentence:

> *That* the flight was going to be delayed didn't come as a big surprise.

The *that* clause can easily be moved to the end with a dummy *it* in the subject position:

> **It** didn't come as a big surprise *that* the flight was going to be delayed.

Here are some more examples of shifted *that* clauses:

Original:	*That* I couldn't remember his name was only to be expected.
Shifted:	**It** was only to be expected *that* I couldn't remember his name.
Original:	*That* they could actually win almost seemed too good to be true.
Shifted:	**It** almost seemed too good to be true *that* they could actually win.
Original:	*That* the cost of college is rapidly rising is beyond question.
Shifted:	**It** is beyond question *that* the cost of college is rapidly rising.

Exercise 7.2

Underline the subject *that* clauses and then move them to the end of the sentence, putting a dummy *it* in the empty subject position.

> That they would even consider doing it seems a little out of character.
> *It* seems a little out of character that they would even consider doing it.

1. That it was over so quickly came as a big relief.

_____

2. That the road was impassable soon became obvious.

_____

3. That we had made a good decision would appear to be the case.

_____

4. That the workers would need more time seemed certain.

_____

5. That they should address the problem quickly was apparent to everyone.

_____

6. That we would have to reschedule the meeting seemed increasingly likely.

_____

7. That I would have to cancel the meeting became clear after all.

_____

8. That the risk was getting too great to accept was likely.

_____

9. That they had forgotten to confirm our reservation became embarrassingly obvious.

_____

10. That she had to leave so soon was a great disappointment to all her fans.

_____

Noun clauses that begin with *that* superficially resemble adjective clauses that also begin with *that*. For example, compare the uses of *that* in the following pair of sentences:

Noun clause:	I know *that* we should change the designs.
Adjective clause:	I know designs *that* we should change.

The simplest way to distinguish the two different types of clauses is to replace the noun clause with *it*:

$$\text{it}$$

Noun clause: I know *that* <u>we should change the designs.</u>

We cannot use *it* to replace the adjective clause beginning with *that*:

$$\textbf{X}\ \text{it}$$

Adjective clause: I know designs *that* <u>we should change.</u>

Another simple way to tell the two uses of *that* apart is to see if you can replace *that* with *which*. *That* and *which* are usually interchangeable in adjective clauses:

Adjective clause: I know designs *that* <u>we should change.</u>
Adjective clause: I know designs *which* <u>we should change.</u>

We cannot replace the *that* in a noun clause with *which*.

Noun clause: I know *that* <u>we should change the designs.</u>
Noun clause: **X** I know *which* <u>we should change the designs.</u>

Exercise 7.3

The following sentences contain a mixture of noun clauses and adjective clauses. Underline the clauses and label them *Noun* or *Adjective (Adj) as* appropriate. Confirm your answer by using the *it* replacement test for noun clauses and the *which* substitution for adjective clauses.

$$\text{Noun}$$

The photographer called and suggested <u>that we postpone the session.</u>
The photographer called and suggested *it.*

$$\text{Adjective}$$

The session *that* <u>we postponed</u> will be rescheduled next Wednesday.
The session *which* <u>we postponed</u> will be rescheduled next Wednesday.

1. The coach claimed that the referee had made a mistake.

_____

2. Did you hear that we are going to get a big snowstorm this weekend?

_____

3. The experiment that we had proposed was finally approved.

_____

4. I almost forgot that we were going to the Smiths' tonight.

_____

5. They will never forget the trip that they took to New Zealand.

_____

6. We finally picked a design that we could all agree on.

_____

7. Everybody felt that the discussion had gone as well as it could.

_____

8. I am very worried about the meeting that we will have this afternoon.

_____

9. We quickly discovered that we could not get a cab in a rainstorm.

_____

10. The cab that we had ordered never showed up.

_____

When a *that* clause is used as the object of a verb, we often delete the word *that* from the beginning of the noun clause. Here are some examples with the deleted *that* represented by Ø in the underlined *that* clauses.

> We knew Ø it was getting pretty late.
> Do you understand Ø we may not be able to hold your reservation?
> The manager said Ø the hotel will be full this weekend.
> I suggest Ø we look for another restaurant closer by.
> The waiter said Ø we would need to wait at least twenty minutes.

Deleting the introductory *that* from the beginning of *that* clauses poses a special problem for nonnative speakers because the introductory word *that* is the obvious clue that signals the beginning of a *that* clause. *That* clauses are unique in this respect: no other type of noun clause has the option of deleting its introductory word. Consequently, anytime we recognize a noun clause that does not begin with a distinctive introductory word, we know by default that it must be a *that* clause with the *that* deleted.

Exercise 7.4

Many of the following sentences contain a *that* clause with a deleted *that*. Underline the *that* clause and confirm your answer by inserting *that* at the beginning of the clause.

We decided <u>we should call a taxi.</u>
We decided *that* <u>we should call a taxi.</u>

1. He claimed he had been working at home all afternoon.

_____

2. I wouldn't have guessed it would have cost so much.

_____

3. His son showed us he could ride his bicycle without using his hands.

_____

4. We quickly discovered the roads were nearly impassable.

_____

5. I suggest we stay at the airport hotel and fly out in the morning.

_____

6. Did you notice Senator Blather was wearing one brown shoe and one black shoe?

_____

7. They concluded the proposal was going to need a lot more work.

_____

8. The coach told the team they would have to practice much harder.

_____

9. As I have gotten older, I have found I need to take better notes at meetings.

_____

10. The defendant denied he had ever been to Chicago.

_____

Wh- clauses

The second type of noun clause always begins with a *wh-* word. The term **wh- word** refers to a special group of words, most of which happen to begin with the letters *wh-*. Here are the most common *wh-* words that begin noun clauses, classified by their parts of speech:

NOUNS

what	whatever
which	whichever
who	whoever
whom	whomever
whose	

ADVERBS

when	whenever
where	wherever
why	how

The fact that *wh-* clauses can begin with adverbs does not change the fact that these introductory words are used to create noun clauses. Here are some examples of adverb *wh-* words used to create noun phrases functioning as objects of verbs, followed by substitution of *it* to verify the function of the noun phrase:

         it

I don't know *when* they will be here.

        it

We saw *where* they were going.

        it

They soon discovered *why* we had packed our umbrellas.

        it

Did you ever learn *how* they were able to finish so quickly?

Wh- clauses can play all four noun roles of subject, object of verb, object of preposition, and predicate nominative (complement of a linking verb). Here are some examples:

Subject

    It

Whatever you want to do is OK with me.

            It
Whose child started the quarrel makes no difference.

          It
When the awards will be announced will have to remain confidential.

        It
Whom they were talking about was not at all clear.

Object of verb

            It
They didn't tell me *who* you were.

              it
Do you know *where* John left our cell phone?

           it
I ate *what* everybody else was eating.

                it
Tomorrow we will learn *where* our new assignment is.

Object of preposition

                      It
The students couldn't help wondering about *what* they had been told.

              it
The hikers looked back at *where* they had been.

       it
After *what* they had been told, they were no longer sure of anything.

                   it
We were finished except for *whatever* clean-up tasks remained to be done.

Predicate nominative

        It
The job is *whatever* you want to make of it.

             it
Their gratitude was *why* all of our work was worth the effort.

> it
> The question is *whose* idea was it in the first place?

> it
> The best technique is *whatever* gets the job done.

Exercise 7.5

Underline the *wh-* clauses in the following sentences. Confirm your answers by replacing the noun clause with *it*.

> <u>What you are entitled to</u> remains to be seen.
> *It* remains to be seen.

1. We never learned where all those copies of the report went.

_____

2. They will do whatever you want them to do.

_____

3. Why they behaved the way they did is a complete mystery to me.

_____

4. I wondered whose approval was necessary for the project to get started.

_____

5. They parked the trucks not far from where the boxes were stacked up.

_____

6. Ask not for whom the bell tolls.

_____

7. After all, that was why we did it in the first place.

_____

8. Did you ever find out whose car was blocking the driveway?

_____

9. Whenever they want to start is OK with me.

_____

10. She showed us how she wanted us to do it.

_____

11. You will never guess what the problem was.

_____

12. We had to settle for whatever they would pay us.

_____

13. The new CEO is whomever the board appoints.

_____

14. The secretary will record whatever is said at the meetings.

_____

15. What you see is what you get.

_____

Up to this point, we have looked only at how *wh-* clauses are used as nouns inside the main sentence. As we have seen, *wh-* clauses can play all four noun roles (subject, object of verb, object of preposition, and predicate nominative) inside the larger (main) sentence.

Now we will examine in some detail the *internal* structure of *wh-* clauses. That is, we will see how *wh-* noun clauses are constructed. *Wh-* clauses, as opposed to the much simpler *that* clauses, require some complicated internal rearrangements of sentence parts.

All *wh-* clauses are formed according to the following two rules:

1. Replace a noun or adverb with the appropriate *wh-* word. We replace nouns with *who, whom, whose* + noun, *what, which, whoever, whomever, whatever,* and *whichever.* We replace adverbs of time with *when* and *whenever*; adverbs of place with *where* and *wherever*; adverbs of cause with *why*; and adverbs of manner with *how.*

Here is an example applied to a *wh-* word that plays the role of object of a verb. In this example, the *wh-* word *what* plays the role of the object of the verb *said.* As usual, the entire noun phrase is underlined.

I know he said *what*.

2. Move that *wh-* word to the first position inside the noun clause. Moving *what* out of its original position leaves behind an empty space or gap (marked with the symbol ∅) where the original object was:

I know *what* he said ∅.

When we hear or read the noun clause *what he said*, we understand that *what* is playing the role of the now missing object of the verb *said*. In other words, we automatically interpret the *wh-* word as filling a gap in the clause.

Here is a second example, only this time the *wh-* word is the adverb *where*:

I know they went *where*.

Rule 2 requires us to move the *wh-* word to the beginning of the noun clause:

I know *where* they went Ø.

When we hear or read the noun clause *where they went*, we understand that *where* is playing the role of a missing adverb at the end of the clause.

Here is an example of a *wh*-word in each of the four possible roles:

Wh- word as subject
I know *who* you are.

In this case only, Rule 2 is meaningless or invalid, depending on how you look at it, because the *wh-* word is already in the first position of the noun clause.

Wh- word as object of a verb
I know you mean *whom*. ⇒ I know *whom* you mean Ø.

Wh- word as object of a preposition
I know you spoke to *whom*. ⇒ I know *whom* you spoke to Ø.

In very formal written English, *to* would move with *whom* to the beginning of the clause:

I know you spoke to *whom*. ⇒ I know to *whom* you spoke Ø.

Wh- word as predicate nominative
I know the outcome was *what*. ⇒ I know *what* the outcome was Ø.

Wh- word as adverb of time
I know you left *when*. ⇒ I know *when* you left Ø.

Wh- word as adverb of place
I know you went *where*. ⇒ I know *where* you went Ø.

Wh- word as adverb of cause

I know <u>you did it</u> *why.* ⇒ I know *why* <u>you did it</u> ∅.

Wh- word as adverb of manner

I know <u>you did it</u> *how.* ⇒ I know *how* <u>you did it</u> ∅.

Exercise 7.6

Use Rule 2 to move the *wh-* word to the beginning of the noun clause. Mark the gap where the *wh-* word came from with ∅.

> We discussed <u>they were doing the job *how.*</u>
> We discussed <u>*how* they were doing the job ∅.</u>

1. I told them <u>I needed *what.*</u>

   _____

2. We did <u>*what* seemed to please them.</u>

   _____

3. The police asked them <u>they did it *why.*</u>

   _____

4. The only thing that counts is <u>you actually do *what.*</u>

   _____

5. I was really impressed by <u>you were trying to accomplish *what.*</u>

   _____

6. You can make it <u>*whenever* will be fine with us.</u>

   _____

7. I can't remember <u>it was *whose suggestion.*</u>

   _____

8. We were confused by <u>they said *what.*</u>

   _____

9. My friends were trying to guess <u>they would pick</u> *which one*.

_____

10. I had no idea about <u>we should do</u> *what*.

_____

11. <u>I voted for</u> *whom* is nobody's business but mine.

_____

12. <u>They had to say</u> *what* about the economy was pretty convincing.

_____

13. The car was parked <u>they said it would be</u> *where*.

_____

14. You will be tested only on <u>you have learned</u> *what* in this class.

_____

15. <u>John gave Mary</u> *what* for her birthday came as a complete surprise to her.

_____

Probably the most common error that nonnative speakers make when they use *wh-* clauses is that they mistakenly use the inverted verb word order of information questions. Since information questions are much more common than *wh-* clauses, it is natural that many nonnative speakers associate all *wh-* words with the inverted verb word order used in information questions. Here are some examples, first with an information question, then a *wh-* clause mistakenly using the same question word order, and finally the correct *wh-* clause word order. The *wh-* word is in italics, and the verb (or first verb if there is more than one) is in bold:

Information question:	*Who* **is** that man?
Incorrect *wh-* clause:	**X** I know *who* **is** <u>that man</u>.
Correct *wh-* clause:	I know *who* <u>that man</u> **is**.

Information question:	*Where* **are** we going?
Incorrect *wh-* clause:	**X** I know *where* **are** <u>we going</u>.
Correct *wh-* clause:	I know *where* <u>we</u> **are** going.

Information question:	*Whom* **should** we ask?
Incorrect *wh-* clause:	**X** I know *whom* **should** <u>we ask</u>.
Correct *wh-* clause:	I know *whom* <u>we</u> **should** ask.

Information question:	*What **have** they done?*
Incorrect *wh-* clause:	**X** I know *what **have** they done.*
Correct *wh-* clause:	I know *what* they **have** done.

Information question:	*Why **would** they want to do that?*
Incorrect *wh-* clause:	**X** I know *why **would** they want to do that.*
Correct *wh-* clause:	I know *why* they **would** want to do that.

Information question:	*What **does** he mean by that?*
Incorrect *wh-* clause:	**X** I know *what **does** he mean by that.*
Correct *wh-* clause:	I know *what* he means by that.

Notice in this last example that the incorrect *wh-* clause (in imitation of the question form) uses the helping verb *does*. In the correctly-formed *wh-* clause, the helping verb *does* is not used.

The mistake is more likely to happen in speaking than in writing. It is more likely to occur in rapid conversation or when the situation is stressful. Nonnative speakers who tend to make this mistake need to be aware of their tendency and consciously monitor themselves for the error.

Exercise 7.7

Many of the following sentences contain *wh-* clauses that incorrectly use information question word order. Cross out these incorrect *wh-* clauses and write the corrected form in the space provided. If the *wh-* clause is correct, write *OK*.

I didn't understand ~~what was he saying~~.
I didn't understand *what he was saying*.

1. It is not clear what were they arguing about.

_____

2. We need to find out how much will it cost.

_____

3. Who will be the speaker depends on the budget.

_____

4. Their expert advice is what are we paying the big bucks for.

_____

5. They were naturally curious about what we had decided to do.

_____

6. How well will he succeed remains to be seen.

_____

7. We couldn't decide what should we wear to the party.

_____

8. I was surprised at what did she say.

_____

9. What were they serving for lunch was fine with us.

_____

10. I certainly understand how do you feel.

_____

11. When should we go hasn't been decided yet.

_____

12. I'll have what are you having.

_____

13. What you say may be used against you.

_____

14. The question is who will be the next president.

_____

15. Our limited time determined where could we go for lunch.

_____

Part 2

Verb Phrases

Basic Verb Forms

This chapter deals with the six basic verb forms that are used as the raw material to make up the tense system of English. The six basic verb forms are the **base**, the **present tense**, the **past tense**, the **infinitive**, the **present participle**, and the **past participle**. The next chapter covers the formation and meaning of the tenses created from these six verb forms and from the modal auxiliary verbs.

All verbs (with the important exceptions of *be* and the **modal auxiliary** verbs *can*, *may*, *must*, *shall*, and *will*) have all six of the forms mentioned above. The six forms are illustrated below by the regular verb *walk* and the irregular verb *run*:

VERB FORMS

Base form	Present tense	Past tense	Infinitive	Present participle	Past participle
walk	walk/walks	walked	to walk	walking	walked
run	run/runs	ran	to run	running	run

We will now look at each of these six forms in detail, seeing how each is formed.

Base form

The base form is the form of the verb that is entered into the dictionary. For example, if you were to look up *ran* in the dictionary, it would refer you to the base form *run*. Since the base form is identical in nearly all cases to the present tense, it is difficult at first to see how one could tell the base form and present tense apart. Fortunately, there is one verb in which the base form and present-tense forms are different, the verb *be*:

BE

Person	Present-tense form
I	am
you (singular)	are
he/she/it	is
we	are
you (plural)	are
they	are

We can use the fact that the base form of *be* is different from all its present-tense forms to determine when base forms are used. There are four places in which the base form is used: (1) to form infinitives, (2) after helping verbs when we talk about the future, (3) in imperative sentences (commands), and (4) as part of the complement of some verbs.

Infinitives

All infinitives are formed by putting *to* in front of the base form. For example:

> to *have*
> to *go*
> to *talk*
> to *sing*

We can show that these verbs are indeed in the base forms by using the verb *be*. If we substitute any of the present-tense forms of *be*, the results are ungrammatical:

> to *be*
> **X** to *am*
> **X** to *are*
> **X** to *is*

Future tenses

The future tense is formed by using a base form after the helping verb *will* (and other modal auxiliary verbs *can*, *may*, *must*, and *shall*):

> will *have*
> can *go*
> must *talk*
> should *sing*

We can show that these verbs are in the base forms by again using the verb *be*. If we substitute any of the present-tense forms, the results are again ungrammatical:

will *be*
X will *am*
X will *are*
X will *is*

Imperatives (commands)

Imperative sentences use the base form of the verb. Here are some examples:

Go away!
Oh, *stop* that!
Answer the question, please.

When we use the verb *be*, we again see that present-tense forms are ungrammatical when used in imperatives:

Be careful what you wish for!
X *Am* careful what you wish for!
X *Are* careful what you wish for!
X *Is* careful what you wish for!

Verb complements

Some verbs use base forms as part of their complements. Here are some examples:

We made them *walk* to school.
I let them *finish* early.
John will have the office *send* you a copy.

When we use the verb *be*, we again see that the present-tense forms are ungrammatical:

I made them *be* quiet.
X I made them *am* quiet.
X I made them *are* quiet.
X I made them *is* quiet.

Exercise 8.1

The verbs in the following sentences contain base forms as well as non-base forms. Underline the base forms and confirm your answer by substituting the verb *be* for the base form. You will need to change the ending of the sentence to be compatible with the meaning of *be*.

The weather forecast said that it would <u>rain</u> tonight.
The weather forecast said that it would <u>*be* rainy</u> tonight.

1. Drive carefully when you go home.

_____

2. My grandmother let the kids help with the cooking.

_____

3. We asked them if they wanted to act in the play.

_____

4. The teacher explained what they would do next.

_____

5. Alice wants to arrive on time for the party.

_____

6. Please make as little noise as you can.

_____

7. I thought that the train would arrive late as usual.

_____

8. My dog hates it when I have to go away.

_____

9. Come early if it is at all possible.

_____

10. I love to get invited to these meetings.

_____

Present tense

With the exception of the verb *be* (and the modal auxiliary verbs that we will discuss later in this chapter), the present tense of all verbs is derived directly from the base form.

However, the present tense differs significantly from the base form in that all verbs in the present tense must enter into a **subject-verb agreement** relationship with their subjects (something that base-form verbs can never do). This agreement is most easily seen in the unique use of the **third-person singular - *(e)s*** when the subject noun phrase is a third-person singular pronoun (*he, she, it*) or any grammatical structure that can be replaced by a third-person pronoun. Here are some examples of structures that can be replaced by third-person pronouns:

Single noun

She

Anita is going to fly to Atlanta next week.

Singular noun phrase

He/She

Any person traveling in the Southeast must eventually fly through Atlanta.

Gerund phrase

It

Going anywhere in the Southeast requires you to go through Atlanta.

Infinitive phrase

It

To go anywhere in the Southeast means flying through Atlanta.

Noun clause

It

Wherever else you want to fly makes no difference.

Exercise 8.2

Replace incorrect base-form verbs with third-person singular present-tense verbs. Confirm your answers by replacing the subject noun phrase with the appropriate third-person pronoun. If the sentence does not require a third-person singular present-tense verb, write *OK*.

The traffic code in this city ~~permit~~ a left turn on a red light.
The traffic code in this city *permits* a left turn on a red light.
It permits a left turn on a red light.

1. The econ class meet in room 103.

   _____

2. Knowing what to do be not the same as actually doing it.

   _____

3. My son always want to eat the same thing every day.

   _____

4. The train on track 2 only stop at Philadelphia and Washington.

   _____

5. What the article said about the economy make a lot of sense to me.

   _____

6. My wife commute to the city by train every day.

   _____

7. The car that he was asking me about be an old Alfa Romeo.

   _____

8. What happened only prove that I was right all along.

   _____

9. The entire company shut down between Christmas and New Year's.

   _____

10. The couple in the apartment above me always play their TV too loud.

    _____

While it is easy to see that third-person singular verbs enter into subject-verb agreement relationships with their subjects, we should not forget that all other forms (other than third-person singular) of the present tense equally enter into subject-verb agreement even though the verb does not change form. For example, the verbs in the following sentences all enter into a subject-verb relationship with their subjects:

> **I** *refuse* to answer the phone. (first-person singular pronoun subject)
> The **books** on the desk *have* to be returned. (plural noun phrase subject)
> **They** *seem* upset about something. (third-person plural pronoun subject)

The third-person singular -*(e)s* is quite regular in pronunciation (the few irregular forms are discussed below). It follows the same rules for pronunciation as the plural endings on regular nouns.

If the base ends in a sibilant sound, the ending is pronounced as a separate syllable /Ez/ rhyming with *buzz*. Here are examples of the most common sibilant sounds that this rule applies to:

/s/ (sometimes spelled -*ce*) pass-passes; discuss-discusses; race-races; rinse-rinses
/š/ wish-wishes; rush-rushes; blush-blushes; splash-splashes
/č/ (spelled -*ch* or -*tch*) watch-watches; switch-switches; branch-branches
/ǰ/ (spelled -*ge* or -*dge*) rage-rages; page-pages; dodge-dodges
/z/ buzz-buzzes; phase-phases; raise-raises; lose-loses; cruise-cruises

If the verb ends in a voiceless consonant sound other than a sibilant, the ending is pronounced /s/. The voiceless consonants are usually spelled *p, t, k, ck, f, gh* (if pronounced /f/). Here are some examples:

back	backs
cough	coughs
cut	cuts
hop	hops
walk	walks

If the verb ends in a vowel or a voiced consonant sound, the ending is pronounced /z/. For example:

call	calls
come	comes
read	reads
run	runs
row	rows
see	sees
snow	snows

There are a few verbs with irregular third-person singular forms. The most common, of course, is *be*, with *is* as its third-person singular form.

The verb *have* is also irregular in the third-person singular:

have	has

Two other verbs have irregular pronunciations in the third-person singular:

do /duw/ (rhymes with *two*)   does /dəz /(rhymes with *buzz*)
say /sey/ (rhymes with *gay*)   says /sɛz/ (rhymes with *fez*)

Exercise 8.3

All of the verbs in the following list form their third-person singular in the regular way with a single sibilant sound pronounced /s/ or /z/ or with a separate unstressed syllable pronounced /əz/. Write the third-person singular form of the noun in the /s/, /z/, or /əz/ column depending on its pronunciation.

Singular form	/s/	/z/	/əz/
reach			*reaches*
1. race	_____	_____	_____
2. send	_____	_____	_____
3. knock	_____	_____	_____
4. shop	_____	_____	_____
5. eat	_____	_____	_____
6. mention	_____	_____	_____
7. rush	_____	_____	_____
8. approach	_____	_____	_____
9. contain	_____	_____	_____
10. doubt	_____	_____	_____
11. cause	_____	_____	_____
12. clash	_____	_____	_____
13. hedge	_____	_____	_____
14. end	_____	_____	_____
15. freeze	_____	_____	_____

16. show _____   _____   _____

17. fail _____   _____   _____

18. patch _____   _____   _____

19. allow _____   _____   _____

20. sign _____   _____   _____

The spelling of the third-person singular is quite regular, following the same spelling rules as the plural of regular nouns.

If the verb ends in a sibilant sound, the ending is spelled *-es* (unless the present-tense verb already ends in an e, in which case just the *-s* is added). For example:

Base	Third-person singular
box	boxes
buzz	buzzes
catch	catches
clutch	clutches
wish	wishes
budge	budges

If the verb ends in any nonsibilant sound (vowels, voiced and voiceless consonants), then we merely add *-s*, for example:

Base	Third-person singular
snow	snows (ends in vowel)
bring	brings (ends in voiced consonant)
result	results (ends in voiceless consonant)

The only possible confusion is with verbs that end in a final silent *e*. For example:

give	gives
strike	strikes
relate	relates
complete	completes

At first glance, the final silent *e* + *-s* looks just like the *-es* ending that is used after sibilant sounds to indicate that the third-person singular *-es* is pronounced as a separate syllable. For example, compare the spelling of *vote-votes* and *push-pushes*. The spelling of *votes* is a final silent *e* + *-s*. The spelling of *pushes* is a sibilant sound /š/ plus a second, unstressed syllable /əz/.

As was the case with the plural of regular nouns, if the verb ends in a consonant + *y*, change the *y* to *i* and add -*es*. For example:

cry	cries
deny	denies
fly	flies
reply	replies
spy	spies
try	tries

However, if the final *y* is part of the spelling of the vowel sound, then just add an *s*. For example:

buy	buys
enjoy	enjoys
obey	obeys
play	plays

Exercise 8.4

Write the third-person singular form of the base-form verbs in the first column.

Base form	**Third-person singular form**
please	*pleases*

1. admit   _____

2. supply   _____

3. go   _____

4. leave   _____

5. annoy   _____

6. kiss   _____

7. have   _____

8. match   _____

9. identify _____

10. declare _____

11. reduce   _____

12. approach   _____

13. destroy   _____

14. eliminate   _____

15. convince   _____

Past tense

There are two different types of past-tense forms: **regular** and **irregular**. The regular verbs form their past tense by adding -*ed* (or -*d* if the word already ends in *e*) to the base form.

The -*(e)d* ending has three different, but completely predictable pronunciations. If the base ends in either *t* or *d*, the -*ed* is pronounced as a separate syllable /əd/ rhyming with *bud*. Here are some examples:

> **-*ed* pronounced as separate syllable**
> fainted
> goaded
> kidded
> mended
> parted
> raided

If the base ends in a voiceless consonant except for *t*, the -*ed* is pronounced /t/. The final voiceless consonants are usually spelled -*p*, -*(c)k*, -*s*, -*sh*, -*(t)ch*, -*x*, -*f*. and -*gh* (when pronounced /f/). Here are some examples:

> **-*ed* pronounced /t/**
> boxed
> capped
> clutched
> coughed
> kissed
> packed

If the base ends in a vowel or voiced consonant except for *d*, the -*ed* is pronounced /d/. Here are some examples:

> **-*ed* pronounced /d/**
> annoyed
> bored

called
fanned
grabbed
played

Exercise 8.5

Write the past-tense form of the following verbs in the appropriate column depending on the pronunciation.

Base	/t/	/d/	/əd/
part			*parted*
1. define	_____	_____	_____
2. wash	_____	_____	_____
3. shout	_____	_____	_____
4. range	_____	_____	_____
5. own	_____	_____	_____
6. test	_____	_____	_____
7. grant	_____	_____	_____
8. save	_____	_____	_____
9. compare	_____	_____	_____
10. approve	_____	_____	_____
11. pick	_____	_____	_____
12. extend	_____	_____	_____
13. rule	_____	_____	_____
14. tax	_____	_____	_____
15. permit	_____	_____	_____

The spelling of the regular past tense follows the normal spelling rules. If the base ends in a stressed syllable with a short vowel, a single final consonant will usually double, according to the normal spelling rules, for example:

Base	Past tense
hop	hopped
rob	robbed
rot	rotted
sin	sinned

If the base form ends in a consonant + -*y*, the *y* will change to *i* before the -*ed* ending. For example:

Base	Past tense
try	tried
supply	supplied
rely	relied
marry	married
justify	justified

If the base form ends in *y* that is part of a vowel sound spelling, keep the *y* and add -*ed*. For example:

Base	Past tense
annoy	annoyed
enjoy	enjoyed
obey	obeyed
play	played
employ	employed

Exercise 8.6

Write the past-tense form of the following base-form verbs.

Base	Past tense
imply	*implied*

1. show   _____

2. deny   _____

3. drop   _____

4. vary   _____

5. occur   _____

6. hope   _____

7. permit   _____

8. stay   _____

9. apply   _____

10. flow   _____

11. slip   _____

12. delay   _____

13. star   _____

14. enjoy   _____

15. dry   _____

Irregular past tenses

The irregular verbs preserve older ways of forming the past tense. In earlier forms of English, the irregular verbs fell into well-defined patterns. By modern times, however, the historical patterns had collapsed together so that today it is not practical to learn irregular verbs according to their historical patterns.

Infinitive

The infinitive is completely regular (even for the verb *be*). The infinitive consists of *to* followed by the base form of the verb. Here are some examples:

Base form	Infinitive
be	to be
do	to do
go	to go
have	to have
sing	to sing
talk	to talk

Present participle

The present participle is also completely regular. It is formed by adding *-ing* to the base form. Here are some examples:

Base form	Present participle
be	being
do	doing
go	going
have	having
sing	singing
talk	talking

The rules of spelling sometimes cause the present participle to be spelled differently from the base form. Here are the most common changes:

Final silent e

If the base form ends in a final silent *e*, the *e* will drop. For example:

Base form	Present participle
enlarge	enlarging
lose	losing
save	saving
tame	taming
time	timing
use	using

Doubled consonant

If the base ends in a single consonant preceded by a short vowel, the consonant will double. For example:

Base form	Present participle
hit	hitting
hop	hopping
rub	rubbing
run	running
skid	skidding
swim	swimming

Exercise 8.7

Write the present participle form of the following base-form verbs.

Base form	Present participle
range	*ranging*

1. skip   _____
2. cry   _____
3. desire   _____
4. vote   _____
5. phrase   _____
6. reply   _____
7. spot   _____
8. admit   _____
9. shake   _____
10. care   _____

Past participle

There are two types of past participles: **regular** and **irregular**. The regular forms are exactly the same as the past tense; that is, they are the base + -(e)d. The rules for spelling and pronunciation are exactly the same as for the past tense.

Irregular past participles

In older periods of English, most irregular past participles ended in -(e)n. Today, only about one-third of irregular past participles still end in -(e)n. About the only generalization we can make now is that if an irregular verb has an -(e)n ending, then it is very likely a past participle. Here are some examples:

Base	Past participle
choose	chosen
eat	eaten
fall	fallen

fly	flown
freeze	frozen
hide	hidden
rise	risen
see	seen
speak	spoken
swear	sworn
tear	torn
wake	woken

As you can see from the examples, the changes in vowels from base form to past participle form are unpredictable.

Two common past participles have unpredictable pronunciations: *been* rhymes with *sin* in American English, but with *seen* in British English. *Done* rhymes with *sun*, rather than *soon* as might be expected.

Exercise 8.8

Complete each sentence by creating the correct irregular past participle.

> She (*choose*) the wrong seat at the theater.
> She *had chosen* the wrong seat at the theater.

1. We skated on the pond after it (*freeze*).

   _____

2. The sun (*rise*) before we left the house.

   _____

3. Once Senator Blather (*speak*), the listeners applauded him.

   _____

4. The baby (*wake*) by the dog's barking.

   _____

5. The secret code (*hide*) by the general.

   _____

Modal Auxiliary Verbs

There are five modal auxiliary verbs: *can*, *may*, *must*, *shall*, and *will*. These verbs have a unique history. They have no base form, no infinitive form, no present participle form, and no past participle form. The modal auxiliary verbs can only be used in the present and past-tense forms (though as we will see in the next chapter, their present and past forms almost never actually mean present or past time). Here is the complete list of forms:

Present tense	Past tense
can	could
may	might
must	—
shall	should
will	would

Notice that the present-tense form *must* has no corresponding past-tense form. This is the only instance in English where there is a present-tense form with no equivalent past-tense form.

The modal auxiliary verbs are also unique in that they do not add an -*s* in the third-person singular form. For example:

Correct third-person singular	Incorrect third-person singular
He *can* go.	X He *cans* go.
He *may* go.	X He *mays* go.
He *must* go.	X He *musts* go.
He *shall* go.	X He *shalls* go.
He *will* go.	X He *wills* go.

The reason for this odd exception to the normal rule is historical. All of the present-tense modal auxiliary verbs are actually derived from past-tense forms, and so they cannot be used with a present-tense ending.

9

Verb Tenses

This chapter deals with the way the basic verb forms discussed in Chapter 8 are used to construct the tense system of English and what the various tenses mean and how they are used.

Traditional classification by time and category

The conventional terminology for describing the tense system of English breaks down verbs by time (present, past, and future) and by category (simple, perfect, and progressive).

	Simple	Perfect	Progressive
Present time	I walk	I have walked	I am walking
	I run	I have run	I am running
Past time	I walked	I had walked	I was walking
	I ran	I have run	I was running
Future time	I will walk	I will have walked	I will be walking
	I will run	I will have run	I will be running

As you can see from this chart, English allows some quite complex string of verbs. However, there are some basic rules that will help you easily classify any verb construction.

1. The first verb, and only the first verb, determines the time of the entire verb construction. For example, if the first verb is in the present-tense form, then the entire construction is present tense. The future tense requires a modal verb (most commonly *will*) followed by a second verb in the base form.

2. Perfect verbs always contain the helping verb *have* in some form followed by a verb in the past participle form.

3. Progressive verbs always contains the helping verb *be* in some form followed by a verb in the present participle form.

The chart is misleading in one aspect: it looks like the three categories of simple, perfect, and progressive are mutually exclusive (in the same way that the three times—present, past, and future—are indeed mutually exclusive). However, it is not only possible, but common for a verb construction to be both perfect and progressive at the same time. For example, the following sentence is a present perfect progressive.

My family *has been living* in California for some time now.

Here are some examples of the three rules applied to sentences. All verb constructions are in italics.

Example 1:   My mother *has called* me a dozen times today.

According to Rule 1, the first verb *have* is a present tense, so we know that the entire construction is present tense.

The verb *have* is a helping verb following by *called*. Is *called* a past tense or a past participle? We know from Rule 1 that only the first verb can be a present or past-tense form. Since *called* is not the first verb, it cannot be a past-tense form. Therefore, *called* is a past participle. Rule 2 tells us that the helping verb *have* (in any tense form) followed by a verb in the past participle form must constitute a perfect tense.

We can conclude that *has called* must be a present perfect construction.

Example 2:   I *will be working* from home all this week.

Will is a modal followed by *be*, a second verb in the base form; therefore *will be* is future time. According to Rule 1, this means the entire construction is future tense.

Be is a helping verb followed by *working*, a verb in the present participle form, meaning that, according to Rule 3, *be working* is a progressive. Therefore *will be working* is a future progressive. Note that *be* plays two roles at the same time: *will* + *be* = future time; *be* + *working* = progressive category.

Example 3:   The kids *had been watching* cartoons all afternoon.

The first verb in the construction, *had*, is a past tense. Therefore, according to Rule 1, the entire verb construction is a past time.

Had as a helping verb is followed by the past participle form *been*. Therefore, according to Rule 2, *had* + *been* indicates a perfect verb.

Been is a helping verb followed by the present participle verb *watching*. According to Rule 3, *been* + *watching* = progressive. The entire verb construction *had been watching* is thus a past perfect progressive.

Exercise 9.1

Classify by time and category the italicized verb constructions in the following sentences.

> past
> progressive
> I *was sleeping* when you called.

1. We *will have finished* by now. *future perfect*

2. They *have charged* my credit card the full amount. *past perfect*

3. *Will* you *tell* him? *simple future*

4. We *have* already *made* a reservation at the restaurant. *past perfect*

5. We *painted* the deck this summer. *simple past*

6. They *will be worrying* about us. *future progressive*

7. The company *is trying* to find a new supplier. *present progressive*

8. I *will introduce* you to the staff. *simple future*

9. The office *has* not *answered* my e-mail yet. *present perfect*

10. We *have stretched* our resources to the limit. *past present*

11. The cat *has been staring* at the dog all afternoon. *past progressive*

12. I *am rescheduling* our vacation. *present progressive*

13. The lake *will have frozen* by now. *future perfect*

14. We *had been renting* an apartment near my wife's job. *past progressive*

15. The committee *has been working* on that problem for a while. *past progressive*

16. They *will have been rethinking* their decision. *future perfect*

17. She *will have made* a decision by now. *future perfect*

18. I *have* always *admired* your work. *present perfect*

19. They *will have been dating* about a year now. *future perfect*

20. The new report *will have made* a decision a little easier.

We will now turn to an examination of what the various combinations of time and category actually mean and how they are used.

Simple category of tenses

In this section we examine the three simple category verbs: simple present, simple past, and future.

Present tense

One of the most confusing features of the present tense for nonnative speakers is that the present-tense verb form does not actually mean present time. The two most common uses of the present tense are for making timeless factual statements and for describing habitual actions.

The present tense is used to state timeless (that is, not bound or limited by time) objective facts. For example:

> In the Fahrenheit scale, water *boils* at 212 degrees.

This statement is not tied to any moment of time. It is a universal generalization that is valid forever. Here is another example in which the timeless nature of the factual statement is not so obvious:

> My grandmother *lives* in a nursing home.

The speaker's grandmother has not always lived in a nursing home, and at some point in the future, she will not be living in the nursing home. The use of the present tense signals that for the *foreseeable immediate future*, the speaker's grandmother is expected to stay in a nursing home. If the speaker had used the present progressive tense:

> My grandmother *is living* in a nursing home.

it would change the meaning completely. The sentence is now tied to the present moment. The grandmother is in a nursing home now, but there is no implication that she is expected to stay there indefinitely. Here are more examples of timeless factual statements in the present tense:

> Christmas *falls* on Sunday this year.
> The moon and the earth *rotate* around a common center of gravity.
> Cucumbers *make* my skin itch.
> My son *lives* in Sacramento.

The present tense is also used for making timeless generalizations, assertions, and observations. For example:

TIMELESS

> Smoking *causes* cancer.
> Everyone *hates* Mondays.
> Airplanes *get* more crowded every day.
> My kids *watch* too much TV.

The present tense is used to describe habitual or repeated actions. For example, in the following sentence:

> Alice *checks* her e-mail first thing when she gets into the office.

the use of the present tense signals that the sentence is describing Alice's habitual or normal activity—not what she is doing at this present moment of time. The sentence does not mean that Alice is checking her e-mail now. The present-tense sentence would still be valid even if Alice has been on vacation and hasn't looked at her e-mail for a month. Typically we use adverbs of frequency (like *usually*, *always*, *every day*, *normally*) in present-tense sentences used for habitual actions. Here are some more examples of this use of the present tense:

> I *have* oatmeal for breakfast every morning.
> He always *returns* his calls promptly.
> They usually *stay* at the Marriott.
> We *don't* eat out very often.

Exercise 9.2

In the following sentences, the italic present-tense forms are all correctly used. Above the present-tense verb, indicate the specific reason why the timeless present tense is appropriate. Write *timeless* to indicate a timeless factual statement or *habitual* to indicate a habitual action.

timeless
The grammar of Japanese *is* very different from the grammar of English.

1. I usually *eat* lunch in my office.   habitual

2. Obama's speeches *focus* on health-care issues.   timeless

3. The Nile *is* one of the few major rivers in the world flowing south to north.   timeless

4. We usually *lock* our doors when we go to bed.   habitual

5. Low interest rates *tempt* many consumers to take on too much debt.   timeless

6.   Sometimes we *go* for long walks on the weekend. *habitual*

7.   In America, rental apartments *come* with all the major kitchen appliances. *timeless*

8.   All too often, debates about global warming totally *ignore* all the scientific evidence. *timeless*

9.   They rarely *watch* TV. *habitual*

10. Mexican food *has* too much fat and salt for me. ~~time~~ *habitual*

11. Paying cash *beats* using your credit card all the time. *timeless*

12. That song certainly *sounds* familiar. *timeless*

13. Most Asian restaurants *have* take-out menus. *timeless*

14. I *sneeze* whenever I step into bright sunshine. *habitual*

15. Many Americans *spend* part of the winter in the Southwest or Florida. *habitual*

Past tense

The past tense is used to refer to events that were completed in the past. The key to using the past tense is to remember that the use of the past tense emphasizes that the events are over and done with *before* the present moment of time. Often the use of the past tense implies that what was true then is not true now. For example, consider the following sentence:

When I was a little boy, I *hated* girls.

The use of the past tense tells us that the speaker's childhood attitude toward girls is confined to the past.

The past tense can be used to refer to a single moment in past time. For example:

I *graduated* in 2004.

The past tense can refer to events that occurred repeatedly in the past. For example:

It *rained* every day during my vacation in Spain.

The implication is that the vacation was over with at some time prior to the present.

The past tense can refer to a span of time in the past. For example:

I *worked* for that company for six years.

The use of the past tense also tells us that the speaker no longer works for that company today. If the speaker were still working for that company today, the speaker would have used the present perfect tense:

> I *have worked* for that company for six years.

Future tense

In traditional grammar, the future tense consists of the helping verb *will* followed by a verb in the base form. For example:

> I *will see* them at the meeting this afternoon.
> It *will rain* all next week.
> The company *will hire* a new personnel director later this year.

The future tense is often combined with a perfect or progressive. For example:

Perfect
My sister *will have* already *left* by now.
They *will have gotten* up early this morning.
The plane *will have landed* by now.

Progressive
They *will be clearing* customs by now.
My family *will be staying* in London over Christmas.
I *will be watching* the game on TV this afternoon.

Perfect tenses

The perfect tenses all consist of some form of the helping verb *have* followed by a verb in the past participle form. The **present perfect** uses the present tense (*has* or *have*). The **past perfect** uses the past-tense form *had*. The **future perfect** uses the future-tense form *will have*.

What's so perfect about the perfect tenses? Nothing. The term *perfect* comes from a Latin phrase *per factus*, which means "completely done." The key idea of the perfect tenses is that they allow us to talk about actions or events that span a period of time up to some final limiting time or other limiting event. The action or event is finished ("perfected") at or before that limiting time or event.

The **present perfect** is used for past-time actions or events whose action or consequences continue up to the present moment of time. The **past perfect** is for past-time actions or events that were finished before some more recent time or event. The **future perfect** is for future time actions or events that will be finished before some later time or event.

Present perfect

The present perfect is formed by the present tense of *have* (*has* or *have*) followed by a verb in the past participle form. Here are some examples:

> I *have known* him all my life.
> We *have* always *shopped* at Ralph's.
> He *has* just *returned.*
> That faucet *has been* leaking for weeks.
> Thanks, but *I have* already had *dinner.*

To understand the meaning of the present perfect, we must contrast it with the meaning of the simple past tense. Compare the following examples:

Past tense:	I *lived* in Tampa for five years. (I don't live there anymore.)
Present perfect:	I *have lived* in Tampa for five years. (I still live there today.)

The use of the past tense in the first example signals that the speaker no longer lives in Tampa. The action was completed at some point in the past that no longer touches the present. The use of the present perfect in the second example tells us just the opposite—that the speaker is still living in Tampa today.

In general, the past tense emphasizes that the actions or events described through the use of the past tense are over with; they do not directly impact the present. The present perfect is just the opposite: it emphasizes the ongoing connection between the past and the present. In the second example sentence above, the speaker has lived in Tampa continuously for the last five years, right up to the present moment. Here are some more examples of the present perfect for events that have spanned an unbroken period of time up to the present moment:

> She *has studied* English since she came to the university.
> They *have shown* that same cartoon for the last three weeks.
> As long as I can remember, I *have* always *hated* broccoli.
> The company *has* never *missed* paying a dividend in its history.

A less obvious use of the present perfect is for single events, even unique ones, that continue to directly impact the present. For example, compare the use of the past tense and the present perfect in the following sentence:

> past
> tense   present perfect
>
> Last year, John *had* an accident that *has* totally *changed* his life.

The accident was a one-time only event in the past. The accident is over and done with, so it was reported in the past tense. However, the consequences of the accident are not tied to that past moment of time; they have continued on to the present. Therefore, the present perfect is appropriate to describe the ongoing nature of the consequences.

Exercise 9.3

Select either the past tense or the present perfect form in the following sentences.

> The children *behaved/have behaved* well since they stopped watching so much TV.

1. Mr. Brown *left/has left* last week for a business trip.

2. Sam *lost/has lost* his car keys and can't get home.

3. The choir *sang/has sung* that song a hundred times.

4. The garage *had/has had* my car for a week now, and it still isn't fixed.

5. We *moved/have moved* there ten years ago.

6. We *lived/have lived* there ever since.

7. We *lost/have lost* the power about noon.

8. Let's go to the arrival section—the plane *landed/has landed* a few minutes ago.

9. I *went/have gone* to Duke University a few years ago.

10. The city *permitted/has permitted* parking on that street for years.

11. After the interview, the personnel director *showed/has shown* me the cafeteria.

12. I *complained/have complained* about that problem a dozen times.

13. Last winter, my grandmother *fell/has fallen* and broke her hip.

14. Since the train strike began, I *drove/have driven* to work every day.

15. I *drove/have driven* my wife's car to work this morning.

Past perfect

The past perfect consists of *had* followed by a verb in the past participle form. The past perfect is used to emphasize that a past-time action or event was completed prior to some more recent (but still past) action or event. Here are some examples:

past perfect   past

They *had* already *graduated* before they *got* married.

past
perfect   past

I *had left* by the time I *got* their message.

past
perfect   past

I *had been* an intern with them for a year before they *made* me a permanent offer.

past
perfect   past

They *had had* a big fight before they *broke* up.

In all the examples that we have looked at so far, the verb in the past perfect form has preceded the verb in the past-tense form. This sequence seems perfectly logical since the past perfect event has to occur before the second past-tense event occurs.

Logical it may be, but that is not the way English works. In fact, the two events can be presented in either order. Here is an example of the same sentence in both orders:

past
perfect   past

He *had taken* out a life insurance policy before he *died*.

past
past perfect

Before he *died*, he *had taken* out a life insurance policy.

The fact that we cannot count on the past perfect event being presented before the more recent past time event makes using the past perfect a great deal more difficult.

Exercise 9.4

In the following sentences, the verbs in italics are all in the base form. The verbs are used to describe two past-time events, one of which precedes the other. Change the verb whose action takes place first into the past perfect form. Change the verb whose action takes place later into the past-tense form. Remember that the two events can occur in either order in the sentence.

The audience *took* their seats before the curtain *go* up.
The audience *had taken* their seats before the curtain *went* up.

1. Apparently, the driver *suffer* a heart attack before the automobile accident *happen*.

   _____

2. After the play *receive* a bad review, the playwright *decide* to make some revisions.

   _____

3. I *make* plans before they *call* with their invitation.

   _____

4. Watson *write* up each case after Sherlock Holmes *solve* the crime.

   _____

5. Before we *go* two miles, my bicycle *get* a flat tire.

   _____

6. After the snow *stop*, we immediately *shovel* off the driveway.

   _____

7. As soon as the rain *let* up, we *dash* out of the building.

   _____

8. After the plane *experience* a sudden drop in cabin pressure, the pilot *request* an unscheduled landing.

   _____

9. Apparently, Shakespeare *write* his first play before he ever *go* to London.

   _____

10. After I *read* the report, I *begin* to understand what the problems were.

    _____

11. I *continue* doing that for some time until I finally *get* some new instructions.

    _____

12. We *vacation* in Hawaii every summer for years until we *have* children.

    _____

13. I *wait* until the office *close* that night at five.

_____

14. We *be* able to start the game after the ground crew *remove* the cover from the field.

_____

15. Before we *settle* on my current job, they *offer* me several other assignments.

_____

Future perfect

The future perfect (FP) consists of *will have* (the future tense of *have*) followed by a verb in the past participle form. The action or event described by the future perfect tense must be completed prior to some other future time or event. The future time can be expressed as an adverb of time. For example:

> FP
> I *will have finished* everything by noon.

>   FP
> By noon, we *will have* already *finished*.

The future time can also be expressed in another clause, which can be in the present tense (PT) or present perfect (Pres P). For example:

>   PT   FP
> By the time you *get* this message, I *will* already *have left*.

>   Pres P   FP
> By the time you *have gotten* this message, I *will* already *have left*.

The two clauses can occur in either order:

>   FP   Pres P
> He *will have packed* all the boxes before she *has printed* all the labels.

>   Pres P   FP
> Before she *has printed* all the labels, he *will have packed* all the boxes.

Exercise 9.5

Replace one of the italicized base-form verbs with the future perfect. Replace the other italicized base-form verb with either the present or present perfect, as appropriate.

The train *leave* the by the time we *get* to the station.
The train *will have left* the station by the time we *have gotten* there.

1. The cement *harden* before we *get* it all poured.

   The cement will have hardened before we get it all poured.

2. Hopefully, the snow plows *clear* the roads before we *leave* the freeway.

   Hopefully, the snow plows will have cleared the roads before we leave the freeway.

3. We *starve* to death before the waiter *bring* us our order.

   We will have starved to death before the waiter brings us our order.

4. Jane *walk* back home before the bus *arrive*.

   _____

5. The audience *forget* the details by the time the speaker *finish*.

   _____

6. They *lock* the gates after they *clear* the parking lot.

   _____

7. The crowd *wonder* what *cause* the delay in getting started.

   _____

8. He *fill* his gas tank as soon as he *locate* the nearest filling station.

   _____

9. The whole group *complete* the test by the time the class *finish*.

   _____

10. The landlord *furnish* the apartment by the time we *move* in.

    _____

Progressive tenses

The progressive tenses are all formed by the helping verb *be* in some form immediately followed by a verb in the present participle form. The **present progressive** uses a present-tense form of *be*, the **past progressive** uses a past-tense form of *be*, and the **future progressive** uses the future tense of *be*. The progressive tenses are all used to describe an action *in progress* (hence the name *progressive*) at some present, past, or future moment of time. The key to using the progressive tenses is that they are always tied to some action that takes place at a specific point or moment in time. Thus the progressive tenses can never be used to make broad timeless generalizations.

Present progressive

The present progressive consists of the present tense of the verb *be* (*am*, *are*, or *is*), followed by a verb in the present participle form. The most common use of the present progressive is to talk about what is happening at the present time. For example, if someone were to go the window and say, "It's *raining*," we know without being told that the speaker is talking about what is happening right now.

The progressive is not limited to just the present moment. It often refers to action that goes beyond just the present moment. For example:

> We *are living* in New Jersey now.
> She's *working* on her degree at NYU.
> The doctor *is seeing* another patient now.

The present progressive often conveys a sense of temporariness. For example, compare the following pair of sentences, the first in the present tense, the second in the present progressive:

> **Present tense:**   They *fly* first-class.
> **Present progressive:** They *are flying* first-class.

In the first sentence, the use of the present tense signals that it is their normal custom to fly first-class. It does not mean that they are flying first-class at the moment. The use of the present progressive in the second sentence means that they are flying first-class on the particular flight we are talking about at the moment. We do not know whether they regularly fly first-class or not.

Not all verbs can be used in the present progressive (or any other progressive tense, for that matter). Of particular importance is a group of verbs called **stative** verbs. We think of a verb as a word used to express action. This is certainly true of most verbs. However, this is not true of stative verbs. Stative verbs do not express action. Instead, stative verbs describe an ongoing condition or "state," which is where the name *stative* derives from. To see the difference, compare the following two sentences:

> **Action verb:**   John *drives* a car.
> **Stative verb:**   John *owns* a car.

The verb *drive* expresses an action; the verb *own* expresses a state or condition.

The practical difference between action and stative verbs is that we can use action verbs in all the progressive tenses, but we cannot use stative verbs in any of the progressive tenses. Here is an example in the present tense:

Action verb:	John *is driving* a car.
Stative verb:	**X** John *is owning* a car.

The meanings of stative verbs make them incompatible with the progressive tenses, since the progressive tenses always describe action that is in progress at some moment of present, past, or future time. Since stative verbs express ongoing, unchanging states, they cannot be used in the time-limited, momentary sense of the progressive.

One of the most common errors of intermediate-level ESL learners is using stative verbs in the progressive tenses.

Here are some more examples of stative verbs incorrectly used in the present progressive:

X I *am hating* spinach.
X They *are doubting* the truth of what you say.
X He *was having* a laptop at the time.
X We *were liking* your proposal.
X She *will be loving* that.
X The company *will be owning* a new office by then.

Stative verbs tend to fall into distinct categories based on meaning:

Emotions:	appreciate, desire, dislike, doubt, feel, hate, like, love, need, prefer, want, wish
Measurement:	consist of, contain, cost, entail, equal, have, measure, weigh
Cognition:	believe, doubt, know, mean, think, understand
Appearance:	appear, be, look, resemble, seem, sound
Sense perception:	feel, hear, see, seem, smell, taste
Ownership:	belong, have, own, possess

Note that some verbs appear twice because they can be used with different meanings.

Exercise 9.6

Examine each verb in italics in the following sentences. If the verb is not a stative verb, rewrite the verb as a present progressive. If the verb is a stative verb, rewrite the verb in the present tense and write *stative* above the verb.

stative
The idea *seem* good to us.
The idea *seems* good to us.

The company *hire* several new accountants. (not stative)
The company *is hiring* several new accountants.

1. The plane *encounter* some resistance.

_____

2. The security guard *unlock* the door.

_____

3. The boss *doubt* that we can finish the project in time.

_____

4. My friend *be* park his car.

_____

5. The entire project *cost* more than a million dollars.

_____

6. You *deserve* the new promotion.

_____

7. We *visit* New York for the first time.

_____

8. The consultant *alter* the size of the project.

_____

9. We *want* to get you input on the proposal as soon as possible.

_____

10. He *undergo* treatment at a hospital in India.

_____

11. Now they *doubt* the wisdom of going ahead so quickly.

_____

12. The design *consist* of three main elements.

_____

13. The clerk *confirm* your reservation.

_____

14. The newlyweds *struggle* to adjust to their new lives together.

_____

15. The briefcase *belong* to that gentleman over there.

_____

16. Captain Brown *command* this aircraft.

_____

17. The entire staff *cooperate* with the study.

_____

18. Her new hairstyle *suit* her very well.

_____

19. The minister *convey* his respects to the convention.

_____

20. We *wait* for the meeting to start.

_____

Past progressive

The past progressive consists of the past tense of the verb *be* (*was* or *were*), followed by a verb in the present participle form. The past progressive is always tied to past time. It can be a specific moment or period in time. For example:

> By 9 A.M. I *was working* at my desk.
> At noon we *were fixing* lunch.
> During the afternoon, we *were having* drinks on the terrace.

Or the past time can be defined by some other event as expressed in a past-tense subordinate clause. For example:

past
progressive   past tense

We *were watching* TV when the lights *went* out.

past   past
tense   progressive

When you *called*, we *were working* in the garden.

past   past
progressive   tense

They *were driving* to Richland when they *had* the accident.

The past progressive can also be used for a past-time action or event that spans a defined period of past time. For example:

All last week, my boss *was meeting* with the sales reps.
From noon on, I *was raking* leaves in the backyard.
All the time he *was talking*, I *was looking* at my watch.

Exercise 9.7

Examine each verb in italics in the following sentences. Rewrite the verb as a past progressive.

At midnight, I *sleep.*
At midnight, I *was sleeping.*

1. The chef *bake* the pie when the guests came.

_____

2. As she *walk* down the street yesterday, she noticed the stray dog.

_____

3. All last month, the teacher *grade* tests.

_____

4. At the time of the hurricane, they *live* on the west side of the city.

_____

5. The police *control* the rioters when the convention began.

_____

Future progressive

The future progressive (F Prog) consists of the future tense (FT) of the verb *be* (*will be*) followed by a verb in the present participle form. The present progressive describes some activity that will be carried out at some future time. The future time can be a specific moment or period in time. For example:

> At noon, I *will be flying* to Houston.
> Next week, the kids *will be staying* with their grandparents.
> During the school year, she *will be living* in a dorm.

Or the future time can be defined as taking place during some future-time event that is expressed in a present-tense subordinate clause. For example:

>   PT   F Prog
> While you *are* in California, I *will be working* on my thesis.

>   F Prog   PT
> He *will be arranging* more interviews while you *enter* the data.

>   F Prog   FT
> I *will be working* from home when they *repaint* my office.

10

Simple Verb Complements

In this chapter we cover basic verb complement terminology and examine simple complements—verbs with no complements (a **zero complement**) or only a single complement.

Overview of basic verb complement terminology.

Verb complements are conventionally classified according to the following hierarchy:

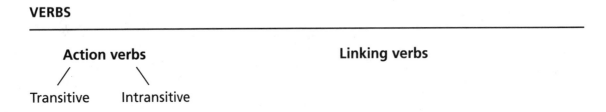

The distinction between action verb and linking verb is determined solely by the nature of the subject-verb-complement relationship. If the complement describes the subject, the verb is a linking verb. If the complement does not describe the subject, then it is an action verb. By far the most common linking verb is *be*. Here are two examples of *be* used as a linking verb:

> Mary's new car *is* a Prius.
> Mary's new car *is* red.

The term **linking** verb refers to the fact that linking verbs connect (link) the words following the linking verb back to the subject. In the two examples above, *is* links the noun phrase *a Prius* and the adjective *red* back to the subject (*Mary's car*). Clearly, the subject, *Mary's car*, is performing no action in these two examples. The subject in linking-verb sentences is the topic of the sentence rather than the doer of any action.

In this book, we will use the term **complement** to refer collectively to any and all grammatical structures that are required by a verb to make a grammatically complete sentence. For example, consider the complement in the following sentence:

Thomas *put* his car in the garage.

This complement contains two components: an object noun phrase (*his car*) and an adverb expression of place (*in the garage*). Both of these components are required by the verb *put* to make a grammatical sentence. If we delete either component, the sentence becomes ungrammatical:

X Thomas *put* his car.
X Thomas *put* in the garage.

In other words, when we use the verb *put*, we have to put something somewhere. Consequently, we would describe the complement of *put* as noun phrase + adverb of place.

Linking verbs have a special terminology for their complements. Consider again our previous examples:

Mary's new car *is* a Prius.
Mary's new car *is* red.

The noun phrase *a Prius* is called a **predicate nominative**, and the adjective *red* is called a **predicate adjective**. Note that the term **object** is not used for noun phrases that are the complements of linking verbs.

Since almost all verbs are classified as action verbs, it is hard to find any very helpful definition of action verbs except negatively: action verbs are those verbs that are not linking verbs. While many action verbs do indeed express action as their name suggests, some so-called action verbs express no action at all. For example, compare the following pair of sentences:

Jackson *bought* a new car.
Jackson *has* a new car.

In the first sentence, Jackson is clearly the performer or doer of an action: he has engaged in the action of buying a new car. In the second sentence, however, Jackson is not engaged in any action at all. He is not doing anything. The sentence is more a statement about Jackson rather than an expression of what Jackson is doing. Nevertheless, both verbs are classified as "action" verbs since they are not linking verbs.

The second distinction in verb terminology is between **transitive** and **intransitive** verbs. (This terminology is normally applied only to action verbs. We do not use these terms in reference to linking verbs.) The term *transitive* is derived from a Latin word meaning "to go across." A transitive verb "goes across" to an object. In other words, a transitive verb controls or "takes" an object. An intransitive verb does not control or take an object. For example, compare the following sentences:

Transitive: The cat *killed* the birds.
Intransitive: The birds *died*.

The verb *kill* is a transitive verb that requires an object. That is, when we kill, we have to kill *something*. Leaving off the object would make the transitive verb *kill* ungrammatical (in the way that the verb is normally used):

X The cat *killed*.

The verb *die* is an intransitive verb that does not take an object. As this pair of examples shows, transitive verbs typically describe what a subject is doing to an object (*killing* it in the case of our example), while intransitive verbs typically describe what is happening to the subject (*dying* in the case of our example).

When you look up a verb in the dictionary, you will notice a little *vi* or *vt* right after the pronunciation guide and the origin of the word but before the definitions begin. *vi* means that the verb is intransitive, and *vt* means that the verb is transitive. It is striking that most verbs can be used both transitively and intransitively. If a verb is used both ways, the dictionary will give all the definitions for the most common use first (either *vi* or *vt*) and then give a second set of definitions associated with the other use.

This chapter and the next one are organized according to the number of complements that verbs require. In this chapter we will address the verbs that take no complements at all (**zero-complement verbs**) and verbs that take only a single complement. The following chapter will address verbs that take multiple complements.

Zero-complement verbs

Verbs that take no complement are called **intransitive** verbs. (All zero-complement verbs are action verbs. Linking verbs are always used with a single complement.) Here are some examples of sentences with intransitive verbs:

The old cow *died*.
My knee *hurts*.
The kids *are sleeping*.

Most of the time we use intransitive verbs with various kinds of optional adverb expressions. For example:

The old cow finally *died* during the night.
My knee *hurts* whenever it rains.
The kids *are sleeping* at my cousin's house tonight.

It is important to realize that these adverb expressions are not part of the complement. In other words, these verbs do not require these adverb expressions for the sentences to be grammatical.

Exercise 10.1

The verbs in the following sentences are in italics. If the verb is intransitive, write *vi* above it. If it is transitive, write *vt* above it. If the verb is intransitive, confirm your answer by deleting all the material that follows the verb.

vi

My nephew just *smiled* ~~when I asked him what he was doing~~.

1. The window *broke* with a loud crash.

2. The kids *broke* the window playing baseball.

3. The cheese sandwich finally *melted* in the toaster oven.

4. The leaky faucet *dripped* all night long.

5. The candidates for city council *spoke* at the meeting.

6. The football team *was practicing* on the athletic field.

7. My ears *rang* for several days after the accident.

8. The head of our company *will retire* at the end of next year.

9. The thin cardboard *tore* when I tried to bend it.

10. Only votes cast before the deadline *counted* in the election.

11. The committee *counted* the ballots.

12. Their application *succeeded* despite all of our misgivings.

13. Real wages *have declined* over the past decade.

14. The kids *laughed* uproariously at the cartoons.

15. The spilled milk *spread* slowly across the floor.

Single-complement verbs

Both action verbs and linking verbs can take a single complement. We will address the two types of verbs separately.

Action verbs

The complement of a transitive action verb is called an **object** or **direct object**. The word *object* normally implies direct object. (There is also an **indirect object**, which we will encounter in the next chapter.) An action verb followed by a single object is by far the most common of all types of complements. All objects are either noun phrases or pronouns. (Compound nouns and pronouns are counted as single complements.) Here are some examples, first with noun phrases, and then with pronouns. Verbs are in italics and objects are in bold.

> **Noun phrase objects**
> John *saw* **Mary**.
> Theo *washed* **his new car**.
> Lois *cashed* **her check**.
> The bright lights *frightened* **the birds**
> We *met* **Susan and her friends**.

> **Pronoun objects**
> I *watched* **them**.
> Ralph *cut* **himself**.
> Someone *called* **you**.
> The children *saw* **us**.

The noun phrase can be any structure that can be replaced by a third-person pronoun: **noun clauses**, **infinitives**, or **gerunds**. Here are some examples:

> **Noun clauses**
>   it
> I loved <u>what they proposed in the new budget</u>
>
>   it
> I loved <u>that they accepted most of our ideas</u>.
>
>   it
> I loved <u>where we went out for dinner</u>.

> **Infinitives**
>   it
> I love <u>to go for long walks in the fall</u>.

             it
I needed <u>to hear what they had to say</u>.

        it
I like <u>to get home early on Fridays</u>.

Gerunds

       it
I love <u>going for long walks in the fall</u>.

       it
I liked <u>hearing what they had to say</u>.

       it
I like <u>getting home early on Fridays</u>.

    The nice thing about using a third-person pronoun to identify objects is that you don't even need to know the technical name for a complex object structure. All you need to know is that it can be replaced by a third-person pronoun.

Exercise 10.2

Underline the objects that follow the italicized transitive verbs. Confirm your answer by showing that a third-person pronoun can substitute for the object.

             it
  I *noticed* <u>that you got a new computer</u>.

1. They *heard* what you said.

2. The lawyers *confirmed* that we needed to consult a patent attorney.

3. They *emphasized* always being on time to meetings.

4. I *anticipated* having to get a taxi to get to work on time.

5. We finally *chose* to look for a new apartment closer to our jobs.

6. The contract *specified* that all the work had to be finished by June 30.

7. We *resumed* what we had been doing before we had to stop.

8. The audience *appreciated* how well they had performed.

9. We *looked into* taking a vacation in Mexico this summer.

10. You *need* to be more careful in the future.

11. The witness *swore* that the defendant had not been at the scene.

12. I couldn't *resist* making fun of such a ridiculous idea.

13. Nobody could *understand* his excited shouting.

14. Finally we *recovered* what we had initially invested in the company.

15. Please *forgive* what I said earlier.

Separable and inseparable phrasal (two-word) verbs. Phrasal (two-word) verbs are an idiomatic combination of verbs and prepositions or adverbs whose meanings are often wildly unpredictable. Phrasal verbs also pose a major problem for nonnative speakers because they have some very unusual grammatical characteristics. In this section we will only examine what are called **separable** and **inseparable** phrasal verbs.

A **separable** phrasal verb is a compound verb consisting of a verb stem and an adverb. (The terminology for phrasal verbs is unsettled. Many books use the term **particle** rather than adverb or preposition. The differences in terminology are not very important since there is no real difference in the description of how phrasal verbs work.) Here are three examples that all involve the verb *call*:

> The CEO *called off* the meetings. (*call off* = cancel or postpone)
> The CEO *called up* the chairman. (*call up* = telephone)
> The CEO *called back* the reporter. (*call back* = return someone's telephone call)

What is so unusual about the grammar of separable phrasal verbs is that the adverb part of the verb compound can be moved to a position following the direct object, breaking the verb compound apart:

> The CEO *called off* the meetings. ⇒ The CEO *called* the meeting *off*.
> The CEO *called up* the chair. ⇒ The CEO *called* the chair *up*.
> The CEO *called back* the reporter. ⇒ The CEO *called* the reporter *back*.

Note that the adverb part of the compound is moved to a position immediately after the direct object, but before any other adverbs:

> The CEO *called off* the meetings <u>yesterday</u> ⇒ The CEO *called* the meetings *off* <u>yesterday</u>.

Sometimes learners make the assumption that the adverb moves to the end of the sentence. This is not correct:

> The CEO *called off* the meetings <u>yesterday</u> ⇒ **X** The CEO *called* the meetings <u>yesterday</u> *off*.

Even more remarkable, if the direct object is a pronoun, then moving the adverb is obligatory. The sentence is ungrammatical if the adverb does not move.

> **X** The CEO *called off* them ⇒ The CEO *called* them *off.*
> **X** The CEO *called up* him/her ⇒ The CEO *called* him/her *up.*
> **X** The CEO *called back* him/her ⇒ The CEO *called* him/her *back.*

Exercise 10.3

Underline the object noun phrase that follows the italicized separable phrasal verb in each sentence and write the appropriate object pronoun substitute above it. Then rewrite the sentence to replace the object noun phrase with the pronoun. Remember to move the adverb portion of the verb compound to a position immediately after the object pronoun.

> them
> We *took down* the Christmas decorations this morning.
> We *took* **them** *down* this morning.

1. I *dropped off* my parents at the station.

_____

2. Jordan *wrote down* the message on a slip of paper.

_____

3. He *looked over* the report carefully.

_____

4. The waiter *brought in* the next course promptly.

_____

5. Susan *read back* the memo to me.

_____

6. I *looked up* the answer on Google.

_____

7. George *thought through* all the complexities very carefully.

_____

8. We *talked over* all the major points before the meeting.

_____

9. Finally, I *got back* my stolen bicycle from the police station.

---

10. She *poured out* her troubles to her closest friend.

---

11. We *picked up* the kids' toys quickly.

---

12. Albert *turned down* the company's generous offer regretfully.

---

13. I *put together* all the loose ends in a neat package.

---

14. Our company *is taking over* their company in a friendly merger.

---

15. The lawyer *summed up* his case simply and forcefully.

We now turn to the second set of transitive phrasal verbs, **inseparable** phrasal verbs. These are verb compounds consisting of a verb stem plus a preposition. (The second element in the compound is called a preposition because, unlike the adverbs in separable compounds, prepositions cannot move.) Here are some examples of inseparable phrasal verbs:

> She *knows about* the meeting.
> I *bumped into* an old friend today.
> John *talked to* Mary.

The second element in the phrasal verb cannot move, even if we replace the object with a pronoun:

> She *knows about* **the meeting**
> She *knows about* **it.** ⇒ **X** She knows **it** *about.*

> I *bumped into* **an old friend** today.
> I *bumped into* **him/her** today. ⇒ **X** I *bumped* **him/her** *into* today.

> John *talked to* **Mary.**
> John *talked to* **her.** ⇒ **X** John *talked* **her** *to.*

The obvious problem for English learners is how to tell which phrasal verbs are separable and which are inseparable. There actually is a way to predict (to a degree at least) which compounds are separable and which are inseparable, but it isn't simple. It turns out that the lists of adverbs and prepositions used in separable and inseparable verb compounds are nearly mutually exclusive. That is, if you know what you are looking for, you can make a good guess based on the second element in the compound whether the compound is separable or inseparable. Here is a list of the most common adverbs and prepositions used in phrasal verbs:

Separable adverbs	Inseparable prepositions
apart	about
away	after
back	against
down	at
in	by
off	for
on	from
out	into
over	of
through	*on*
up	*through*
to	
with	

What is remarkable about the list is that there are only two words, *on* and *through*, that appear on both lists. With the exception of these two words, you can predict with a fair degree of accuracy whether a phrasal verb is separable or inseparable by looking at the second element in the compound. It is probably worth your time to memorize the list of separable adverbs. (You do not need to memorize both lists. The list of separable adverbs is longer, and separable adverbs are much less common than inseparable prepositions.) Sometimes this rule of thumb ("rule of thumb" is an English idiom meaning an imperfect, but nevertheless helpful guide) will be wrong, but it will be right far more often than guessing will be.

Exercise 10.4

Label the italicized phrasal verbs as *Sep* (for separable) or *Insep* (for inseparable). If the verb is separable, confirm your answer by moving the adverb to a position immediately after the object.

> Sep
> They *talked over* their proposal this morning.
> They *talked* their proposal *over* this morning.

1. Please *look after* my plants.

_____

2. James always *played down* the size of the problem.

_____

3. He *consulted with* everybody involved in the project.

_____

4. They *split up* the original team.

_____

5. He *hinted at* the possibility of a new job.

_____

6. They *guarded against* getting over confident.

_____

7. I *pointed out* all the problems.

_____

8. A policeman *pulled over* the red convertible.

_____

9. I *stand by* my original statement.

_____

10. The terrorists *blew up* a gasoline truck.

_____

11. She *learns from* her mistakes.

_____

12. He was trying to *paper over* his involvement.

_____

13. Let's *talk about* our problems.

_____

14. We need to *pare down* our expenses.

_____

15. They *prayed for* a swift recovery.

_____

16. We *set up* the display tables quickly.

_____

17. He hardly *blinked at* his outrageous offer.

_____

18. We *turned in* our badges at the desk.

_____

19. Did you *hear about* the new office?

_____

20. I kept *playing over* the entire conversation.

_____

Linking verbs

In linking verbs, the subject is not an actor performing any action, and the complement is not the recipient of any action. Rather, the complement is used to describe some attribute or characteristic of the subject. The verb is called a **linking verb** because it links the complement back to the subject.

Linking verbs can take three different types of complements: (1) noun phrases (including pronouns), (2) predicate adjectives, and (3) adverbs of place and time.

If the complement of the linking verb (Link) is a noun phrase, it is called a **predicate nominative** (Pred Nom) rather than an object. Here is an example:

subject   Link   Pred Nom
Thomas is a football player.

Note that the subject *Thomas* and the predicate nominative *a football player* are one and the same person:

Thomas = a football player.

This identity of subject and predicate nominative is the key to recognizing a linking verb when the complement is a noun phrase. Here are some more examples:

> Sally *became* a professional tennis player.
> Sally = a professional tennis player.

> Cinderella's coach *turned into* a pumpkin.
> Cinderella's coach = a pumpkin

> I *felt like* a complete idiot.
> I = complete idiot.

In an action verb sentence, of course, the subject and the object do not refer to the same person or thing. For example:

> Sally *met* a professional tennis player.
> Sally ≠ a professional tennis player

> Cinderella's coach *impressed* her sisters.
> Cinderella's coach ≠ her sisters.

> I *talked to* a complete idiot.
> I ≠ a complete idiot.

Exercise 10.5

Label the italicized verbs as *Act* for action verb or *Link* for linking verbs. Confirm your answer by using equal (=) and unequal signs (≠) to indicate whether the subject and the complement refer to each other.

> Link
> The keys *looked like* the ones I lost yesterday.
> The keys = the ones I lost yesterday.

1. The keys *unlock* the storage cabinet.

_____

2. The plan *seemed* a good idea at the time.

_____

3. The board *approved* the plan.

---

4. Richard *became* a highly successful salesman.

---

5. Her new car *is* a Ford.

---

6. Unfortunately, his new mansion *looks like* a cheap motel.

---

7. Louise greatly *resembles* her sister Thelma.

---

8. Louise *called up* her sister Thelma.

---

9. The new nominee really *seems like* a good choice for the job.

---

10. The housing market *has turned into* a complete disaster.

---

11. My first choice *would be* an apartment near where I work.

---

12. Albuquerque *resembles* a typical city in the 1960s.

---

13. The actor *seemed* a man in his midfifties.

---

14. My brother *ended up* a lawyer in a big law firm.

---

15. What you can see *is* all that we have left.

The second complement type that linking verbs can take is a predicate adjective. Here are some examples with the linking verb in italics and the predicate adjective in bold.

> Senator Blather's speech *was* pretty **dull**.
> The soup *is* **cold**.
> John *got* very **angry**.
> The weather *turned* **dark** and **stormy**.
> Terry's chili *is* too **spicy** for me.
> *Stay* **warm**!
> Let's *get* **ready**.

Exercise 10.6

Label the italicized verbs as *Act* for action verb or *Link* for linking verbs. Underline the complements of the linking verbs and label them *Pred Adj* (for predicate adjective) or *Pred Nom* (for predicate nominative) as appropriate.

>   Pred
>   Link Adj
> Our cat *goes* <u>crazy</u> during thunderstorms.

1. On hearing the bad news, Agnes *turned* deathly pale.

2. The note *sounded* flat to me.

3. George *seemed* terribly upset about something.

4. The situation *could* easily *turn* ugly.

5. You *look* ready to go.

6. Everyone *noticed* his strange behavior at the party last night.

7. After his long illness, Jason *looked like* a ghost of his former self.

8. Over the years they *have grown* closer to each other.

9. The day *was getting* terribly warm.

10. Please *remain* calm.

11. The wine *has gone* bad.

12. I *felt* much better after seeing the doctor.

13. They *looked* ready to go.

14. Our simple plan *has turned into* a huge project.

15. All the indicators *appeared* positive.

Many hundreds of true adjectives are derived from the present participle form of verbs. For example, here is the true adjective *amusing* used both as a noun modifier and as a predicate adjective:

Noun modifier:	He told an *amusing* story.
Predicate adjective:	His story was *amusing*.

It is sometimes very difficult to tell predicate adjectives apart from the same word used as part of the progressive tense. Here is an example:

Predicate adjective:	The story was *amusing*.
Progressive verb:	His story was *amusing* the guests.

As you can see, *amusing* is a predicate adjective in the first example, but a main verb in the progressive form in the second example. In both cases, *amusing* follows the verb *be*. The two sentences look alike, but are actually built in different ways:

	main predicate verb + adjective
Predicate adjective:	The story <u>was</u> *amusing*.

	helping main verb + verb
Progressive:	His story <u>was</u> *amusing* the guests.

Fortunately, there are several reliable tests to help us decide when a present participle word form is being used as predicate adjective following a linking verb and when it is being used as a main verb in a progressive verb construction.

If the present participle is being used as a predicate adjective, it can almost always be modified by the word *very*. For example:

His story was **very** *amusing*.

When we try to use *very* with a present participle used as a main verb, the result will always be ungrammatical:

X His story was **very** *amusing* the guests.

If the present participle is being used as the main verb in a progressive construction, we can usually paraphrase the sentence by changing the progressive construction to a simple present tense or past tense, for example:

His story *was amusing* the guests. ⇒ His story *amused* the guests.

When we try to turn a predicate adjective into a main verb, the result will always produce an ungrammatical sentence. For example:

His story was *amusing.* ⇒ **X** His story *amused.* (who?)

Amused is a transitive verb that must have an object.

Here is another pair of examples:

(1) The report was *discouraging.*
(2) The report was *discouraging* everyone.

In (1), we can tell that *discouraging* is a predicate adjective because we can modify it with *very*:

The report was **very** *discouraging.*

When we try the *very* test with (2), the result is ungrammatical:

X The report was **very** *discouraging* everyone.

In (2), we can tell that *discouraging* is part of a progressive verb construction because we can paraphrase the verb construction with a past tense:

The report *was discouraging* everyone. ⇒ The report *discouraged* everyone.

Exercise 10.7

Apply the *very* and paraphrase tests to each sentence in the following pairs of sentences.

The repeated failures were *upsetting.*
The repeated failures were *upsetting* everyone.
Very test: The repeated failures were **very** *upsetting.*
Paraphrase: **X** The repeated failures *upset.* (who?)
Very test: **X** The repeated failures were **very** *upsetting* everyone.
Paraphrase: The repeated failures *upset* everyone.

1. The movie was *frightening*.

The movie was *frightening* the children.

Very test: _____

Paraphrase: _____

Very test: _____

Paraphrase: _____

2. My boss is *demanding*.

My boss is *demanding* an answer.

Very test: _____

Paraphrase: _____

Very test: _____

Paraphrase: _____

3. His suggestions were *surprising*.

His suggestions were *surprising* everyone.

Very test: _____

Paraphrase: _____

Very test: _____

Paraphrase: _____

4. The mistakes were *alarming*.

The mistakes were *alarming* everyone.

Very test: _____

Paraphrase: _____

Very test: _____

Paraphrase: _____

5. The company is *accepting*.

The company is *accepting* applications.

Very test: _____

Paraphrase: _____

Very test: _____

Paraphrase: _____

The third type of complement that linking verbs can take is an adverb of place or time. Here are some examples of both kinds of adverbs:

Adverb of place complement
The picnic *is* **at the beach.**
Our apartment *was* **on 53rd Street.**
We *were* **there.**

Adverb of time complement
The meeting *is* **at ten.**
The game *is* **Saturday afternoon.**
That *was* **then**; this *is* **now.**

One of the differences between adverbs of place and time as complements of linking verbs and ordinary optional adverbs is that we can never delete complements. Complements, by definition, are grammatical structures required by a verb to make a complete sentence. If we delete adverbs that are complements, the resulting sentence will be an ungrammatical fragment. Optional adverb modifiers, on the other hand, can always be deleted without affecting the grammaticality of the sentence. Compare the result when we delete the adverbs from the following sentences:

Complement: The meeting *is* **on the third floor**.
Optional adverb modifier: I *attended* the meeting **on the third floor**.

When we try to delete the adverbs from the two different sentences, the deletion of the complement results in an ungrammatical sentence, while the deletion of the optional adverb from the action verb sentence has no effect on the grammaticality of the sentence:

Complement: **X** The meeting *is* ~~on the third floor~~.
Optional: I *attended* the meeting ~~on the third floor~~.

Multiple Verb Complements

A **complement** is any grammatical structure or structures required by a verb to make a valid sentence. In this chapter we will examine nine different verb complements that contain two components. Since it is easy to get all the complements and terms confused, we will briefly list and label them all (with an example) before going into any detailed descriptions:

1. Indirect object + direct object

Jane *gave* <u>the boss</u> <u>her report</u>.
          IO   DO

2. Object + noun phrase complement

Ralph considers <u>his boss</u> <u>a fool</u>.
       Obj   NP Comp

3. Object + adjective complement

Ralph considers <u>his boss</u> <u>foolish</u>.
       Obj   Adj Comp

4. Object + adverb of place

I *put* <u>the box</u> <u>on the table</u>.
    Obj   Adv of Pl

5. Object + *that* clause

I *told* <u>him</u> *that* <u>his plan was very risky</u>.
     Obj   *that* clause

6. *To* phrase + *that* clause

I mentioned <u>*to him*</u> *that* <u>we needed to leave soon</u>.
      to phrase   *that* clause

7. Object + infinitive

$$\underset{\text{Obj}}{} \qquad \underset{\text{Inf}}{}$$

Ralph *expected* <u>the office</u> *to be* <u>empty on a Sunday morning</u>.

8. Object + base form

$$\underset{\text{Obj}}{} \; \underset{\text{Base form}}{}$$

He *made* <u>me</u> *do* it.

9. Object + present participle

$$\underset{\text{Obj}}{} \qquad \underset{\text{Pres Part}}{}$$

The teacher *caught* <u>several students</u> *cheating* <u>on the exam</u>.

1. Indirect object + direct object

A small but important group of verbs take not one object but two objects. When there are two objects in a sentence, the objects are called the **indirect object (IO)** and the **direct object (DO)**. (In a sentence with a single object, that object is always a direct object, usually shortened to just "object." We can only have an indirect object where there is also a direct object.) The two objects occur in a fixed order: the indirect object always precedes the direct object. Here are two examples of sentences with this type of double complement:

$$\underset{\text{IO}}{} \qquad \underset{\text{DO}}{}$$

Jane *gave* <u>the boss</u> <u>her report</u>.

$$\underset{\text{IO}}{} \qquad \underset{\text{DO}}{}$$

John *got* <u>the kids</u> <u>a pizza</u>.

Exercise 11.1

Underline the indirect and direct objects in the following sentences. Label the indirect object *IO* and the direct object *DO*. Be careful not to include optional adverbs as part of the objects.

$$\underset{\text{IO}}{} \qquad \underset{\text{DO}}{}$$

Jane *sent* <u>her boss</u> <u>an e-mail</u> at work.

1. My brother *teaches* college-prep high school seniors advanced calculus.

2. Please *order* me a toasted bagel with cream cheese.

3. I *offered* a friend a lift to the train station.

4. *Could* you *read* the kids a bedtime story before it gets too late?

5. I *did* him a big favor once.

6. *Pass* us some plates and silverware, will you?

7. We *should give* the people working at the desk a short break.

8. Let's *fix* her a nice dinner for her birthday.

9. Last year we *sold* the Johnston company about a thousand laser-jet printers.

10. Her great uncle *left* me a small bequest in his will.

11. We *saved* you a piece of birthday cake.

12. The car dealership *loaned* us a car while ours is in the shop.

13. We *should write* them a nice thank-you note for their gift.

14. Please *get* me all the current invoices.

15. We *should show* the visitors the new art gallery.

Nearly all complements that have an indirect object + direct object complement have an alternative form that functions as a paraphrase of the original form. We can imagine this paraphrase taking place as a two-step process: (1) the indirect object is turned into a prepositional phrase using *to* or *for*, and (2) the direct object is then moved in front of the prepositional phrase. Here are examples of how this *to/for* paraphrase transforms the original IO + DO complements:

$$\text{Jane } gave \underset{\text{IO}}{\underline{\text{the boss}}} \underset{\text{DO}}{\underline{\text{her report}}}. \Rightarrow \text{Jane gave } \underset{\text{DO}}{\underline{\text{her report}}} \underset{\substack{\text{Prep} \\ \text{phrase}}}{\underline{to \text{ the boss}}}.$$

$$\text{John } got \underset{\text{IO}}{\underline{\text{the kids}}} \underset{\text{DO}}{\underline{\text{a pizza}}}. \Rightarrow \text{John got } \underset{\text{DO}}{\underline{\text{a pizza}}} \underset{\substack{\text{Prep} \\ \text{phrase}}}{\underline{for \text{ the kids}}}.$$

It is reasonably easy to predict which verbs take *to* and which take *for*. In general, *to* is used to describe something being transferred from one person to another, either physically or metaphorically.

Here are some examples of a physical transfer:

$$\text{I } gave \underset{\text{IO}}{\underline{\text{them}}} \underset{\text{DO}}{\underline{\text{the books}}}. \Rightarrow \text{I } gave \underset{\text{DO}}{\underline{\text{the books}}} \underset{\substack{\text{Prep} \\ \text{Phrase}}}{\underline{\textbf{to} \text{ them}}}.$$

$$\text{We } loaned \underset{\text{IO}}{\underline{\text{the neighbors}}} \underset{\text{DO}}{\underline{\text{our truck}}}. \Rightarrow \text{We } loaned \underset{\text{DO}}{\underline{\text{our truck}}} \underset{\substack{\text{Prep} \\ \text{Phrase}}}{\underline{\textbf{to} \text{ the neighbors}}}.$$

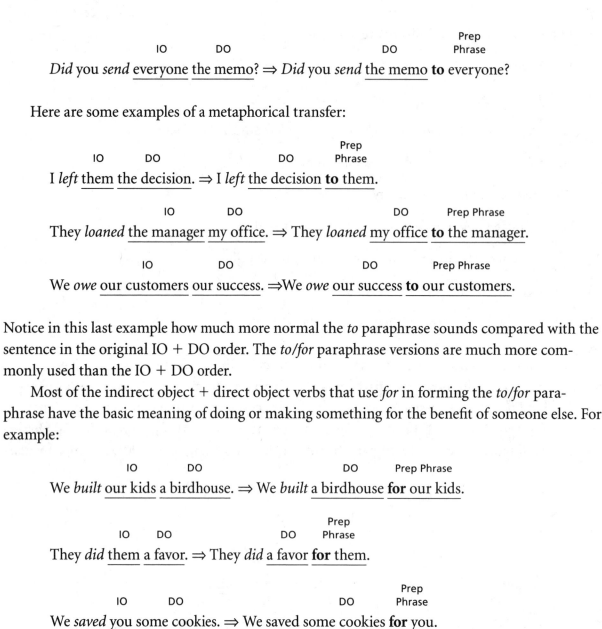

Did you *send* everyone the memo? ⇒ Did you *send* the memo **to** everyone?

Here are some examples of a metaphorical transfer:

I *left* them the decision. ⇒ I *left* the decision **to** them.

They *loaned* the manager my office. ⇒ They *loaned* my office **to** the manager.

We *owe* our customers our success. ⇒We *owe* our success **to** our customers.

Notice in this last example how much more normal the *to* paraphrase sounds compared with the sentence in the original IO + DO order. The *to/for* paraphrase versions are much more commonly used than the IO + DO order.

Most of the indirect object + direct object verbs that use *for* in forming the *to/for* paraphrase have the basic meaning of doing or making something for the benefit of someone else. For example:

We *built* our kids a birdhouse. ⇒ We *built* a birdhouse **for** our kids.

They *did* them a favor. ⇒ They *did* a favor **for** them.

We *saved* you some cookies. ⇒ We saved some cookies **for** you.

Exercise 11.2

The following sentences are the same sentences used in the previous exercise. Using your answers from Exercise 11.1, use the *to/for* paraphrase for all the indirect objects. You will probably be able to choose the correct preposition 90 percent of the time based on the guidelines given previously for selecting *to* or *for*.

Jane *sent* her boss an e-mail at work. ⇒ Jane *sent* an e-mail **to** her boss at work.

1. My brother *teaches* college-prep high school seniors advanced calculus.

2. Please *order* me a toasted bagel with cream cheese.

3. I *offered* a friend a lift to the train station.

4. *Could* you *read* the kids a bedtime story before it gets too late?

5. I *did* him a big favor once.

6. *Pass* us some plates and silverware, will you?

7. We *should give* the people working at the desk a short break.

8. Let's *fix* her a nice dinner for her birthday.

9. Last year we *sold* the Johnston company about a thousand laser-jet printers.

10. Her great uncle *left* me a small bequest in his will.

11. We *saved* you a piece of birthday cake.

12. The car dealership *loaned* us a car while ours is in the shop.

13. We *should write* them a nice thank-you note for their gift.

14. Please *get* me all the current invoices.

15. We *should show* the visitors the new art gallery.

If both the indirect object and the direct objects are pronouns, then the *to/for* paraphrase is obligatory in American English (but not in all dialects of British English). For example:

$$\text{IO} \quad \text{DO} \qquad\qquad\qquad \overset{\text{Prep}}{\text{DO phrase}}$$

X The company *gave* them it. ⇒ The company gave it *to* them.

$$\text{IO} \quad \text{DO} \qquad\qquad\qquad \overset{\text{Prep}}{\text{DO phrase}}$$

X My parents *got* them it. ⇒ My parents got it *for* them.

Exercise 11.3

Replace both the indirect and direction objects with pronouns, and then apply the *to/for* paraphrase to the pronoun objects.

            them   it

I *showed* our friends the new plan for remodeling the kitchen.

I showed *it* **to** *them*.

1. I *owed* my cousin a big favor.

2. The real estate agent *found* my parents a terrific apartment.

3. The agent *handed* my parents the apartment key.

4. The music teacher *taught* Janet a new piano sonata today.

5. The wizard *granted* the princess three wishes.

6. Please *serve* the guests the first course.

7. The owner very kindly *saved* our friends the last big table.

8. *Throw* George a towel, will you?

9. The boss *promised* Dorothy the first new opening.

10. *Would* you *read* everybody the message again, please?

11. John *bought* his kids a playground set.

12. We *prepared* the new vice president a revised organization chart.

13. Please *give* Mrs. Stoddard our best wishes.

14. We *ordered* the entire staff a catered lunch.

15. *Ship* the office in Dayton the new routers.

Let us now look at each type of object complement in more detail.

2. Object + noun phrase complement

The term **complement** refers to a noun phrase or adjective that follows an object and renames that object. That is, the object (Obj) and the object complement must refer to the same person or thing. The object complement can be a noun phrase complement (NP Comp) or an adjective complement (Adj Comp).

                  NP
        Obj   Comp

Ralph considers <u>his boss</u> <u>a fool</u>.

                  Adj
        Obj   Comp

Ralph considers <u>his boss</u> <u>foolish</u>.

In both sentences, the object complement refers back to the object:

> his boss = a fool (noun phrase complement)
> his boss = foolish (adjective complement)

Here are some more examples of noun phrase complements:

Obj = NP Comp
The Supreme Count *declared* George Bush president.

Obj = NP Comp
I *pronounce* you husband and wife.

Obj = NP Comp
Politicians always *believe* themselves great natural leaders.

One of the problems with object complements is that they look so much like the more common indirect objects in an indirect object + direct object complement construction. Both object complements and direct objects follow other noun phrases. How can we tell them apart?

We can easily tell them apart because in an object complement sentence, the person or object in the object complement must be the same person or object as the preceding noun (the object). In an indirect object + direct object sentence, they are never the same person or object. Compare the following two sentences:

Obj   NP Comp
Object + noun phrase complement: The outcome made John a happy man.
John = a happy man

IO   DO
Indirect object + direct object: The kids made John a birthday present.
John ≠ a birthday present

A second way to tell them apart is to use the *to/for* paraphrase. This paraphrase will work for indirect object + direct object complements, but it will never work for object + object complement sentences. For example:

IO + DO:	The kids made John a birthday present.
To/for paraphrase:	The kids made a birthday present *for* John.
Obj + NP Comp:	The outcome made John a happy man.
To/for paraphrase:	**X** The outcome made a happy man *to/for* John.

Exercise 11.4

Underline and label the noun phrases that follow the verbs in the following sentences, using *Obj + NP Comp* and *IO + DO* for the two complement types. Confirm your answer by showing both tests: the =/≠ test and the *to/for* paraphrase.

>   Obj   NP Comp
> The critics *considered* her latest book a great success.
> =/≠ test: her latest book = a great success
> *to/for* paraphrase: **X** The critics considered a great success *to/for* her latest book.

1. I *have* often *wished* myself a better person.

2. The board *considers* the CEO a great natural leader.

3. We *told* them the truth.

4. The President *appointed* her Undersecretary of State for Latin Affairs.

5. The newspaper *named* AMPEX Corporation the company of the year.

6. Senator Blather *considered* himself an expert on foreign affairs.

7. I *told* them my name.

8. The minister *wished* them a long and happy life.

_____

_____

9. The magazine *ranked* him one of the best young golfers in the state.

_____

_____

10. Bruce *confessed* himself a junk-food addict.

_____

_____

11. The press *called* her a rising star in the industry.

_____

_____

12. I *found* us a terrific apartment.

_____

_____

13. I *found* John a bit of a bore.

_____

_____

14. He *made* himself a cheese sandwich.

_____

_____

15. He *made* himself a first-rate bridge player.

_____

_____

3. Object + adjective complement

Some verbs, including many (but not all) of the verbs that take noun phrase + noun phrase complements, take object + adjective complements. Here are some examples:

Adj

Obj = Comp

He drives <u>me</u> + <u>crazy</u>.

Adj

Obj = Comp

The proposal *left* <u>us</u> = <u>cold</u>.

Obj = Adj Comp

The jury *found* <u>them</u> + <u>innocent</u> of all charges.

Obj = Adj Comp

I *like* <u>my steak</u> + <u>medium-rare</u>.

Most uses of this complement type are phrases that allow very little substitution for the adjective object complement. For instance, in the four examples of this complement type given above, few of the adjectives will allow other adjective complements to be used with that verb.

In the first example

He *drives* me **crazy**.

we can only substitute a few close synonyms for *crazy*:

He *drives* me <u>mad</u>.
He *drives* me <u>nuts</u>.

In the second example

The proposal *left* us <u>cold</u>.

about the only substitute for *cold* is *lukewarm*:

The proposal *left* us <u>lukewarm</u>.

The same is true of the remaining two examples. We can only substitute *guilty* for *innocent* in the third example. In the fourth example, we can only substitute words for describing meat (such as *rare, well-done, juicy,* and *pink*) for *medium-rare*.

As is the case with noun phrase object complements, we can easily recognize adjective object complements because they *must* refer to the object. In the first example above, for instance:

He drives <u>me</u> <u>crazy</u>.

the adjective complement *crazy* can only refer to the object *me*.

Parallel to what we did with noun phrase object complements, we can represent the relationship between the adjective object complement and object by an equal sign (=). For example:

The proposal *left* <u>us</u> <u>cold</u>.
us = cold

The jury *found* <u>them</u> <u>innocent</u> of all charges.
them = innocent

I *like* <u>my steak</u> <u>medium-rare</u>.
my steak = medium-rare

Exercise 11.5

Underline and label the objects (*Obj*) and adjective complements (*Adj Comp*) in the following sentences. Confirm your answer by using an = sign to connect the adjective complement to the object.

Obj =   Adj
       Comp
We usually *find* <u>their suggestions</u> quite <u>helpful</u>.

1. The senator always *gets* his opponents angry at his absurd claims.

2. The insulated cover *will keep* the food cold for hours.

3. I *like* my chili blazing hot.

4. The press *finds* him quite entertaining.

5. I *consider* him trustworthy.

6. I *need* them ready by noon.

7. We *painted* the deck a light blue.

8. The evidence *proves* the original hypothesis correct.

9. I *would rate* their food only so-so.

10. We *would like* the presentation light and upbeat.

Many verbs that can take objects and object complements (both noun phrase and adjective complements) will also allow an alternate form with *to be* in front of the object complement. For example, in addition to the following object complements:

Obj   NP Comp

I always *imagined* <u>him</u> <u>a wealthy man</u>.

Adj
Obj Comp

I always imagined <u>him</u> <u>taller</u>.

we have an alternative form with *to be*:

Obj   NP Comp

I always *imagined* <u>him</u> **to be** <u>a wealthy man</u>.

Adj
Obj   Comp

I always imagined <u>him</u> **to be** <u>taller</u>.

The forms with and without *to be* mean exactly the same thing. In fact, often native speakers would prefer to use the version with *to be*. While not every object complement can be used with the *to be* paraphrase, most can.

Exercise 11.6

Underline and label the objects and type of object complements (*NP Comp* or *Adj Comp*) in the following sentences, then insert *to be* between the object and the object complement.

Obj   NP Comp

The board *chose* <u>her</u> <u>the next CEO of the company</u>.
The board *chose* <u>her</u> **to be** <u>the next CEO of the company</u>.

1. We always *found* them kind and considerate.

2. I *believed* myself ready.

3. The jury *must presume* the defendant innocent.

4. I *consider* you a fair person.

5. The treasurer *showed* himself a wizard of financial control.

6. We just *assumed* the budget a done deal.

7. It is a mistake to *think* him a fool.

8. The court *found* the plaintiff's claim valid.

9. I always *maintained* them one of the best companies in the business.

10. I *confessed* myself totally ignorant of what they were talking about.

4. Object + adverb of place

A few verbs require an expression of place after the object. For example:

I *put* the box on the table.

The verb *put* requires an expression of place. When you *put* something, you have to put it somewhere. If we delete the expression of place, the sentence becomes ungrammatical:

X I *put* the box.

The expression of place can be an adverb prepositional phrase (as in the example), or merely a single-word adverb. For example:

I *put* the box there.
I *put* the box down.
I *put* the box back.

The adverb of place can also include adverbs that have a sense of motion or direction toward a place. For example:

I *pushed* a coin into the slot of the vending machine.
I *drove* the car into the garage.
I *drove* the car around the parking lot.

All of the verbs that take this complement type have a sense of causing someone or something to be placed somewhere or to be moved to some place. Here are some more examples:

Can you *take* me to the airport?
Carefully, I *laid* the eggs in the carton.
You can *lead* a horse to water, but you can't make him drink. (Saying)
Show me where to go.
Send any mail that comes to my home address.

One particular pair of verbs that take this complement type causes some nonnative speakers a problem: *bring* and *take*. In English, as in many languages, *bring* and *take* are directional words. *Bring* means "toward the speaker," and *take* means "away from the speaker." For example:

Please *bring* the books to me. (toward the speaker)
Please *bring* the books here. (toward the speaker)
Please *take* the books to his office. (away from the speaker)
Please *take* the book there. (away from the speaker)

Exercise 11.7

Decide whether *bring* or *take* is more appropriate in the following sentences.

Can you (~~bring~~/*take*) me to the airport?

1. Can you (*bring/take*) me home after the meeting?

2. Did you (*bring/take*) the visitors to the Art Gallery in Old Town?

3. I can (*bring/take*) them back here, if you like.

4. The van will (*bring/take*) you to where the ship will dock.

5. Let me (*bring/take*) you out to dinner tonight.

6. Please (*bring/take*) the kids back here after the movie.

7. (*Bring/Take*) your umbrella if you go out to lunch.

8. Why did you (*bring/take*) them there?

9. The trash collectors finally (*brought/took*) away the old Christmas tree.

10. Look at the trash along the shoreline that the high tide (*brought/took*) in.

5. Object + *that* clause

Some verbs can take an object followed by a *that* clause. For example:

      Obj   *that* clause
I *told* him *that* his plan was very risky.

           Obj   *that* clause
We *reminded* the kids *that* it was time to go to bed.

That clauses are the simplest type of noun clauses. They consist of the introductory word *that* + a sentence in its normal statement word order. As is often the case with *that* clauses used in nonsubject roles, the word *that* is often omitted, especially in casual speech. For example:

> Obj   *that* clause
> I *told* <u>him</u> Ø <u>his plan was very risky.</u>

> Obj   *that* clause
> We *reminded* <u>the kids</u> Ø <u>it was time to go to bed.</u>

The deletion of *that* from a *that* clause poses special problems for nonnative speakers because the deletion erases one of the key signals that we rely on to identify *that* clauses. From this point on, we will put *that* in parentheses to remind us that we often delete it.

The verbs that take this complement type have a restricted range of meaning. Most of the verbs express some form of communication: for example, *convince, tell, warn, write.* Here are some example sentences using these verbs:

> We *convinced* them (*that*) it was a bad idea.
> I *told* you (*that*) I needed to leave early.
> The lifeguards *warned* the swimmers (*that*) the tide was dangerous.
> My parents *wrote* me (*that*) they were coming for Christmas.

Exercise 11.8

Underline and label the object + *that* clause complements in the following sentences. Note that all of the introductory *that*s have been deleted. Confirm that these are *that* clauses by inserting the missing *that*.

> Obj   *that* clause
> I *bet* <u>you</u> / <u>New England will win the Superbowl this season.</u>

1. My boss *told* me I would have to work late tonight.

2. We *satisfied* them our emergency plans met all state and federal requirements.

3. I *urged* the company they reconsider their decision.

4. We *will inform* them the meeting has been cancelled.

5. The consultant *advised* the union the contract would have to be rewritten.

6. The salesman *assured* us the car was in perfect running order.

7. I'll *bet* you we can't get a taxi at this time of day.

8. *Convince* me I'm wrong.

9. We *instructed* everyone they would have to fill out new payroll forms.

10. I *e-mailed* them we would be back a day early.

11. *Don't remind* me this was my idea to begin with.

12. Man, that really *taught* me I should get everything in writing.

13. *Promise* me you will be careful.

14. My boss finally *persuaded* the company they should revise the policy.

15. I *warned* them they would get into trouble.

6. *To* phrase + *that* clause

A few verbs that express communication have an unusual feature: they use a prepositional phrase beginning with *to* (a *to* phrase) instead of the expected object. Using the verb *say* as an example, where we would expect

               Obj   *that* clause
X I said **him** *that* we needed to leave soon.

we find instead a *to* phrase in place of the object:

         to phrase   *that* clause
I said **to him** *that* we needed to leave soon.

Using an object with verbs that take a *to* phrase is a common error for nonnative speakers. Here are some more examples of both the incorrect and correct forms:

Wrong:	**X** He *mentioned* **us** that his son was moving to Chicago.
Right:	He mentioned **to us** that his son was moving to Chicago.
Wrong:	**X** They explained **us** that our cost estimates were too low.
Right:	They explained **to us** that our cost estimates were too low.
Wrong:	**X** We pointed out **them** *that* they were behind schedule.
Right:	We pointed out **to them** *that* they were behind schedule.

Even though the verbs that take the *to* phrase + *that* clause complement are all verbs of communication, we cannot conclude that therefore all verbs of communication take *to* phrases. Some do, but some don't. For example, compare *say* and *tell*:

> I *said* **to Jane** that we would have to leave a little early.
> I *told* **Jane** that we would have to leave a little early.

Say takes a *to* phrase, but *tell* takes an object. Unfortunately, you just have to know which verbs take the *to* phrase and learn them as variations of the normal object + *that* clause complement types. Here are the most common verbs that take a *to* phrase instead of the expected object complement:

acknowledge	explain	remark
admit	mention	report
announce	point out	say
complain	propose	signal
confess	prove	state
declare	recommend	suggest

Exercise 11.9

Many of the following sentences incorrectly use objects where they should use *to* phrases instead. If the sentence is incorrect, replace the object with a *to* phrase. If the sentence is correct as it is, write *OK* above the object.

> to you
> Let me *prove* ~~you~~ that my plan will work.

1. He pulled me aside and *remarked* me that the meeting was going very well.

2. In no uncertain terms, they *stated* us that they were upset about what had happened.

3. Please *suggest* them that they should take their conversation out into the hall.

4. You should *point out* the committee that they have already approved the proposal.

5. I *confessed* him that I didn't really like sports.

6. We *reminded* them that we were already pretty late.

7. Senator Blather *acknowledged* the reporters that he had never actually voted on the bill.

8. She *explained* them that the hotel did not have any more available rooms.

9. They *informed* us that our flight had been cancelled.

10. We *complained* them that we had confirmed reservations.

11. The committee *will report* them that they recommend moving the plant to Ohio.

12. We *admitted* them that we had probably made a mistake in our recommendations.

13. They *said* me that I should wait here.

14. They *reminded* me that I should wait here.

15. I *proposed* them that they should accept the offer.

7. Object + infinitive

In this construction, the object is followed by an infinitive (together with all the infinitive's complements and modifiers, if any). For example:

Obj   Infinitive phrase

Ralph *expected* <u>the office</u> <u>*to be* empty on a Sunday morning</u>.

Many verbs take this complement type. Fortunately, the verbs tend to fall into four distinct groups based on meaning. Here are the four groups with some examples of each:

Verbs of permission:	allow, enable, help, inspire, permit, require The company *authorized* the project team *to go* ahead.
Verbs of cognition:	assume, expect, feel, imagine, know, understand John *considered* his job *to be* vital to the company's success.
Verbs of causation:	cause, drive, force, get, intend, lead, mean, prompt I *got* a friend *to drive* me to the station.
Verbs of naming:	appoint, choose, elect, name, vote They *chose* Alice *to lead* the new task force.

Exercise 11.10

Underline and label the object (*Obj*) and infinitive phrase (*Inf*) in each sentence (include the infinitive's complement). Above the italicized verb classify the verb as *permission*, *cognition*, *causation*, or *naming*.

causation   Obj   Inf
I *asked* <u>a friend</u> <u>to take notes at the meeting for me</u>.

1. We *expected* them to be ready by now.

2. The government *permitted* the project to go ahead under certain restrictions.

3. Roberta *wanted* the kids to go to summer school this year.

4. The coupon *entitles* you to buy a second ticket at half price.

5. *Remind* me to get some gas on the way home.

6. I *believed* myself to be entirely in the wrong.

7. They *used* the loan to buy some much-needed equipment.

8. The news *prompted* us to reconsider what we were planning.

9. The VP *asked* Anne to head up the new division in Europe.

10. Please *allow* us to help you with that.

11. His parents *encouraged* her to apply to Duke.

12. I *knew* them to be better players than they had first appeared.

13. He *inspired* us to try even harder.

14. The CEO *picked* an outsider to head the review committee.

15. The results *forced* us to reevaluate all of our plans.

8. Object + base form

Only a few verbs take this complement type, but they are commonly used. Here is an example:

Obj   Base form
He *made* <u>me</u> <u>do</u> it.

The term **base form** is also called an **unmarked** or **bare infinitive**. All of these terms refer to the same thing: a verb phrase that contains a base-form verb followed by that verb's complements and modifiers (if any). We can see that this complement type is indeed a base form by using the verb *be*. For example:

DO   Base form
They *let* <u>Mary</u> **be** the leader in the new project.

If the verb *be* were not in its base form, it would be *is* to agree with its subject *Mary*:

> **X** They *let* Mary **is** the leader in the new project.

Nonnative speakers commonly make mistakes with this complement type because it is easily confused with the much more frequent object + infinitive complement. That is, nonnative speakers sometimes overgeneralize the *to* of the object + infinitive complement to the less-common object + base form complement. For example, compare the following two sentences:

Object + infinitive: We *allowed* them to finish.
Obj + base form: **X** We *let* them **to** finish.

In the second example, the *to* has been added to the base form in mistaken analogy to the more common infinitive complement.

Here are some more examples of the correct and incorrect use of the object + base form complement and object + infinitive complement:

                                                  Obj Base form
Correct: Please *let* <u>me</u> <u>help you</u>.

                                           Obj   Inf
Incorrect: **X** Please *let* <u>me</u> **to** <u>help you</u>.

                                           Obj   Base form
Correct: I once *saw* <u>Pelé</u> <u>play football</u>.

                                           Obj   Inf
Incorrect: **X** I once saw <u>Pelé</u> **to** <u>play football</u>.

Most of the verbs in the group refer to sense perception: for example, *hear*, *see*, and *watch*. Another common group refers to causation: for example, *cause* and *make*. A particularly common verb in this group is *have*, which in this context means to "cause someone to do something." For example:

I *had* my assistant *take* notes during the meeting.

Here is a list of the more common verbs that take the base-form complement:

feel	let	observe
have	listen to	overhear
hear	make	see
help	notice	watch

Exercise 11.11

Choose the correct complement type (base form or infinitive) from the two forms in parentheses.

I heard them (*come in*/~~*to come in*~~) late last night.

1. The doctor *felt* the patient's pulse (*flutter/to flutter*) irregularly.

2. *Would* you *call* them and *have* them (*make/to make*) a reservation for us?

3. Please *watch* the kids (*play/to play*) in the backyard for a few minutes, will you?

4. *Did* you actually *hear* him (*say/to say*) that we might quit?

5. I *consider* them (*be/to be*) ready to go.

6. We *listened to* them (*discuss/to discuss*) what they should do.

7. You *will notice* the car's performance gradually (*get/to get*) worse over time.

8. I need to *help* the kids (*get/to get*) ready for bed.

9. *Have* them (*give/to give*) me a call.

10. We couldn't help overhearing them (*talk/to talk*) about the incident.

9. Object + present participle

This type uses a present participle verb phrase (Pres Part VP) as a complement. For example:

            Obj   Pres Part VP
We *watched* him ***fixing*** his bicycle.

            Obj   Pres Part VP
She *found* them ***watering*** the garden.

            Obj   Pres Part VP
I couldn't help *hearing* the group ***discussing*** their project.

The verb *catch* often has the negative implication of discovering somebody doing something improper. For example:

The teacher *caught* several students *cheating* on the exam.
The manager *caught* some employees *sleeping* on the job.
The audit *caught* several offices *overcharging* customers.

Get and *have* both mean to cause somebody to do something. For example:

> The police have *got* volunteers *searching* the woods.
> We *have* the interns *searching* the records.

One of the difficulties in recognizing this complement type is that present participle verbs look just like present participles used as **gerund phrases**. (Gerund phrases are discussed in detail in Chapter 6.) Gerund phrases are *-ing* forms of the verb used in noun phrases. For example, consider the following sentence:

> NP
> *Working* on his report kept Rudolph up all night.

The gerund phrase *working on his report* is a noun phrase playing the role of subject. Fortunately, there is a simple and highly reliable way to identify gerund phrases: they can always be replaced by *it*:

> It
> *Working* on his report kept Rudolph up all night.

When we try to substitute *it* for a present participle verb phrase, the result will always be ungrammatical. For example:

> X it
> I *saw* him *working* on his report.

The object + present participle complement type is very close in meaning and usage to the object + base form complement type. For example, compare the following sentences:

Object + base: We watched him *fix* his bicycle.
Object + present participle: We watched him *fixing* his bicycle.

There is little difference in meaning between these two sentences. There probably is some slight emphasis on the process of repairing the bicycle in the object + present participle complement as compared to the object + base form complement, but it would be easy to overstate how significant that difference is.

A practical problem for nonnative speakers is that the two different complement types use many of the same verbs. For example, the following verbs are freely used with both complement types: *feel, have, hear, listen to, notice, observe, overhear, see, spot, spy, watch.*

Some verbs can be used with the object + present participle complement but not the base-form complement: *catch, discover, find, get, leave, smell.* For example:

Object + present participle: We found them *working* in the back office.
Object + base form: **X** We found them *work* in the back office.

Only one common verb can be used in the object + base form but not with the object + present participle: *make*. For example:

Object + base-form: We *made* them *fix* the bill.
Object + present participle: **X** We *made* them *fixing* the bill.

Here is a list of the verbs that are commonly used with object + present participle complements. Note that most of these are verbs of sense perception:

catch	hear	see
discover	leave	smell
feel	notice	spot
find	observe	spy
get	overhear	watch
have	perceive	

Exercise 11.12

Choose the correct complement type (present participle, base form, or both) from the two forms in parentheses. If both are correct, write *both* above the verbs.

both
We *will have* the workers (*painting/paint*) the hallway tomorrow.

1. We *left* the painters (*finishing up/finish up*) the trim in the dinning room.

2. *Listen to* her (*playing/play*) that piano.

3. He *made* me (*doing/do*) it.

4. We *discovered* the kitten (*hiding/hide*) in the attic.

5. I *heard* the kitchen faucet (*dripping/drip*) all night.

6. Fortunately, I *smelled* the brakes (*smoking/smoke*) on the rear axle.

7. After a bad beginning, we *got* the two sides (*talking/talk*) to each other.

8. During the earthquake, we all *felt* the building (*shaking/shake*) a little.

9. Finally, we *spotted* a white sail (*flashing/flash*) in the afternoon sun.

10. I *found* myself (*worrying/worry*) about tomorrow's presentation.

11. We *made* Johnny (*finishing/finish*) his homework before he watched any TV.

12. They *must have overheard* us (*talking/talk*) about it at lunch.

13. We *were watching* our daughter's team (*playing/play*) soccer.

14. I *caught* myself (*dozing off/doze off*) during the performance.

15. We saw them (*getting into/get into*) a taxi on 53rd Street.

Exercise 11.13

Underline the complements in the following sentences. Label the type of complement using the following terms: *IO + DO* for indirect object + direct object; *Obj + NP Comp* for object + NP complement; *Obj + Adj Comp* for object + adjective complement; *Obj + Adv of Pl* for object + adverb of place; *Obj + That* for object + *that* clause; *To + That* for *to* phrase + *that* clause; *Obj + Inf* for object + infinitive; *Obj + Base* for object + base form; or *Obj + Pres Part* for object + present participle.

           Obj   that
Don't tell <u>me</u>/<u>we were right all along</u>?

1. Please *let* me help you with that.

2. The test *proves* the suspect innocent.

3. I *noticed* them leaving during the meeting.

4. They *appointed* her chief counsel.

5. He *is putting* the leftovers into the refrigerator.

6. My parents *sent* the kids some books.

7. Fortunately, the board *considered* my idea quite promising.

8. I *told* them they needed to get prior approval before going ahead.

9. Sadly, I *put* the iPhone back on the counter.

10. We *thought* the outcome a big disappointment, to tell the truth.

11. *Can* you *give* my friend a lift to the airport?

12. Let us *prove* to you that we can do the job.

13. We *moved* the kittens out of the kids' bedroom.

14. I *wanted* my parents to stay with us this Christmas.

15. I *drove* the car over to my mother's house.

16. I *had* the waiter set an extra place for you.

17. We *helped* them to get ready to leave.

18. I *told* them that we would be a little late for dinner.

19. Jane *baked* Sarah a birthday cake.

20. I *considered* our project a success.

21. What *prompted* John to change his mind so suddenly?

22. The oven *will keep* food hot for hours.

23. She *explained* to us that her parents would need to use the apartment that week.

24. I *caught* my son watching TV while studying.

25. I *confess* to you that I am more than a little nervous.

Adverbs

The term **adverb** is used both narrowly to refer to single-word adverbs and broadly to refer to any grammatical unit (word, phrase, or clause) that functions as an adverb. In this book, unless specified otherwise, we will use the term **adverb** broadly to include all types of adverbs. If we need to be more specific, we will use the terms *single-word adverb*, *adverb phrase*, or *adverb clause*.

Adverbs are conventionally defined as grammatical elements (words, phrases, or clauses) that "modify verbs, adjectives, and other adverbs." Since 99 percent of the time, adverbs are used to modify verbs, from this point we will focus exclusively on adverbs that modify verbs.

This chapter is divided into two parts. In the first part, we will discuss how adverbs are formed. In the second part, we will discuss how adverbs are used.

How adverbs are formed

In this section we will examine how adverbs are formed at the word level, at the phrase level, and at the clause level.

Word-level adverbs

Adverbs fall into two distinct groups: (1) a small number of mostly single-syllable words that are used with very high frequency, and (2) the great majority of adverbs that are derived from adjectives, for example *deep/deeply*; *true/truly, sad/sadly.*

Here are the twenty-five most commonly used adverbs (note that not one of the very high frequency adverbs is derived from an adjective by adding *-ly*):

1. only

2. then

3. now

4. also

5. even

6. just

7. here

8. back

9. still

10. never

11. well

12. again

13. so

14. there

15. away

16. always

17. once

18. however

19. often

20. over

21. perhaps

22. thus

23. yet

24. too

25. almost

One of the fundamental identifying features of modifying adverbs is that they are by definition optional elements. Unlike the other major parts of speech—nouns, adjectives, and verbs—adverbs can always be deleted without affecting the grammaticality of the sentence. For example, consider the following sentence:

We had dinner then.

The adverb *then* can be deleted without making the rest of the sentence ungrammatical:

> We had dinner ~~then~~.

Exercise 12.1

Underline the single-word adverbs in the following sentences. Confirm your identification by deleting the adverb.

> It ~~always~~ costs a fortune to eat at Gordy's.

1. I usually *don't have* that much trouble printing documents.

2. We *went* to Mexico City once.

3. I simply *couldn't understand* what they were saying.

4. The audience suddenly *became* quiet.

5. We often *see* them on the weekends.

6. They *knocked* on the door again.

7. We *have made* our decision, too.

8. She really *plays* the piano well.

9. Perhaps we *will see* you at the conference.

10. I always *take* the bus to work.

11. *Are* we *done* already?

12. We probably *can't get* to the meeting by ten.

13. Let's *arrange* a meeting soon.

14. We always *see* them over the holidays.

15. My parents often *discuss* moving to a smaller place.

Ninety-five percent of adverbs are formed from adjectives by adding an *-ly* suffix. Here are some examples:

Adjectives	Adverbs
abrupt	abrupt<u>ly</u>
eager	eager<u>ly</u>
first	first<u>ly</u>

honest	honest<u>ly</u>
jealous	jealous<u>ly</u>
last	last<u>ly</u>
quick	quick<u>ly</u>
sad	sad<u>ly</u>
slow	slow<u>ly</u>
soft	soft<u>ly</u>
suspicious	suspicious<u>ly</u>

Even adjectives formed from the **present** and **past participle** of verbs can be changed to adverbs by adding *-ly*. Here are some examples:

PRESENT PARTICIPLE

Adjectives	Adverbs
amusing	amusing<u>ly</u>
frightening	frightening<u>ly</u>
interesting	interesting<u>ly</u>
laughing	laughing<u>ly</u>
pleasing	pleasing<u>ly</u>
revealing	revealing<u>ly</u>

PAST PARTICIPLE

Adjectives	Adverbs
assured	assured<u>ly</u>
bemused	bemused<u>ly</u>
learned	learned<u>ly</u>
marked	marked<u>ly</u>
reported	reported<u>ly</u>

Exercise 12.2

Change the adjective in the underlined phrase into a single-word adverb. Then rephrase the sentence using the adverb in place of the underlined phrase.

honestly
He answered the question ~~in an honest manner~~.

1. He drove home <u>in a safe manner</u>.

2. She completed the Haydn piano sonata <u>in a perfect manner</u>.

3. The audience applauded <u>in a warm manner</u>.

4. They did the job <u>in a barely adequate manner</u>.

5. We acted <u>in a reasonable manner</u>.

6. We went out of the children's room <u>in a very quiet manner</u>.

7. They have always done their work <u>in a highly capable manner</u>.

8. I have always tried to behave <u>in a proper manner</u>.

9. The rain was falling <u>in a soft manner</u>.

10. The meal was prepared <u>in an excellent manner</u>.

11. He talked to the group <u>in a quite engaging manner</u>.

12. She took care of her children <u>in a devoted manner</u>.

13. He framed the terms of the discussion <u>in a clear manner</u>.

14. He replaced the money <u>in a telling manner</u>.

15. She turned away from the accident <u>in a disgusted manner</u>.

The spelling of *-ly* adverbs is largely what we would expect when we add a suffix beginning with a consonant. Adjectives ending in a final silent *e* retain the *e*. For example:

Adjectives	Adverbs
accurate	accurate<u>l</u>y
complete	complete<u>l</u>y
desperate	desperate<u>l</u>y
entire	entire<u>l</u>y

Adjectives that end in a consonant + *y* change the *y* to *i* before the *-ly* suffix. <u>For</u> example:

Adjectives	Adverbs
fussy	fuss<u>il</u>y
hardy	hard<u>il</u>y
merry	merr<u>il</u>y
mighty	might<u>il</u>y

There are only a few exceptional spellings for *-ly* adverbs:

Adjectives	Adverbs
due	duly
gay	gaily
true	truly

Truly is one of the most commonly misspelled words in English.

Exercise 12.3

In the right column, write the *-ly* adverb form of the adjective in the left column.

Adjective	**Adverb**
loose	*loosely*

1. sleepy _____

2. rare _____

3. needy _____

4. hardy _____

5. immediate _____

6. greedy _____

7. true _____

8. sketchy _____

9. scary _____

10. gay _____

Like adjectives, adverbs form their comparative and superlative forms in two fundamentally different ways: (1) by adding an *-er* and *-est* ending, and (2) by using the helping words *more* and *most*. For example:

-er/-est
George finished *fast*.
George finished *faster* than Frank.
George finished the *fastest* of all the runners in his age group.

more/most
George finished *quickly*.
George finished ***more*** *quickly* than Frank.
George finished the ***most*** *quickly* of all the runners in his age group.

However, as we will see below, the basis for deciding which adverbs use the *-er/-est* patterns and which use the *more/most* pattern is completely different from the basis for deciding between *-er/-est* and *more/most* in adjectives.

Only simple, uncompounded adverbs can use the *-er/-est* endings. For example:

high
The ball went *higher* and *higher*.
John's kite went the *highest* of anyone's.

loud
The bells rang *louder* as we came nearer.
The old church bell rang the *loudest* of all.

sharp
I answered *sharper* than I had intended.
His criticisms stung the *sharpest* of all.

tight
She smiled *tighter* and *tighter*.
She smiled the *tightest* at Bill's stupid comments.

Adverbs that are formed from adjectives by the *-ly* suffix (the vast majority of all adverbs) must use *more* and *most*. For example:

amusingly
He spoke ***more*** *amusingly* than ever.
He spoke the ***most*** *amusingly* of all the presenters.

brightly
The light shone more *brightly* as it grew darker.
The stars shone the *brightest* that dark night.

charmingly
They laughed ***more*** *charmingly* than ever.
They laughed the ***most*** *charmingly* about their own mistakes.

completely

The plan was discussed *more completely* after dinner.

The plan was discussed the *most completely* by the review staff.

eagerly

I spoke *more eagerly*.

I spoke the *most eagerly* on the topics I knew most about.

suspiciously

They behaved *more suspiciously* than ever.

The butler behaved the *most suspiciously* of all the suspects.

A few adverbs have historically irregular forms:

Base form	Comparative	Superlative
badly	worse	worst
far (distance)	farther	farthest
far (other meanings)	further	furthest
little	less	least
much	more	most
well	better	best

Farther and *farthest* refer to physical distance. For example:

His golf ball went *farther* than mine did.

His shot went the *farthest* from the tee.

Further and *furthest* are used in all other meanings. For example:

His comments on the incident went *further* than the other's.

His comments went the *furthest* of anybody's in explaining what happened.

Exercise 12.4

Supply the comparative and superlative forms of the following adverbs.

Base form	Comparative form	Superlative form
suddenly	*more suddenly*	*most suddenly*

1. soon   _____   _____

2. late   _____   _____

3. frequently   _____   _____

4. raw   _____   _____

5. firmly   _____   _____

6. brilliantly   _____   _____

7. long   _____   _____

8. honestly   _____   _____

9. critically   _____   _____

10. low   _____   _____

11. bitterly   _____   _____

12. well   _____   _____

13. heavily   _____   _____

14. tight   _____   _____

15. badly   _____   _____

Adverb phrases

Two types of phrases play the role of adverbs: **adverb prepositional phrases** and **adverbial infinitive phrases**. Here is an example of each type of phrase:

Adverbial prepositional phrase:	Sally met her friends <u>after work</u>.
Adverbial infinitive phrase:	Sally met her friends <u>to plan the reception</u>.

Adverb prepositional phrases consist of prepositions followed by noun phrase objects. The noun phrase objects are nouns (with or without modifiers), pronouns, gerunds (Chapter 6), or noun clauses (Chapter 7). Here are examples of adverb prepositional phrases with various types of objects. The entire prepositional phrase is underlined, and the object noun phrase is in italics:

Noun phrase:	We had dinner <u>at *that new restaurant on 88th Street*</u>.
Pronoun:	There is a drug store <u>by *us*</u>.
Gerund:	We only finished on time <u>by *everyone's working overtime*</u>.
Noun clause:	They have an apartment <u>near *where we live*</u>.

Exercise 12.5

Underline the adverb prepositional phrases in the following sentences and label the type of object that follows the preposition: *noun phrase*, *pronoun*, *gerund*, or *noun clause*.

> noun phrase
> They handled the situation <u>with the greatest possible care</u>.

1. They opened a window in the back room.

2. The kids ruined the rug by spilling food.

3. The moon was shining on us.

4. We improved the operation by simplifying the entire process.

5. He upset his neighbors by how loudly he played the TV.

6. They got married over the holidays.

7. We finally sold it after we placed an ad in the local paper.

8. We visited some friends near Cleveland.

9. I was a little confused by what he said.

10. We enjoyed the food in Italy.

Adverb infinitive phrases consist of the **infinitive** form of the verb together with that verb's complements and/or modifiers (if any). Here are some examples of infinitive phrases used as adverbs. The entire infinitive phrase is underlined, and the infinitive verb itself is in italics:

> We went to the post office <u>*to get* some stamps</u>.
> You need a prescription <u>*to get* your medicine at the drugstore</u>.
> You must practice hard <u>*to win*</u>.
> He raised the issue just <u>*to cause* an argument</u>.
> We turned off the water <u>*to fix* a leak in a pipe</u>.

Adverbs used as an infinitive always have the basic meaning of explaining *why* somebody does (or needs to do) something. In fact, we can paraphrase all infinitives used as adverbs with *in order*. Here is the *in order* paraphrase applied to all the example sentences given above:

> We went to the post office **in order** <u>*to get* some stamps</u>.
> You need a prescription **in order** <u>*to get* your medicine at the drug store</u>.
> You must practice hard **in order** *to win*.

He raised the issue just **in order** *to cause* an argument.

We turned off the water **in order** *to fix* a leak in a pipe.

Exercise 12.6

Underline the adverb infinitive phrases in the following sentences. Confirm your answer by adding *in order* to the infinitive phrase.

                                                     in order
You *must sell* the stock / <u>to get the tax credit for the loss.</u>

1. We *ended* the interview to save the candidate any further embarrassment.

2. The doctors *operated* to reduce the risk of infection.

3. We *reduced* the price to attract a larger market.

4. We *made* a quick trip back home to pick up some things for the picnic.

5. I *wore* some heavy pants to protect my legs from the thorns.

6. We *acted* quickly to minimize the possible damage.

7. We *hired* a lawyer to file the estate papers.

8. The family *made* a down payment to ensure that they would have a place to stay.

9. We *audited* the books to ensure compliance with federal regulations.

10. I *smiled* to show that there were no hard feelings.

Adverb clauses

Clauses are grammatical constructions that contain both a subject and a verb that enter into a subject-verb relationship with that subject. Adverb clauses are dependent clauses that are attached to the main or independent clause as adverb modifiers. While adverb clauses can modify adjectives and other adverbs, the vast majority of adverb clauses modify verbs. This is the only kind of adverb clause we will be concerned with. Compared to adjective and noun clauses, adverb clauses have a simple and uniform structure: an introductory **subordinating conjunction** + a statement—a complete sentence in a statement form. Together, the subordinating conjunction and the complete statement make up an adverb subordinate clause. In the following examples, the subordinating conjunctions are in bold and the complete statements are underlined:

             Sub
             Conj   statement

I'*ll give* them a call **when** + <u>I get a chance.</u>

             Sub
             Conj   statement

Go get a cup of coffee **while** + <u>I finish up here.</u>

           Sub Conj   statement

I *went* home **because** + <u>I wasn't feeling well.</u>

              Sub Conj   statement

We *decided* to go ahead, **although** + <u>we certainly had our doubts about it.</u>

             Sub Conj   statement

We *could go* to a movie **unless** + <u>you would rather stay home.</u>

Exercise 12.7

Underline the entire adverb clause; label the subordinating conjunction (*Sub Conj*) and statement.

                      Sub Conj   statement

The children *enjoyed* themselves **everywhere** <u>we went.</u>

1. He *will do* it if he can.

2. We *need* to leave before it gets too dark.

3. They *will finish* by six unless there is an unexpected problem.

4. The theater always *gets* quiet when the curtain goes up.

5. We *got* together for coffee after we had finished the presentation.

6. We *warned* them about it as soon as we could.

7. *Order* a pizza when the waiter comes, will you?

8. I'*ll give* you a call after I get back to the office on Monday.

9. We *saw* signs of the problems everywhere we looked.

10. They *will meet* with us whenever we want them to.

11. Bob *might change* his mind if we made a good argument.

12. He *won't do* it unless there is a good reason.

13. It *cost* quite a bit extra because we had to rush the job.

14. We *had* a good time everywhere we went.

15. They *have lived* there since they first moved to the city in the late eighties.

The use and meaning of adverbs

In the previous section we saw that there are three different forms of adverbs: single-word adverbs, adverb phrases, and adverb clauses. All of these forms of adverbs are used to modify verbs. Virtually all adverbs that modify verbs have a single point of origin in the sentence. They are the final component of the verb phrase, following the verb and its complement as shown in the following diagram:

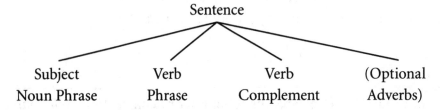

Optional adverbs can be single-word adverbs, adverb prepositional phrases, adverb infinitive phrases, or adverb clauses. For example:

Single-word adverb:	John met Mary *recently*
Adverb prepositional phrase:	John met Mary *on the weekend*
Adverb infinitive phrase:	John met Mary *to borrow her computer*
Adverb clause:	John met Mary *when he was on campus*

One of the defining characteristics of adverbs that modify verbs is that they are moveable. All of the other grammatical components (including adverbs used as complements) are fixed in place. Only adverbs that modify verbs can be shifted forward to other positions in the sentence. For example:

Single-word adverb

Original:	John met Mary *recently*.
Shifted:	*Recently* John met Mary.
Shifted:	John *recently* met Mary.

Adverb prepositional phrase

Original:	John met Mary *on the weekend*.
Shifted:	*On the weekend*, John met Mary.

Adverb infinitive phrase

Original:	John met Mary *to find out what was going on at school.*
Shifted:	*To find out what was going on at school,* John met Mary.

Adverb clause

Original:	John saw Mary *when he was on campus.*
Shifted:	*When he was on campus,* John saw Mary.

Exercise 12.8

Underline the adverb at the end of each sentence. Confirm your answer by shifting the adverb to the beginning of the sentence.

Jason *located* the missing computer <u>later that same afternoon</u>.
<u>Later that same afternoon</u>, Jason located the missing computer.

1. Sally *gained* five pounds between Christmas and New Year's.

   _____

2. The zookeeper *replaced* the cover quickly.

   _____

3. I *had* everything ready before I went into the meeting.

   _____

4. We *took* a later train to avoid the morning rush.

   _____

5. The public health department *was* able to halt the disease by a rigid quarantine.

   _____

6. There *is* a report of a serious forest fire in the mountains to the east of us.

   _____

7. He *will undergo* treatment sometime during the winter.

   _____

8. We *have decided* to drop the suit after getting advice from counsel.

   _____

9. The streets *flood* whenever we get a heavy spring rain.

_____

10. We *have made* significant improvements over the past six months.

_____

11. The roads *were* nearly impassable after the last ice storm.

_____

12. We *could afford* a new car if I got a raise this year.

_____

13. The company *rented* another office to get more storage space.

_____

14. The family *goes* for a drive on nice Sunday afternoons.

_____

15. We *got* some good news finally.

_____

Adverbs categorized by meaning

All adverbs fall into four broad categories of meaning: **time**, **place**, **reason**, and **manner**. Here are some examples (single-word, prepositional phrase, and adverb clause) of each type:

Adverbs of time (single word)
They went home Tuesday.
I came to the office early.
I haven't been feeling well recently.

Adverb prepositional phrase
I only work on weekends.
We will be on vacation during the last two weeks in August.
They left here about six o'clock.

Adverb clause
We visit my sister's family whenever we get the chance.
They were in Chicago when John gave his talk at the conference.
I'll stay as long as I am needed.

Adverbs of place (single word)

I just had lunch there.
I talked to Gary outside.
We finished exercising indoors.

Adverb prepositional phrase

A problem has come up at the office.
I could hear people talking in the living room.
There is a big oak tree behind the garage.

Adverb clause

Let's talk where it is quieter.
I need to sit down where I can rest for a minute.
They advertised the concert everywhere they could put up a poster.

Adverbs of reason (single word)

There are no single-word adverbs of reason.

Adverb prepositional phrase

We only did it out of a sense of duty.
I took the job for the benefits.
Ralph went to the wedding because of family obligation.

Adverb infinitive phrase

I went back to the office to get my briefcase.
We approached them to see if they would consider an offer.
I shook the tree to get the last walnuts off.

Adverb clause

He went home because he wasn't feeling well.
I bought a video recorder so that I could take pictures of the party.
We did it since it was part of our job description.

Adverbs of manner (single-word)

They turned down the offer politely.
He acted alone.
She acknowledged the reward gracefully.

Adverb prepositional phrase

We made the plane <u>with time to spare</u>.
We only succeeded <u>through good teamwork</u>.
They took the bad news <u>without complaint</u>.

Adverb clause

They did it <u>as well as anyone could have</u>.
We rowed <u>as if our lives depended on it</u>.
John reacted <u>as though he had never heard of the idea before</u>.

Exercise 12.9

Underline the adverbs in the following sentences. Above each adverb write the meaning of the adverb (*time*, *place*, *reason*, or *manner*).

manner   time

George *sprained* his back <u>badly</u> <u>this weekend</u>.

1. I *bought* lunch at the station before getting on the train.

2. We *searched* the Internet to find the cheapest fares.

3. He *works* in the office most mornings.

4. You *must practice* hard every day.

5. I *completed* the course at the university this spring.

6. You *managed* a difficult situation quite well today.

7. She *watched* thoughtfully for a few minutes.

8. She *ordered* a book from Amazon today because the local store didn't have it.

9. Charles *measured* the space carefully to make sure the rug would fit.

10. The kids *were* disappointed this morning because they couldn't go.

11. We *made* everyone happy recently by extending the deadline.

12. I *loaned* a friend your book last week because he needed it for a research project.

13. The kids *were playing* noisily in the backyard all afternoon.

14. The dog *registered* his displeasure by growling at us every time we came near him.

15. We *shared* a cab this morning because we were all going to the same place.

Order of adverbs

There is a strong tendency to use the different classes of adverbs in a certain left-to-right order. People usually follow this order when they use more than one class of adverb: (1) manner, (2) place, (3) time, (4) reason.

Here are some examples:

	Manner	Place	Time	Reason
I bought some sandwiches		at the grocery	this morning	for lunch
You need to practice	seriously		every day	to get any better
The plane circled the field	with its engine roaring		all afternoon	
It rained	heavily	in the mountains	during the night	due to a warm front
I found an apartment for Anne	by advertising	in the paper	Sunday	
Fred did the dishes			after breakfast	because there wasn't a clean dish in the house
The pipe started leaking	badly	under the sink	this morning	

Exercise 12.10

Move the adverbs in each of the following sentences to follow the proper manner-place-time-reason left-to-right order.

because it was so hot in our kitchen last night at a restaurant We *ate* dinner.
We *ate* dinner at a restaurant last night because it was so hot in our kitchen.

1. over the weekend at the gym I *hurt* my knee.

   _____

2. this afternoon by replacing the circuit board They *fixed* my computer.

   _____

3. because the flow is so restricted loudly all the time The river *roars*.

   _____

4. at the Marriott since our offices were being repainted We *had* our sales presentation.

   _____

5. because he was calling from his cell phone so loudly He *talked*.

   _____

6. to keep current with their needs every year carefully We *survey* all of our customers.

   _____

7. since we had dealt with that issue before at once I *recognized* the problem.

   _____

8. for their generous leave policy a lot Everyone *liked* the company.

   _____

9. before we took any action thoroughly We *investigated* the problem.

   _____

10. this afternoon at the gym because it was so hot I *got* very tired.

   _____

11. for a few minutes to give them time to get organized *Can* you *postpone* the meeting?

   _____

12. every weekend at school Our son *is taking* advanced placement courses.

   _____

13. because the material was new to us a great deal Everyone *enjoyed* the lecture.

   _____

14. to get any real compliance seriously You *must enforce* your policies.

_____

15. to collect antiques every year We *tour* Italy.

_____

16. when we explained to him again perfectly He *understood* the idea.

_____

17. in order to head off a bigger problem later right now You *must solve* the problem.

_____

18. since it has major cost implications carefully They *will review* your proposal.

_____

19. when you leave in order to save electricity Please *turn off* the lights in the office.

_____

20. tonight to take Anne to a movie *Can* I *borrow* the car?

_____

Part 3

Sentences

13

Questions and Negatives

Every language has ways of forming questions and negatives. In English, the processes of forming questions and negatives are closely related. First we will examine how English forms questions, and then we will turn to negatives.

Questions

In all languages there are two fundamentally different types of questions: **yes-no questions** and **information questions**.

Yes-no questions ask for "yes" or "no" answers. Information questions, on the other hand, ask for specific information and cannot be answered with a simple yes or no. Here are some examples of each type:

Here are some roughly comparable *yes-no* and information questions:

Yes-no questions	Information questions
Is there a staff meeting today?	When is the staff meeting?
Do you know his wife's name?	What is his wife's name?
Can I go, too?	Where are you going?
Will you be late?	When will you get back?

Obviously, the answers to the *yes-no* questions only anticipate an answer of yes or no, while the information question requires a specific piece of information. A mere yes or no to the question, "When is the staff meeting?" would be inadequate and inappropriate.

Exercise 13.1

Underline the verbs in the following questions and label each question as either *yes-no* or *information*.

> yes-no
> <u>Will</u> you <u>mail</u> the letters at the post office for me?

1. Can you determine the exact cost?

2. Whom did the police finally arrest for the crime?

3. How much can we afford?

4. Have they decided yet?

5. Was the ending of the movie really surprising?

6. Why should they want that?

7. Is the phone ringing?

8. Has it been raining all day?

9. Must they insure it for the full amount?

10. Will you be ready by six?

11. How much would it cost?

12. Will my using my cell phone disturb you?

13. Why should we care about it?

14. Has Lois approved it yet?

15. How often will we be meeting over the next couple of weeks?

Yes-no questions

There are two different ways that English forms *yes-no* questions: **yes-no questions** and **tag questions**. Here is an example of each:

> **Yes-*no* question:**   Are you ready to go?
> **Tag question:**   You are ready to go, aren't you?

Since tag questions always involve negatives, we will postpone dealing with them until the next section on negatives.

The basic characteristic of *yes-no* questions is that the subject and verb are inverted. In a statement, the normal word order is subject + verb. In *yes-no* questions, the subject and verb have been inverted so that the word order is verb + subject.

Here are some more examples with the subject in italics and the verb in bold:

Statement	Inverted *yes-no* question
We **should** call them.	**Should** *we* call them?
Bill **is** sick.	*Is* **Bill** sick?
I **can** come, too.	**Can** *I* come, too?
They **will** be home late.	**Will** *they* be home late?
You **are** leaving tonight.	**Are** *you* leaving tonight?
He **has** lost his mind.	**Has** *he* lost his mind?

Only a handful of verbs can be used in forming inverted *yes-no* questions. The vast majority of verbs cannot be inverted. For example:

Statement word order	Inverted word order
John **works** in New York.	X **Works** *John* in New York?
He **commutes** from Princeton.	X **Commutes** *he* from Princeton?
His parents **live** in California.	X **Live** *his parents* in California?

(If you think these inverted questions have a vaguely Shakespearean or King James Bible ring to them, you are absolutely correct. Up until the beginning of the eighteenth century, it was perfectly grammatical to form *yes-no* questions by inverting the first verb with the subject, no matter what the first verb was: helping verbs and main verbs alike both inverted with the subjects.)

There is no standard name in traditional grammar for the verbs in modern English that can be inverted to form *yes-no* questions. The verbs that can be inverted are made up of just the following three groups of verbs:

1. **Modal auxiliary verbs**: These include *can, could, may, might, must, shall, should, will,* and *would*. Here are some examples of questions formed with modal auxiliary verbs:

Statement word order	Inverted word order
We **can** drive there.	**Can** *we* drive there?
I **may** see you later.	**May** *I* see you later?
You **would** like them.	*Would* *you* like them?

Note: In traditional grammar *will* is singled out from the other modal auxiliary verbs as part of the future tense. Actually, there is nothing special about *will* from a grammatical point of view—it is just another one of the modal auxiliary verbs.

2. **Helping verbs**: The helping verbs are *be* and *have*. They help to form the progressive and perfect tenses.

Progressive:	*be* (*am*, *is*, *are*, *was*, *were*)
Perfect:	*have* (*have*, *has*, *had*)

Here are some examples of questions formed with helping verbs:

Statement word order	**Inverted word order**
He **is** leaving soon.	**Is** *he* leaving soon?
John **was** staying there.	**Was** *John* staying there?
They **have** been very busy.	**Have** *they* been very busy?
She **had** returned his e-mail.	*Had* *she* returned his e-mail?

3. **Main verbs**: In American English, the only main verb that can be used to form *yes-no* questions is *be* (*am*, *is*, *are*, *was*, *were*). Here are some examples of questions formed with the main verb *be*:

Statement word order	**Inverted word order**
The kids **are** at school.	**Are** *the kids* at school?
Jane **is** an accountant.	**Is** *Jane* an accountant?
He **is** here.	**Is** *he* here?

Note: In British English *have* used as a main verb can also be inverted to form *yes-no* questions. We will discuss the difference between the British and American use of *have* as a main verb later in this chapter.

Exercise 13.2

Turn the following statements into *yes-no* questions. Underline the verb(s) in the question and identify whether the first verb is a *modal auxiliary*, *helping verb*, or *main verb*.

John has locked the gates.

helping
verb
<u>Has</u> John <u>locked</u> the gates?

1. We are ready to leave soon.

2. You can translate that into Spanish.

_____

3. The kids were very happy with their presents.

_____

4. I should decline a second helping of your terrific dessert.

_____

5. They will be able to finance it by themselves.

_____

6. The French filmmakers have influenced his movies a lot.

_____

7. Her criticism is of great concern to the board.

_____

8. I'm working on it.

_____

9. He should postpone his trip.

_____

10. They are just kidding.

_____

11. It has gone on too long.

_____

12. He could have done it differently.

_____

13. They are in big trouble about this.

_____

14.   That will stain the carpet.

---

15.   We are turning around at the next corner.

To this point, we have formed *yes-no* questions from statements that contained verbs that can be inverted: the nine modal auxiliary verbs, the two helping verbs (*be* and *have*) and the main verb *be* (ignoring the British use of the main verb *have* for the moment).

What happens, however, when the statement does not contain any of these verbs? The answer is unique to English: we insert into the sentence what amounts to a dummy auxiliary verb. This dummy verb takes away the tense marker from the main verb (just like any modal auxiliary or helping verb) so that the main verb becomes an uninflected base form. The dummy verb, in its present or past tense form, is then inverted with the subject just like any other auxiliary verb. This dummy verb, is, of course, the verb *do*. Here are some examples using this dummy auxiliary verb.

Let's start with a simple sentence:

John **smiled**.

We cannot invert the verb *smiled* because it is neither an auxiliary verb nor a helping verb. What we do instead is insert the dummy auxiliary verb *do* in front of the main verb *smiled*. We will call this process the ***do* insertion rule**.

After *do* has been inserted just in front of the verb, we will automatically transfer the tense marker from that verb to *do*. (All we are really saying is that the first verb must always carry the present or past tense marker.) In our example, *do* picks up the past-tense marker from *smiled* so that *do* becomes *did* and *smiled*, having lost its past-tense marker, reverts back to its base form *smile*. The *do* insertion rule has now produced this intermediate sentence:

John ***did*** smile.

This is a perfectly grammatical sentence. It is a kind of emphatic version of the original sentence. It emphasizes that John really did smile, even though it is not something that we would normally expect of John. (This emphatic use of *do* as a kind of special-purpose auxiliary verb is the actual historical source of the *do* used in *yes-no* questions and negatives in modern English.)

This intermediate sentence now contains an auxiliary verb that can be inverted in the normal way to produce an ordinary *yes-no* question:

John **did** smile. ⇒ **Did** *John* smile?

Here are some more examples of changing statements to *yes-no* questions using the intermediate step of forming an emphatic *do* statement:

Statement	Emphatic *do* statement	*Yes-no* question
The TV **works**.	*The TV* **does** work.	**Does** *the TV* work?
She **got** the answer.	*She* **did** get the answer.	**Did** *she* get the answer?
He **returned** it.	*He* **did** return it.	**Did** *he* return it?
It **rained**.	*It* **did** rain.	**Did** *it* rain?
I **care**.	*I* **do** care.	**Do** *I* care?

Exercise 13.3

Turn the following statements into *yes-no* questions using the *do* insertion rule to form an emphatic *do* statement.

He shut the window.

Emphatic *do* statement	*Yes-no* question
He *did* shut the window	*Did* he shut the window?

1. He installed the program.

_____ _____

2. Tom fell down.

_____ _____

3. Ralph bought a camera.

_____ _____

4. Ruth swims every day.

_____ _____

5. The meeting lasted hours.

_____ _____

6. They trust each other.

_____ _____

7. The boss quit yesterday.

_____ _____

8. They tried really hard.

_____ _____

9. The wind damaged it.

_____ _____

10. Bob retires soon.

_____ _____

11. She loaned him her car.

_____ _____

12. He wrecked her car.

_____ _____

13. She got really angry.

_____ _____

14. He paid for the damages.

_____ _____

15. She still talks to him.

_____ _____

Exercise 13.4

Change the following sentences directly to their corresponding *yes-no* questions. Notice that some verbs will require *do* and some will not. Underline all the verbs in both the statement and the *yes-no* question.

Statement	**Yes-no question**
The CEO <u>has</u> <u>approved</u> the deal.	<u>Has</u> the CEO <u>approved</u> the deal?
The CEO <u>approved</u> the deal.	<u>Did</u> the CEO <u>approve</u> the deal?

1. They guessed the right answer.   _____

2. You can combine the results.   _____

3. That eliminated the problem. _____

4. That is stretching the material. _____

5. They will hire a consultant. _____

6. We have gathered enough material. _____

7. You can get away this weekend. _____

8. They questioned the results. _____

9. Ruth can convince them of anything. _____

10. The kids are making too much noise. _____

11. This seat is occupied. _____

12. It will rain this afternoon. _____

13. I should ignore his advice. _____

14. They have examined the issue carefully. _____

15. The photographer is ready. _____

There are not many differences in grammar between British and American English, but the use of *have* as a main verb is one of them. In American English, *have* as a main verb is just like any other main verb (except *be*, of course). To form a *yes-no* question, we must use the dummy helping verb *do*. For example:

Statement	**Inverted *yes-no* question**
She **has** a cold.	**Does** *she* **have** a cold?
They **had** a good time.	**Did** *they* **have** a good time?
I **have** a question.	**Do** *you* **have** a question?
The program **had** a bug.	**Did** *the program* **have** a bug?

In British English, however, *have* can also be treated like the main verb *be*: it is inverted with the subject without the use of *do*. For example:

Statement	**Inverted *yes-no* question**
She **has** a cold.	**Has** *she* a cold?
They **had** a good time.	**Had** *they* a good time?
I **have** a question.	**Have** *you* a question?
The program **had** a bug.	**Had** *the program* a bug?

According to some studies, in British English the use of *do* with *have* as a main verb is becoming more common in informal situations so that, for example, you would hear both of these in conversation in England:

> **Has** *she* a cold?
> **Does** *she* **have** a cold?

Likewise, the British use of **have** as a main verb is much more commonly heard in American English that it was a few generations ago.

Exercise 13.5

Change the following statements containing *have* into both British and American English.

We have a problem.

British English	**American English**
Have we a problem?	Do we have a problem?

1. You have a glass.

_____

2. The car has a flat tire.

_____

3. You have your ticket.

_____

4. She has a good chance.

_____

5. Your cat has a name.

_____

6. The house has a pool.

_____

7. The picture has a frame.

_____

8. The book has an index.

_____   _____

9. The letter has a stamp.

_____   _____

10. The car has a GPS.

_____   _____

One problem nonnative speakers may have with *yes-no* questions is that in informal conversational English, nobody seems to follow the rules. In listening to casual conversation, you will be surprised at how frequent nonstandard, informal *yes-no* questions are. One study of conversational English found that informal questions made up an astonishing 41 percent of the total number of questions.

By far the most common informal *yes-no* question is one in which an inverted verb (or *be* as a main verb) has been deleted. In the following examples, the deleted verb is represented by ∅:

Standard *yes-no* question	Elliptical *yes-no* question
Are *they* going to the meeting?	∅ *They* going to the meeting?
Are *you* ready?	∅ *You* ready?
Do you know where the sugar is?	∅ You know where the sugar is?
Have you had lunch yet?	∅ You had lunch yet?

Notice the deleted verb is either a helping verb (some form of *be* from a progressive tense; some form of *have* from a perfect tense; or some form of the dummy helping verb *do*) or it is some form of *be* used as a main tense. We cannot delete modal auxiliary verbs. For example:

Standard *yes-no* question	Elliptical *yes-no* question
Can *I* come with you?	X ∅ *I* come with you?
Will *we* get there on time?	X ∅ *We* get there on time?
Should they call a cab?	X ∅ *They* call a cab?

Exercise 13.6

Change the statements in the left column to the corresponding informal *yes-no* question in the right column. Use a ∅ to represent the position of the missing verb. If you cannot change the statement into an informal *yes-no* question, write *Invalid*.

Statement	Informal *yes-no* question
You are taking a break.	∅ You taking a break?

1. The group is working on it.   _____

2. They are redoing the office again.   _____

3. We have been opening new stores.   _____

4. You can locate the Smith file.   _____

5. The cat is staring at the goldfish.   _____

6. You have been sleeping badly lately.   _____

7. They should try to finish today.   _____

8. Harry was very upset about it.   _____

9. There have been some questions.   _____

10. You miss me. (Tricky!)   _____

Information questions

The other major type of question is **information questions**. They are called information questions because (unlike *yes-no* questions) they begin with **interrogative pronouns** that ask for specific kinds of information. For example, information questions that begin with the interrogative pronoun *where* ask for information about place. For example, the question

> **Where** did Charlie go?

must be answered with information about the places where Charlie could have gone. For instance:

> He went to Chicago.
> He went home.
> He went where he could get a good latte.

Here is a list of the main single-word interrogative pronouns arranged by the part of speech that the interrogative pronoun plays:

Pronoun	Part of speech	Example
Who, whom	Noun phrase	**Who** are you?
		Whom did you meet?
What, which	Noun phrase	**What** did you find?
		Which did you pick?
Whose, which	Possessive	**Whose book** is on the desk?

	Noun phrase	**Which book** do you want?
Where	Adverb of place	**Where** are you going?
When	Adverb of time	**When** will you get there?
Why	Adverb of reason	**Why** do you want to go there?
How	Adverb of manner	**How** will you get there?

In addition, there are a number of interrogatives compounded with *how*. All of these are adverbs. For example:

How often	Frequency	**How often** do you go there?
How long	Length in time/space	**How long** will you stay?
How far	Distance	**How far** is it?
How much	Quantity	**How much** does it cost to go there?
How soon	Quickness	**How soon** can you get there?

Sometimes these adverbs are called **interrogative adverbs**, and sometimes they are merely lumped together with the other interrogative pronouns, as we will do here.

Exercise 13.7

Underline the interrogative pronouns and label their part of speech: noun, possessive noun, or type of adverb.

Adv of
frequency
<u>How often</u> do you come here?

1. Who are you?

2. Whom did you say you were?

3. How much gasoline do we need to buy?

4. Whose advice should we take?

5. When shall we three meet again?

6. Why do we want to do that?

7. Whom did they finally pick?

8. How did your team do this weekend?

9. Whose dog is that in the backyard?

10. How much longer do we have to wait?

If you look at the ten information questions in Exercise 13.7, you will immediately notice one thing: all information questions begin with an interrogative pronoun. Clearly, one part of forming information questions is to move the interrogative pronoun to the first position in the sentence (unless it was already in the first position to begin with). To get a sense of how this process works, let us begin with a simple example:

Where *shall* we eat?

Underlying every question, no matter whether it is a *yes-no* question or an information question, there is a corresponding statement. The statement that underlies this information question is

Adv of
place

We *should* eat **where**.

Here the interrogative pronoun *where* originates as an adverb of place following the verb *eat*.

We change this underlying statement into something approximating the final information question by moving the interrogative adverb to the beginning of the sentence:

We *should* eat **where**. ⇒ **Where** we *should* eat?

In many languages in the world,

Where we *should* eat?

would be a perfectly grammatical sentence. English, of course, makes the process more complicated.

Information questions must also undergo the same rule that we saw for *yes-no* questions: we must invert the first verb with the subject. In other words, there is a general rule that holds equally for both *yes-no* and information questions. In our example, the final step in converting the underlying statement to a question is inverting the verb *should* and the subject *we*:

Where we *should* eat. ⇒ **Where** *should* we eat?

As you can see, there is a two-step process for converting underlying statements into information questions:

1. Move the interrogative pronoun to the first position in the sentence.

2. Invert the verb and subject.

Here are some more examples showing the application of the two rules:

<table>
<tr><td></td><td style="text-align:center">Adv
of time</td></tr>
</table>

Underlying statement:	They *will* be back **when**.
Rule 1:	They *will* be back **when**. ⇒ **When** they *will* be back.
Rule 2:	**When** they *will* be back. ⇒ **When** *will* they be back**?**

Adv of
frequency

Underlying statement:	You *have* seen it **how often**.
Rule 1:	You *have* seen it **how often**. ⇒ **How often** you *have* seen it.
Rule 2:	**How often** you *have* seen it. ⇒ **How often** *have* you seen it**?**

NP

Underlying statement:	We *should* give them **what**.
Rule 1:	We *should* give them **what**. ⇒ **What** we *should* give them.
Rule 2:	**What** we *should* give them. ⇒ **What** *should* we give them**?**

Poss noun

Underlying statement:	That *is* **whose car**.
Rule 1:	That *is* **whose car**. ⇒ **Whose car** that *is*.
Rule 2:	**Whose car** that *is*. ⇒ **Whose car** *is* that**?**

Note that the possessive noun *whose* can never be separated from *car*, the word *whose* modifies. In other words the possessive noun + noun unit makes up a single noun phrase that cannot be broken up.

Exercise 13.8

Change the following statements to information questions. Apply the two rules step by step.

We *are* leaving **how soon**.

Rule 1:	We *are* leaving **how soon**. ⇒ **How soon** we *are* leaving.
Rule 2:	**How soon** we *are* leaving. ⇒ **How soon** *are* we leaving**?**

1. They *will* finish on time **how**.

2. We *should* ask **whom**.

_____

_____

3. They *are* staying **where**.

_____

_____

4. The matter with him *is* **what**.

_____

_____

5. We *can* see her **how soon**.

_____

_____

6. They *are* staying **how long**.

_____

_____

7. They *had* planned to leave **when**.

_____

_____

8. The meetings *are* **how long** usually.

_____

_____

9. I *should* pay **how much** for it.

_____

_____

10. They *would* meet with us **how often**.

_____

_____

11. He *had* given **what** to them for Christmas that year.

_____

_____

12. We *should* care **why** what he thinks about it.

_____

_____

13. They *would* park the car **where** if the lot is closed.

_____

_____

14. Robert *is* doing **what on earth** in Cleveland.

_____

_____

15. We *should* call him **what**.

_____

_____

To this point we have only worked with information questions that have been formed with verbs that can be inverted: modal auxiliary verbs, helping verbs, and *be* as a main verb. Now we will look at information questions that require *do*. There is nothing actually different about these questions, except that having to insert *do* adds one more step to the process. Let us start again with the two movement rules:

1. Move the interrogative pronoun to the first position in the sentence.

2. Invert the verb and subject.

Between these two rules, we need to apply the **do insertion rule**. That is, we insert *do* before the first verb and transfer the tense of that first verb to *do*. We then apply Rule 2 in the normal way. Here is an example:

Statement:	They *left* **when**.
Rule 1:	**When** they *left*.
***Do* insertion:**	**When** they *did* leave.
Rule 2:	**When** *did* they leave?

Note that *did* has picked up the past tense from *left*, causing *left* to revert back to its base form, *leave*.

Here are several more examples using the *do* insertion rule:

Statement:	You *want* to go **where**.
Rule 1:	**Where** you *want* to go.
***Do* insertion:**	**Where** you *do* want to go. (Note that *do* is in the present tense)
Rule 2:	**Where** *do* you want to go?

Statement:	They *turned* the offer down **why**.
Rule 1:	**Why** they *turned* the offer down.
***Do* insertion:**	**Why** they *did* turn the offer down.
Rule 2:	**Why** *did* they turn the offer down?

Statement:	You *called* them **how often** about the meeting.
Rule 1:	**How often** you *called* them about the meeting.
***Do* insertion:**	**How often** you *did* call them about the meeting.
Rule 2:	**How often** *did* you call them about the meeting?

Exercise 13.9

Change the following statements to information questions using *do* insertion and the two movement rules.

I *missed* **what**.

Rule 1:	**What** I *missed*.
***Do* insertion:**	**What** I *did* miss.
Rule 2:	**What** *did* I miss?

1. They *claimed* **how much** in damages.

_____

_____

_____

2. He *demanded* to see **whom**.

_____

_____

_____

3. The decision *depends* on **what**.

_____

_____

4. Your cats *reacted* to your new dog **how**.

_____

_____

5. The kids *want* to do this weekend **what**.

_____

_____

6. You *rented* **which movie**.

_____

_____

7. She *got* to the office **when**.

_____

_____

8. Roberta *picked* **whom** for the advisory committee.

_____

_____

9. You *think* that you will pick **whose health plan**.

_____

_____

10. They *plan* to stay in Los Angeles **how long**.

_____

_____

_____

The way information questions in English are formed differs in two important respects from the way information questions are formed in nearly all other languages. Most languages convert statements to information questions by moving an interrogative pronoun to the first position in the sentence. However, as you know, English also requires that the subject and verb be inverted and that we insert *do* if there is no other suitable helping verb to be the tense-carrying verb. Thus English requires two extra steps, both of which are complicated. Given that the process of forming information questions in English is both unusual and complicated, it is not surprising that mistakes in information questions are among the most common mistakes of nonnative speakers, even fluent ones who rarely make other kinds of mistakes. In the following examples, the subject noun phrase is in italics and the helping verb is in bold.

Error	**Standard**
X Where *you* **are** going?	Where **are** *you* going?
X When *they* **will** be back?	When **will** *they* be back?
X What *they* **have** done?	What **have** *they* done?
X Why *he* **said** that?	Why **did** *he* say that?

All of these mistakes result from stopping the process of converting statements to information questions after doing only Rule 1: move the interrogative pronoun to the first position in the sentence. To correct these errors, speakers need to apply the *do* insertion rule (if necessary) and then, most critically, apply Rule 2 and invert the subject and the first, tense-carrying helping verb.

Exercise 13.10

Correct the errors in the left column and put the corrected form in the right column.

Error	**Standard**
Why I *should* believe you?	Why *should* I believe you?
1. **When** the program *will* start?	_____
2. **How** I *am* doing?	_____
3. **What** we *have* missed so far?	_____
4. **How much** they *are* charging for it?	_____

5. **Why** he *had* so much trouble? _____

6. **How early** we *could* finish here? _____

7. **Where** we *sign* up for the program? _____

8. **Whose advice** you *are* going to follow? _____

9. **What song** they *were* singing? _____

10. **How many parts** I *should* order now? _____

11. **What subject** you *teach*? _____

12. **What** the problem *was* with my phone? _____

13. **How** they *will* recognize you? _____

14. **When** they *should* take the test? _____

15. **Why** the government *requires* that form? _____

Up to this point we have ignored one type of information question: questions in which the interrogative pronoun plays the role of subject. Here are some examples with *who* playing the role of subject with all the different types of verbs:

Modal:	**Who** *can* take the dog for a walk?
	Who *will* take care of the children?
Helping verb:	**Who** *is* working on the Smith papers?
	Who *has* had lunch already?
Be **as main verb:**	**Who** *is* the visitor?
	Who *was* Alfred Smith?
No helping verb:	**Who** *reported* the accident?
	Who *answered* the phone?

As you can see, these information questions seem to break all the rules: there is no inversion of subject and helping verb, and in the last pair of examples, *do* is not used when there is no helping verb. Obviously, there is something special that happens when the interrogative pronoun plays the role of subject.

Basically, the two rules do not apply when the interrogative pronoun is the subject. To see why this is the case, let's start with the following statement and try to apply the two rules:

Who *should* go next.

Rule 1 does not apply because the interrogative pronoun is already in the first position in the sentence. If we apply Rule 2, we will produce an ungrammatical question because we will put the subject after the verb as though we were trying to create some strange form of *yes-no* question:

   X *Should* **who** *go next?*

Thus, we cannot apply either Rule 1 or Rule 2 when the interrogative pronoun is the subject of the sentence. When the interrogative pronoun plays the role of subject, the underlying statement is already in the correct final form for an information question and no further changes are needed (or even possible). Since only nouns can play the role of subject, the kinds of interrogative pronouns that can be subjects are necessarily limited to the following:

Nouns:	*who*, *what*, *which*
Possessive nouns:	*whose*, *which* + noun

Here are some more examples:

Nouns
Who *told* you the answer?
What *do* you mean by that?
Which *is* the right one?

Possessive nouns
Whose computer *did* you use?
Which train *should* we take?

A particularly difficult problem for native and nonnative speakers alike is choosing between *who* and *whom* in information questions. For example, which of the following is correct?

   Who did you want to see?
   Whom did you want to see?

To determine which one is correct, we have to undo Rule 1 and move the interrogative pronoun back to where it came from:

   Rule 1:   **Who** *did* you want to see? ⇒ You wanted to see **who**.

By undoing Rule 1 we can see that *who* is the object of the verb *see*. Since it is an object pronoun, we must use *whom* rather than *who*. Thus, the correct form of the information questions is

   Whom did you want to see?

Here is a second example. Which of the following is correct?

> **Who** wanted to see you?
> **Whom** wanted to see you?

This is an easier question because there is no other noun besides *who* that is able to play the role of the subject of *wanted*. *You*, the only other noun in the sentence, is locked in place as the object of the verb *see*.

Exercise 13.11

Choose the correct form. If *whom* is the correct answer, rewrite the underlying sentence to show where *whom* came from.

> (~~Who~~/<u>Whom</u>) have they decided on for the job?
> They have decided on whom for the job?

1. (*Who/Whom*) did they nominate for the award?

_____

2. (*Who/Whom*) did she draw a picture of?

_____

3. (*Who/Whom*) has been waiting the longest?

_____

4. (*Who/Whom*) was involved in the project?

_____

5. (*Who/Whom*) had he been seeing before he met her?

_____

6. (*Who/Whom*) should we send the invitations to?

_____

7. (*Who/Whom*) will they trust the most, George or Fred?

_____

8. (*Who/Whom*) could have taken the money?

_____

9. (*Who/Whom*) do we give the money to?

_____

10. (*Who/Whom*) have we not heard from recently?

_____

Negatives

The rules for forming negatives are similar to the rules for forming questions. We will begin by looking at the process for forming negative statements. *Not* is inserted immediately after modal auxiliary verbs, helping verbs, and *be* used as a main verb. For example:

	Positive	**Negative**
Modals	John *can* meet with us.	John *can* **not** meet with us.
	They *should* leave now.	They *should* **not** leave now.
	It *might* rain today.	It *might* **not** rain today.
Helping	He *is* writing a book now.	He *is* **not** writing a book now.
	I *have* seen that movie.	I *have* **not** seen that movie.
	They *were* talking.	They *were* **not** talking.
Be	The car *is* ready.	The car *is* **not** ready.
	The water *is* cold.	The water *is* **not** cold.
	The game *was* over.	The game *was* **not** over.

Exercise 13.12

Change the positive statements in the left column into negative statements in the right column.

Positive
I was looking at them.

Negative
I was *not* looking at them.

1. You should buy a new cell phone. _____

2. They are adopting the new plan. _____

3. We can arrange a meeting. _____

4. I have driven Anne's new car. _____

5. They were upset by the outcome. _____

6. They have ignored the problem. _____

7. I am counting on it. _____

8. Richard might be able to come. _____

9. The replacement is a standard size. _____

10. I could unlock the file cabinet. _____

In writing, *not* is sometimes contracted and sometimes left uncontracted. In works of fiction, *not* is usually contracted to give a sense of what the spoken language actually sounds like. In nonfiction writing, especially if the writing is at all formal, *not* is usually left uncontracted.

In speech, *not* is almost always contracted, unless the speaker is strongly asserting the fact that the sentence is negative. Since the normal expectation in the spoken language is that *not* will be contracted, when *not* is left uncontracted it gives the sentence a special negative emphasis even without any extra stress on the pronunciation of *not*. (Although, in fact, *not* usually is stressed.)

Here are the contracted forms of the modals and the helping verbs *be* and *have*. Note that many verbs do not have contracted forms.

Uncontracted	Contracted
can	can't
could	couldn't
may	may not (no contraction)
might	might not (no contraction)
must	mustn't
shall	shall not (no contraction)
should	shouldn't
will	won't (highly irregular)
would	wouldn't
am	am not (no contraction)
is	isn't
are	aren't
was	wasn't
were	weren't
has	hasn't
have	haven't
had	hadn't

Exercise 13.13

Underline the verb and *not*. If the verb and *not* have a contracted form, draw a line through the verb and *not* and write the contracted form above them. If there is no contracted form, write *OK* above them.

can't
I ~~can not~~ imagine doing it any other way.

1. We should not get stuck in traffic this time of day.

2. They must not do that.

3. They will not identify themselves.

4. The kids have not flown by themselves before.

5. The time allotted for the presentations was not equally divided.

6. I might not be able to come to the reception.

7. Unfortunately, we were not prepared for such an emergency.

8. They may not have the necessary documentation.

9. It probably would not make any difference anyway.

10. We can not get the authorization to hire the new staff.

When a sentence does not have a modal auxiliary, helping verb, or *be* used as a main verb, we must insert the dummy auxiliary verb *do* immediately in front of the first verb. By exactly the same process we saw with questions, *do* takes the present or past tense marker from the first verb, leaving that verb in the uninflected, base form. Again, we will call this the *do* insertion rule. The *do* insertion rule creates an emphatic version of the sentence. Here is an example:

Underlying positive statement:	Most people today *smoke*.
***Do* insertion rule:**	Most people today *do* smoke.

Next, we need to use the *not* insertion rule to insert *not* immediately after the first verb just as we did in sentences with auxiliary and helping verbs:

***Not* insertion rule:**	Most people today *do* **not** smoke.

Here are some more examples:

Underlying positive statement:	I *like* living in New York.
Do insertion rule:	I *do* like living in New York.
***Not* insertion:**	I *do* **not** like living in New York.

Underlying positive statement:	They know where it is.
Do insertion rule:	They do know where it is.
***Not* insertion:**	They *do* **not** know where it is.

Exercise 13.14

Convert the underlying positive statements into negative statements by using the *do* and *not* insertion rules.

> The waiter *charged* us for the extra coffee.
> **Do** insertion: The waiter *did* charge us for the extra coffee.
> *Not* insertion: The waiter *did* **not** charge us for the extra coffee.

1. I *remembered* where I parked the car.

   _____

   _____

2. You *called* the office.

   _____

   _____

3. It *happened* the way we thought it would.

   _____

   _____

4. He *passed* the exam on the first try.

   _____

   _____

5. We *stayed* until the meeting was over.

   _____

   _____

6. Jim *believed* what his staff was telling him.

   _____

   _____

7. I *walked* to work this morning.

   _____

   _____

8. They *came* to a satisfactory agreement.

_____

_____

9. The manager *explained* all of the office procedures.

_____

_____

10. The documents in question actually *exist*.

_____

_____

11. The regulations *apply* to this situation.

_____

_____

12. They *prepared* enough food for everybody.

_____

_____

13. She *felt* very good this morning.

_____

_____

14. Jason's family *went* home for Christmas this year.

_____

_____

15. The SEC *stopped* the merger from going ahead as planned.

_____

_____

Given how difficult it is to form both questions and negatives, it is surprisingly easy to form negative questions. It is simply a matter of applying the *not* insertion rule to an already formed question. The *not* insertion rule places the *not* immediately after the first verb. No further changes are needed, except of course the contraction of the verb + *not* if that is appropriate. Here are some examples:

Yes-no questions

Can they get ready in time? ⇒ *Can* **not** (*Can't*) they get ready in time?
Will the kids be back for dinner? ⇒ *Will* **not** (*Won't*) the kids be back for dinner?
Should we tell them? ⇒ *Should* **not** (*Shouldn't*) we tell them?
Are you coming? ⇒ *Are* **not** (*Aren't*) you coming?
Have you finished yet? ⇒ *Have* **not** (*Haven't*) you finished yet?
Am I right? ⇒ *Am* **not** (*Aren't*) I right?
Do you know the answer? ⇒ *Do* **not** (*Don't*) you know the answer?

Information questions

Who *is* going with us? ⇒ Who *is* **not** (*isn't*) going with us?
What *have* we done? ⇒ What *have* **not** (*haven't*) we done?
Why *did* we do that? ⇒ Why *did* **not** (*didn't*) we do that?
Who *will* be able to go? ⇒ Who *will* **not** (*won't*) be able to go?

Exercise 13.15

Turn the following statements into negative questions. Show the contracted forms of the negative (if any).

The lawyers *could* prove that the defendant was at the scene of the crime.
Couldn't the lawyers prove that the defendant was at the scene of the crime?

1. You should report the accident to the police.

   _____

2. Bob could get a license for his antique car.

   _____

3. They were a well-established firm.

   _____

4. She has been doing her French homework.

   _____

5. You like rap music.

   _____

6. She is wearing her coat.

_____

7. He could ask for a new assignment.

_____

8. It might cause a real argument.

_____

9. He filled the car up with gas.

_____

10. You watched the game last night?

_____

11. He is retiring next year.

_____

12. She just bought a new car seat for Timmy.

_____

13. He reminded everyone about the meeting on Monday.

_____

14. You hate going on long trips these days.

_____

15. They have already guessed what they are getting for Christmas.

_____

Question tags

A tag is a word or phrase added onto an otherwise already complete sentence. Most languages have what is called a **question tag**. Question tags are not genuine requests for information where the speaker is seeking new information. Question tags are short phrases added to the ends of sentences by speakers to get confirmation that their audience is following and/or agreeing with what the speakers are saying. A simple question tag is _right_. For example:

You know how to fill out these forms, _right_?

Often a question tag is a single fixed phrase like *right* in English or *nicht wahr* in German. The most common and important question tag in English is unusually complex because the form of the question tag is not fixed. It depends entirely on the grammar of the main sentence. Here is a pair of examples:

> You are coming tonight, *aren't you?*
> You are not coming tonight, *are you?*

The form of the question tag is determined by the grammar of the main sentence in four different ways:

1. Most obviously, there is a positive-negative reversal between the main sentence and the question tag. If the main sentence is positive, then the question tag must be negative. If the main sentence is negative, then the question tag must be positive.

2. The verb in the question tag is determined by the verb in the main sentence. If the verb in the main sentence is a modal auxiliary or helping verb, then the tag must be that same modal auxiliary or helping verb. For example:

Modal

They *should* go, *shouldn't* they?

We *will* be ready, *won't* we?

Alice *can* play the oboe, *can't* she?

Be

We *are* going soon, *aren't* we?

The boss *wasn't* upset, *was* he?

Have

Joan *has* finished the job, *hasn't* she?

The office *hadn't* closed early, *had* it?

If the verb in the main sentence is *be* used as a main verb, then *be* is repeated in the question tag. For example:

They *were* happy with our work, *weren't* they?

It *isn't* a good time to meet, *is* it?

(As you have doubtless noticed, these same verbs—modals, helping verb, and *be* used as a main verb—also figure prominently in forming questions and negatives without using *do*.)

If the main sentence does not use a modal auxiliary, helping verb, or *be* as a main verb, then the question tag must use *do*. For example:

Roger missed the bus again, *didn't* he?

I predicted the outcome of the game, *didn't* I?

Senator Blather speaks after dinner, *doesn't* he?

If *do* (usually in the negative) is used in the main sentence, then *do* must be repeated in the question tag. For example:

He *didn't* mean it, *did* he?

I *don't* know, *do* I?

3.   The tense of the tag question must be the same as the tense in the main sentence. If the tense in the main sentence is past, then the tag must also be past. If the tense in the main is present, then the tag must also be present. For example, consider the following sentence:

John and Mary *are* sailing to the island tomorrow, *aren't* they?

The question tag is in the present tense because the verb in the main sentence is in the present tense. If the tag were in a different tense, the sentence would be ungrammatical:

X John and Mary *are* sailing to the island tomorrow, *weren't* they?

4.   The noun phrase in the question tag is based on the subject noun phrase in the main sentence. If the subject noun phrase is a pronoun, then that pronoun must be repeated in the question tag. For example:

They are going to rewrite the letter, aren't *they*?

However, if the subject noun phrase in the main sentence is not a pronoun, the noun phrase in the question tag must be a pronoun that replaces the subject noun phrase in the main sentence. Here are some examples with various kinds of noun phrases in the main sentence:

Proper noun:	*Barbara* called again, didn't *she*?
Compound nouns:	*Tom and Barbara* will be there, won't *they*?
Abstract noun:	*The conflicts in the Middle East* are not a simple matter, are *they*?
Gerund:	*Going to school* takes a lot of money, doesn't *it*?
Infinitive:	*To graduate this fall* has always been his goal, hasn't *it*?
Noun clause:	*Where they should live* has been an issue with them, hasn't *it*?

Exercise 13.16

Add a question tag to each of the following sentences.

You need a pillow.
You need a pillow, don't you?

1. We won't get over this easily.

___

2. The group can count on us.

___

3. What he said really made an impact on everyone.

___

4. The CEO and the Board issued a press release.

___

5. The new staff members are sadly lacking in experience.

___

6. The gate agent can't change our seat assignments.

___

7. Working all the time really wears you down.

___

8. The fire department couldn't get there in time.

___

9. To run such a large operation requires a big support staff.

___

10. The article in the *Times* wasn't very accurate.

___

11. The doctors might have to operate.

___

12. This year's graduates were all looking for jobs in finance.

_____

13. The consultants don't know what to suggest.

_____

14. Who reports to Mrs. Johnston won't be decided till later.

_____

15. Trying your best is the important thing.

_____

14

The Passive

In most sentences, the subject of the sentence is also the **agent** or performer of the action of the verb. For example, consider the following sentence:

> Mary answered the phone.

The subject, *Mary*, is also the agent, the person who performs the action of answering the phone.

Sometimes, however, we want to use sentences in which the subject is not the agent. For example, consider the following sentence:

> Mary was promoted last week.

Mary is still the nominal subject (the verb *was* is in the third-person singular to agree with the singular noun *Mary*), but *Mary* is not the agent. In other words, *Mary* is not the person doing the promoting. Instead, she is the *recipient* of the action of the verb *promote*. She did not promote anyone; somebody promoted her. Accordingly, the sentence is a **passive** sentence.

Passive sentences in English have a unique grammatical structure: they must contain what we will call the **passive helping verb** *be*. There are actually two different helping verbs that use *be* in some form: one that is used to form the progressive, and one that is used to form the passive. How can we tell them apart? The answer is by looking at the form of the verb that immediately follows the helping verb *be*. Compare the following sentences:

	present participle be + verb
Progressive:	We <u>were cleaning</u> out the garage yesterday.

	past participle be + verb
Passive:	The garage <u>was cleaned</u> out yesterday.

As you can see,

> *be* + present participle = progressive
> *be* + past participle = passive

A sentence can even be both progressive and passive so long as it meets the requirements: *be* + present participle (Pres Part) for the progressive and *be* + past participle (Past Part) for the passive. Here is an example of a sentence with both:

> The job <u>is</u> <u>being</u> <u>contracted</u> out to a firm in Singapore.
> *be* + Pres Part *be* + Past Part

In order to have both a progressive and a passive, the sentence must contain two different *be*'s: one for the progressive, and one for the passive. What is tricky is that the verb *being* plays a role in both constructions: it is the present perfect tense form that is required for the progressive, and it is also the helping verb for the passive.

Only sentences that contain the sequence *be* + a past participle verb are passive. All other sentences are called **active** sentences. That is, by default, sentences that do not contain the sequence of *be* + a past participle are automatically classified as **active**.

Here are some examples of passive sentences with the helping verb *be* and the past participle in bold. Note that the passive helping verb can be used in combination with other helping verbs (in italics), sometimes producing rather long and complicated verb sequences:

> The movie **was filmed** in Spain.
> I **was reminded** that we have to go to Chicago tomorrow.
> The contract *will* **be signed** Tuesday.
> Your car *has* **been parked** on the lower level.
> The meeting *should have* **been finished** by now.
> The accident *is* **being reported** to the insurance company.

Exercise 14.1

Write *active* or *passive* above the verbs in the following sentences as appropriate. If the sentence is passive, confirm your answer by underlining the verb *be* and the past participle.

> passive
> We should have <u>been warned</u> of the risk before we started.

1. Mrs. Johnston was appointed to the district court.

2. The present was wrapped in bright red paper.

3. Finally, the mystery has been solved!

4. John has retired from his position at the university.

5. The remodeling is costing us a fortune.

6. Your salary will be adjusted to reflect the higher cost of living in Tokyo.

7. The gate is always locked at 6 P.M.

8. The company's success has been noticed by the financial press.

9. My car was previously owned by a reckless teenager.

10. The operation has just emerged from bankruptcy.

11. Senator Blather was elected in 1996.

12. The alarm was first sounded by a security guard in the early morning.

13. I should have listened more carefully.

14. The product should have been recalled earlier.

15. The play is being directed by Joan Ridgeway.

Virtually every passive sentence has an active sentence counterpart. In order to use a passive sentence effectively, we need to be able compare the passive and active forms of the same sentence to see which version best suits our purpose. To make this comparison, we need to understand how to convert a passive sentence into its counterpart active form, and vice versa, how to convert an active sentence into its counterpart passive form. Unfortunately this conversion back and forth between the active and passive forms is one of the most complicated operations in English grammar.

Let us begin by looking closely at how we change the active sentence "John saw Mary" into its passive counterpart, "Mary was seen by John." The first and most important step is to insert the passive auxiliary verb *be* immediately in front of the main verb in the active sentence. Adding the passive auxiliary verb *be* automatically triggers the following changes in verb forms: the original tense of the main verb passes over to *be*, and the main verb changes to its past participle form.

John *saw* Mary. ⇒ John *was seen* Mary.

The next two steps are both complicated and unique to the passive. The subject in the active sentence is turned into a prepositional phrase beginning with *by*:

John *was seen* Mary. ⇒ **by** John *was seen* Mary.

Then this new prepositional phrase switches place with the original object:

by John *was seen* Mary. ⇒ Mary *was seen* **by** John.

The most important thing to understand about the process that converts the active to the passive is that it does not change the meaning of the sentence. The passive means exactly the same thing as the original active. The purpose of the shift from active to passive is to change the focus or emphasis of the sentence. In the active form of the sentence, the focus is on what the subject does. In the passive form of the sentence, the focus is on what happens to the object. In our example, the active version of the sentence tells us what John did (he saw Mary). The passive version of the sentence tells us what happened to Mary (she was seen by John).

Here are some more examples of the three-step process of changing an active sentence to its passive counterpart:

Active:	Kathy *postponed* the meeting.
Insert passive auxiliary:	Kathy *was postponed* the meeting.
Insert *by*:	**by** Kathy *was postponed* the meeting.
Switch subject and object:	The meeting *was postponed* **by** Kathy.
Active:	The joke *amused* the audience.
Insert passive auxiliary:	The joke *was amused* the audience.
Insert *by*:	**by** the joke *was amused* the audience.
Switch subjects and objects:	The audience *was amused* **by** the joke.
Active:	The Senator *denies* all charges.
Insert passive auxiliary:	The Senator *is denied* all charges.
Insert *by*:	**by** the Senator *is denied* all charges.
Switch subjects and objects:	All charges *are denied* **by** the Senator.

Did you notice that we had to make one final adjustment when we switched the subject and object in the last example? When the old object in the active sentence became the new subject in the passive sentence, we had to adjust the form of the verb *be* to agree with the number of the new subject since it was different from the number of the old subject. That is, we had to change *is denied* to *are denied* to agree with the new plural subject *all charges* rather than the old singular subject *the Senator*.

Exercise 14.2

Use the three-step process shown previously to convert the following active sentences into their passive sentence counterparts.

McGraw-Hill published the books.

Insert passive auxiliary:	McGraw-Hill *was published* the books.
Insert *by*:	**by** McGraw-Hill *was published* the books.
Switch subjects and objects:	The books *were published* **by** McGraw-Hill.

1. Janet answered my questions.

_____

_____

_____

2. The press office issued a statement.

_____

_____

_____

3. Everybody supported the proposal.

_____

_____

_____

4. A visitor taught my economics class today.

_____

_____

_____

5. What happened proved my point.

_____

_____

_____

6. Somebody made a big mistake.

_____

_____

_____

7. Our law firm represents the union.

_____

_____

_____

8. Many companies use our software programs.

_____

_____

_____

9. The new process obtains much better results.

_____

_____

_____

10. The government recognizes the problem.

_____

_____

_____

Fortunately, adding the passive auxiliary to other sentences with other helping or auxiliary verbs is not at all difficult because the passive auxiliary is always added at the end of any sequence just in front of the main verb so that adding the passive auxiliary does not cause changes in any of the other auxiliary or helping verbs. Here are some examples:

Perfect
Active:	Mary has seen John.
Passive:	John has *been seen* by Mary.

Active:	The rug had covered most of the floor.
Passive:	Most of the floor had *been covered* by the rug.

Progressive
Active:	Mary is seeing John.
Passive:	John is *being seen* by Mary.

| Active: | Ralph was offering me the job. |
| Passive: | I was *being offered* the job by Ralph. |

Modal auxiliary

| Active: | Mary might see John. |
| Passive: | John might *be seen* by Mary. |

| Active: | They will pay the bill. |
| Passive: | The bill will *be paid* by them. |

As you can see from the preceding examples, the forms of *be* and the main verb are completely predictable: the passive auxiliary *be* always takes on whatever tense the main verb originally was: if the main verb was in the past tense, *be* is in the past tense; if the main verb was in the progressive, *be* is in the progressive, and so on. The main verb then always changes to its past participle form.

Exercise 14.3

Use the three-step process to convert the following active sentences into their passive sentence counterparts.

My parents are watching the kids.

Insert passive auxiliary:	My parents are *being watched* the kids.
Insert *by*:	**by** my parents are *being watched* the kids.
Switch subjects and objects:	The kids are *being watched* **by** my parents.

1. The waiter is calculating the bill.

_____

_____

_____

2. The police will solve the crime.

_____

_____

_____

3. The merchants were displaying summer clothing.

_____

_____

_____

4. The mosquitoes might bother you this time of year.

_____

_____

_____

5. Everybody had accepted his offer.

_____

_____

_____

6. We are hiring some new employees.

_____

_____

_____

7. The union could have sued the company.

_____

_____

_____

8. The secretary had delayed the merger.

_____

_____

_____

9. Jackson should have seen them.

_____

_____

_____

10. They are talking about what happened.

_____

_____

_____

Going from the passive to the active is relatively easy. A quick way to do it is to move the noun phrase inside the *by* prepositional phrase to the subject position and turn the main verb (the last verb in the chain of verbs) into a simple present or past tense and then use the subject of the passive sentence as the object. Here is an example:

Passive:	The motion was made by Mr. Brown.
Active:	Mr. Brown made the motion.

With a little practice, it is relatively easy to change a passive sentence back to its active counterpart in your head. See how quickly you can do the following exercise in your head, without using pen or pencil to work it out.

Exercise 14.4

Without working though the process step-by-step, see how fast you can convert the following passive sentences to their active forms.

The manuscript was examined by an expert from the university.
An expert from the university examined the manuscript.

1. Alice was discouraged by the weak response to the ads.

_____

2. The estate was evaluated by a professional appraiser.

_____

3. Smoke was detected by a sensor in the lab.

_____

4. The hotel room had been cleaned by the maid.

_____

5. A new hearing was requested by the defendant's lawyer.

_____

6. The carpet had been badly faded by the sun.

    _____

7. The material had been snagged by a splinter.

    _____

8. A new plan was being developed by Roberta.

    _____

9. The entire project has been coordinated by a special task force.

    _____

10. The idea was critiqued by the entire staff.

    _____

11. The clock was wound up by my grandfather once a week.

    _____

12. The rocks were lifted onto the truck by a loader.

    _____

13. The rocket had been launched by a team from NASA.

    _____

14. Unfortunately, the house had been badly neglected by the previous owners.

    _____

15. The pool is being cleaned by a neighbor's son.

    _____

15

Indirect Quotation

There are two forms of quotation: **direct** and **indirect**. Direct quotation uses quotation marks to signal that we are repeating someone's words exactly as the person said or wrote them. In this chapter we will discuss how to correctly use indirect quotation—quotation without the use of quotation marks. An indirect quotation is putting someone else's words into your own sentence. While indirect quotation allows a certain amount of freedom in how the writer reports the words of someone else, this freedom of expression does not release the writer from full responsibility for accurately reporting the content of what is being reported.

Indirect quotations consist of a verb of reporting followed by a noun clause beginning with *that* (a *that* clause—see Chapter 7). For example:

Pinker argues *that* the brains of mammals follow a common general plan.

In this example, the *that* clause is the object of the verb *argues*.

Indirect quotation is very different from direct quotation. To see the differences, compare the following quotes:

Direct:	Tom said, "My parents are going to Malta this summer."
Indirect:	Tom said that his parents were going to Malta this summer.

If you look closely, you will see a number of differences between the two types of quotations.

• The most obvious and important difference is the use of quotation marks. If a quotation is in quotation marks, it is a direct quote. If it is not in quotation marks, it is an indirect quotation.

• Both direct and indirect quotations use the same verb *said* to introduce the quote, but in the case of direct quotation, *said* is separated from the quoted material by a comma. No comma is used in the indirect quote.

•   The indirect quotation uses *that* to introduce the quoted material. Direct quotation cannot use *that* in this manner.

•   In the direct quotation, the quoted material begins with a capital letter; in the indirect quotation, the paraphrased material begins with a lowercase letter.

•   The tenses in the two quotations are different. The direct quotation is in the present tense. The indirect quotation is in the past tense.

•   There is a difference in pronouns. The *my* in the direct quotation shifts to *his* in the indirect quotation.

The use of *that* is especially significant because sometimes it is the only way we can tell the difference between direct and indirect quotation. For example, could you use quotation marks with the following sentence?

Bill said that his parents had enjoyed their trip to Malta.

The answer is that you could not because *that* signals an indirect quotation. We can never use *that* with direct quotation. One of the characteristics of *that* clauses (including *that* clauses used in indirect quotation) is that we may optionally delete *that*. However, deleting *that* in indirect quotation is a really bad idea because *that* is one of the best ways to distinguish direct and indirect quotation. Accordingly, in the following discussion, we will always retain *that* in indirect quotation.

Compare the following direct and indirect quotations:

Direct: She said, "I *am* going home soon."
Indirect: She said that she *was* going home soon.

The direct quotation is in the present progressive tense (***am going***). In the indirect quotation, the verb has shifted to the past progressive tense (***was going***). The standard name for this is **backshifting**. Moving from direct quotation to indirect quotation involves a surprisingly elaborate set of backshifts from present tenses to past tenses, and from past tenses to past perfect tenses. The basic rule is this:

Present tenses ⇒ past tenses
Past tenses ⇒ past perfect tenses

Here are some examples of present tenses backshifting to past tenses:

Present tense ⇒ past tense
Direct: He said, "I ***have*** to go."
Indirect: He said that he ***had*** to go.

Present progressive ⇒ past progressive

Direct:	He said, "I *am leaving* soon."
Indirect:	He said that he *was leaving* soon.

Present perfect ⇒ past perfect

Direct:	He said, "We *have been gone* a long time."
Indirect:	He said that they *had been gone* a long time.

Present modal ⇒ past modal

Direct:	They said, "We *will see* him tomorrow."
Indirect:	They said that they *would see* him tomorrow.

Exercise 15.1

Convert the following direct quotations to indirect quotations. Be sure to use *that* in the indirect quotations.

> Jim said, "The computer paper is stored in the bottom drawer."
> Jim said *that* the computer paper *was* stored in the bottom drawer.

1. Alice said, "The company hosts the annual meeting in Las Vegas this year."

   _____

2. Tom said, "Francine has decided to move to Chicago."

   _____

3. I said, "Tom will meet us as soon as possible."

   _____

4. Ralph said, "Everyone has enjoyed the visit."

   _____

5. The TV said, "The storm may move up the coastline."

   _____

6. My mom said, "Everyone is looking forward to meeting Barbara."

   _____

7. Bill said, "The keys are kept next to the backdoor."

   _____

8. Terry said, "We can still get reservations for the weekend."

_____

9. The contractor said, "The electricians will finish the wiring Friday."

_____

10. I said, "I know you are right."

_____

Here are some examples of backshifted past tenses:

Past tense ⇒ past perfect tense
Direct: I said, "I **was** a little disappointed."
Indirect: I said that I **had been** a little disappointed.

Past progressive ⇒ past perfect progressive
Direct: She said, "I **was** _looking_ forward to it."
Indirect: She said that she **had been** _looking_ forward to it.

Past perfect: no change possible because sentence is already in past perfect tense
Direct: They said, "Bill **had** _made_ a reservation."
Indirect: They said that Bill **had** _made_ a reservation.

Past modal: no change possible because there are no past perfect modals
Direct: We said, "Sam **would** _take_ care of it."
Indirect: We said that Sam **would** _take_ care of it.

Exercise 15.2

Convert the following direct quotations to indirect quotations. Be sure to use _that_ in the indirect quotations.

She said, "Ron already filled out the forms."
She said _that_ Ron **had** already filled out the forms.

1. He said, "They have really done a great job."

_____

2. I said, "We were busy all afternoon."

_____

3. Rudy said, "We saw a terrific movie Saturday."

_____

4. Mom said, "The rain was pouring down all afternoon."

_____

5. The mechanic said, "Jack was working on our car."

_____

6. The bank said, "The check has been deposited already."

_____

7. Alice said, "They have already made plans for dinner."

_____

8. He said, "We helped our kids move into their new apartment."

_____

9. Marion said, "I was watching TV when you called."

_____

10. Francis said, "Bob pulled a muscle exercising."

_____

Indirect quotation requires a number of adjustments in the reference of first and second person pronouns. Here are the most common shifts that may cause problems for nonnative speakers:

First person to third
Direct:	He said, "*I* will introduce Sally to the group at lunch."
Indirect:	He said that *he* would introduce Sally to the group at lunch.

Second person to third
Direct:	She said, "*You* are making a big mistake."
Indirect:	She said that *he/she* was making a big mistake.

We see the same kind of shift in reflexive and possessive pronouns. For example:

First person to third
Direct:	He said, "*I* just cut *myself* on *my* arm."
Indirect:	He said that *he* had just cut *himself* on *his* arm.

Second person to third

Direct: She said, "*You* made a fool of *yourself* in *your* memo."

Indirect: She said that *he/she* had made a fool of *himself/herself* in *his/her* memo.

Exercise 15.3

Convert the following direct quotations to indirect quotations.

Sue said, "I am worried about meeting my deadline."
Sue said *that* she *was* worried about meeting *her* deadline.

1. He said, "I may be able to arrange a meeting with my manager."

_____

2. I said, "It was a good idea to talk to you."

_____

3. The postman said, "You need to mail your package before five."

_____

4. Bob said, "The paint in my living room is drying properly."

_____

5. Jane said, "I was just talking to my mother."

_____

6. He said, "I will be staying at home tomorrow."

_____

7. She told Paul, "You can count on me."

_____

8. Ruth told me, "I am not ready to get rid of my car yet."

_____

9. Alice told her son, "You have been staying up too late talking to your friends."

_____

10. My wife reminded me, "I am having dinner with my friend after work."

_____

In many languages, indirect questions merely repeat the original direct questions after the verb of reporting. Speakers of those languages sometimes carry over into English that way of forming indirect questions. Here is an example of such an error with a *yes-no* question:

Direct:	He asked, "Are you finished?"
Indirect:	**X** He asked are you finished?

English uses *if* and (less commonly) *whether* in forming indirect *yes-no* questions. For example:

Direct:	He asked, "Are you finished?"
Indirect:	He asked *if* you were finished.
Indirect:	He asked *whether* you were finished.

Notice that the indirect question is punctuated with a period rather than a question mark.

There are also two other changes between direct and indirect questions. One of the changes is not new: the backshifting of *is* to *was*.

The other change in the indirect question is new: changing the question word order of verb + subject (*are you* in this example) in the direct quotation to the statement word order of subject + verb (*you were*) in the indirect quotation.

Here are some more examples of the changed word order of indirect *yes-no* questions with the first verb in bold and the subject in italics:

Direct:	He asked, "**Can** *we* go now?"
Indirect:	He asked if *we* **could** go now.

Direct:	He asked, "**Have** you finished?"
Indirect:	He asked if *you* had finished.

Direct:	He asked, "**Are** they OK?"
Indirect:	He asked if *they* were OK.

If the *yes-no* question uses the dummy helping verb *do*, the form of the indirect question changes in a surprising way. For example:

Direct:	He asked, "**Does** *John* know where we are going?"
Indirect:	He asked if *John* **knew** where we were going.

The dummy helping verb *do* has disappeared from the indirect question. The reason is essentially a side effect of changing the question word order of verb + subject in the direct question back to the statement word order of subject + verb in the indirect question. Here in slow motion is what happens when we reverse the positions of the dummy helping verb *do* and the subject in our example sentence:

> **Does** *John* know . . . ⇒ *John* **does** know . . .

Now the dummy helping verb *do* and the present tense marker it carries have been put back in front of the main verb *know*. Since the present tense marker is now next to a real verb (*know*), there is no longer any need for the dummy verb *do* to carry the present tense marker, and so *do* disappears.

> *John* **does** know . . . ⇒ *John* ∅ **knows**

Finally, we have to change *knows* to *knew* according to the basic rule of backshifting in indirect questions.

> *John* ∅ knows . . . ⇒ *John* **knew**

Here are some more examples with the helping verb *do*:

Direct:	She asked, "**Does** *Sally* plan to join us?"
Indirect:	She asked if *Sally* **planned** to join them.
Direct:	They asked, "**Did** *Fred* call the meeting?"
Indirect:	They asked if *Fred* **had** called the meeting.

Exercise 15.4

Change the following direct quotation *yes-no* questions to their corresponding indirect question forms.

> He asked Tim, "Are you tired after your trip?"
> He asked Tim if he were tired after his trip.

1. He asked me, "Will you be able to come to the reception?"

   _____

2. I asked the kids, "Did you set the table for six people?"

   _____

3. He asked, "Has Ruth written her essay yet?"

   _____

4. They asked Bob, "Is it true that you are moving to Dallas?"

_____

5. She asked me, "Do you work at J.P. Morgan?"

_____

6. They asked us, "Is the reception starting at six?"

_____

7. I asked, "Has the coach announced when the game starts?"

_____

8. She asked me, "Will you turn off the lights in your office?"

_____

9. I asked them, "Did you hear the news?"

_____

10. He asked, "Is Tina leaving for Seattle Sunday?"

_____

11. The waiter asked me, "Did you have a reservation?"

_____

12. The receptionist asked me, "Are we holding your mail while you are away?"

_____

13. He asked me, "Do you have any idea how late you are?"

_____

14. I asked Sarah, "Can you return the book to the library for me?"

_____

15. I asked my brother, "Did Mom give you a call about the party?"

_____

The formation of indirect information questions is much like the formation of indirect *yes-no* questions. Here is an example:

Direct:	He asked, "Where **are** *the kids* going?"
Indirect:	He asked where *the kids* **were** going.

The one difference is that indirect information questions do not use *if* or *whether*. Everything else is the same: the verb + subject word order of the direct question changes to the statement word order of subject + verb.

Here are two more examples:

Direct:	She asked, "Why **is** *it* so hot in here?"
Indirect:	She asked why *it* **was** so hot in there.

Direct:	They asked, "Whom **should** *we* contact?"
Indirect:	They asked whom *we* **should** contact.

If the interrogative pronoun happens to play the role of the subject, then the direct question has a special word order in which the subject (the interrogative pronoun) and the verb are already in statement word order (rather than the expected question word order). For example:

Direct:	He asked, "*Who* **gave** us the information?"

The subject *who* is in front of the verb *gave*. In other words, the word order of the direct question is exactly the same as the word order of the indirect question:

Indirect:	He asked *who* **had given** us the information.

The peculiar word order results from the fact that the interrogative pronoun is also the subject. In all other cases, the interrogative pronoun plays the role of object or adverb, and as such, the interrogative pronoun plays no role in subject + verb word order issues.

As we would expect, when the direct question uses the dummy helping verb *do*, the *do* will disappear from the indirect question for exactly the same reasons it disappears from indirect *yes-no* questions. For example:

Direct:	He asked, "When **does** *the movie* start?"
Indirect:	He asked when *the movie* **started**.

When the tense marker is moved back to the first real verb, there is no need for the dummy *do* to continue to carry the tense marker, and so *do* disappears.

Here are some more examples involving *do*:

Direct:	John asked, "What **did** *Sally* say?"
Indirect:	John asked what *Sally* **said**.

Direct:	John asked, "Whom **did** *Bob* want to see?"
Indirect:	John asked whom *Bob* **wanted** to see.

Exercise 15.5

Change the following direct quotation information questions to their corresponding indirect question forms.

Kerry asked, "Why did you want to know that?"
Kerry asked why I wanted to know that.

1. Sam asked Harriet, "When will she begin the lesson?"

_____

2. I asked him, "How often do you go shopping?"

_____

3. They asked me, "Why did you want to move back to the city?"

_____

4. She asked him, "Where did you park the car?"

_____

5. I asked her, "Whom were you looking for?"

_____

6. He asked the waitress, "How long will we wait before getting a table?"

_____

7. She asked the children, "What story do you want to hear?"

_____

8. He asked us, "How come the class broke up so early?"

_____

9. She asked us, "Who knows where the library is?"

_____

10. The cabdriver asked me, "Where do you want me to take you?"

_____

Final Review

Use the following exercises to test your comprehension of all the lessons in this book.

Exercise 16.1 (Chapter 1: Proper and common nouns)

The following pairs of nouns contain one uncapitalized proper noun and a related common noun. Put the two nouns in the correct columns and capitalize the proper noun.

	Proper noun	**Common noun**
movie, star wars	*Star Wars*	*movie*
1. soccer player, david villa	_____	_____
2. airplane, boeing	_____	_____
3. burger king, restaurant	_____	_____
4. nation, canada	_____	_____
5. erie, lake	_____	_____
6. simba, lion	_____	_____
7. company, disney	_____	_____
8. wuthering heights, book	_____	_____
9. london, city	_____	_____
10. schwinn, bicycle	_____	_____

Exercise 16.2 (Chapter 1: Noncount nouns)

All of the underlined nouns in the following sentences are in the plural. Some plurals are correctly used with count nouns. However, many plurals are incorrectly used with noncount nouns. Draw a line through each incorrectly used noncount noun and write the corrected form above it. If the plural is correctly used with a count noun, write **OK** above the noun.

                         wood   OK

      Please be careful of the ~~woods~~ on the desks.

1. Traveling through spaces takes a lot of times.

2. The teacher's knowledges of electricities is immense.

3. Did you put peppers on those pizzas?

4. The baseball team had bloods on their uniforms.

5. Astronauts need oxygens in their spacecraft.

6. What hopes do they have of succeeding?

7. The basketball team lost their luggages at the airport.

8. Our government is investigating the power of winds for energies.

9. My mother and father cannot eat cheeses or milks.

10. Police officers enforce justices.

Exercise 16.3 (Chapter 1: Plural and possessives of nouns)

Fill in the following chart with all of the forms for each noun.

Singular	Possessive only	Plural only	Plural and possessive
wife	*wife's*	*wives*	*wives'*
1. boy	_____	_____	_____
2. boss	_____	_____	_____
3. friend	_____	_____	_____
4. plane	_____	_____	_____
5. city	_____	_____	_____
6. deer	_____	_____	_____

7. company   _____   _____   _____

8. thief   _____   _____   _____

9. mouse   _____   _____   _____

10. beach   _____   _____   _____

Exercise 16.4 (Chapter 3: Using indefinite and definite articles)

In each blank space, use an indefinite article (*a* or *some*), or the definite article *the* if the noun is defined by modifiers.

> There is ____*a*____ cat on top of your car.

1. The presidential candidates debated _____ interesting issues last night.

2. The presidential candidates debated _____ issue of inflation last night.

3. She tried to learn _____ Spanish vocabulary in class.

4. She tried to learn _____ Spanish vocabulary that she was assigned.

5. There is _____ way to avoid traffic.

6. What is _____ shorter way to get to his house?

7. His cousin adopted _____ dog.

8. His cousin adopted _____ dog that you saw at the shelter.

9. Would you like _____ apples?

10. We would like to hear _____ joke you think is so funny.

Exercise 16.5 (Chapter 3: Using indefinite articles)

Fill in the blanks with the indefinite articles *a*, *an*, or *some* as appropriate.

> Would you turn ____*a*____ light on?

1. I need _____ accounting textbook for class tomorrow.

2. There was _____ confusion in the airport.

3. The boss needs _____ answer from you.

4. Be careful, there is _____ wasp in the house.

5. I heard that you had _____ good time.

6. That is _____ ugly dress in the store.

7. I borrowed _____ tools for my project.

8. That radio needs _____ antenna.

9. There was _____ pit in that cherry.

10. Do you need _____ water?

Exercise 16.6 (Chapter 3: Using indefinite and definite articles)

Use the appropriate article in the blank spaces in the following sentences. If the sentence is making a generalization, put a ∅ in the blank space to show that no article is used.

_____∅_____ olives are usually too salty for me.

1. _____ cats are curious animals.

2. My boss hates _____ meetings.

3. At the airport, her son watched _____ planes from New York land.

4. _____ oranges are their favorite fruit.

5. He sat on the couch to read _____ travel guide he had ordered.

6. Without _____ rain, _____ crops will not grow.

7. _____ punctuality is valued in that office.

8. In this city, _____ parks are always planted with flowers.

9. _____ sandals like that give me _____ blisters.

10. _____ hurricanes always seem to strike in September.

Exercise 16.7 (Chapter 4: Noun phrases)

Underline all the noun phrases in the following sentences. Show that your answer is correct by writing the appropriate third-person pronoun under the noun phrase that you have underlined.

        It
The book you asked for finally came in.

1. I asked the new worker you hired to come to my office.

2. The car that he wrecked is in the workshop.

3. Where is the laptop that I ordered?

4. My mother and her friends went to the movies.

5. The mascot of that university is a tiger.

6. Our office manager ordered the most expensive copy machine.

7. All players, trainers, and coaches must register at the field.

8. Their wildlife organization protects animals on the endangered species list.

9. I am not used to driving a car that runs on ethanol.

10. My aunt reads to all the little girls in her neighborhood.

Exercise 16.8 (Chapter 4: Adjective clauses)

The adjective clauses in the following sentences have been underlined. Replace the word(s) in parentheses with the appropriate relative pronoun (*who, whom,* or *whose*).

> whom
> The actor (~~the actor~~) I met last year is now starring in a new movie.

1. That teacher, (teacher) we nominated for an award last year, is moving to a new school.

2. The teacher (teacher's) students are best prepared for exams will get an award.

3. Give your statistics to Mr. Walker, (Mr. Walker) is a teacher of economics.

4. The Tigers, (Tigers') fans are the loudest in the league, often win home games.

5. His mother, (his mother) we sang to last night, just celebrated her birthday.

6. Jane, (Jane) is the first doctor in her family, started her own practice.

7. I took that stray dog, (dog's) leg was injured, to the veterinarian.

8. The catering company, (catering company's) chefs studied in France, will be handling the reception.

9. He complained to his boss, (boss) always gets results.

10. The CEO, (CEO) addressed his comments directly to the board members, finished his speech early.

Exercise 16.9 (Chapter 4: Adjective clauses and relative pronouns)

All of the following sentences contain at least one adjective clause with the relative pronoun deleted. Underline the adjective clause and restore an appropriate relative pronoun.

                                  that
The equipment / <u>you ordered last week</u> has just arrived.

1. That poem you memorized for class is inspiring.

2. The clothes hung on the clothesline have blown away.

3. Dorothy went to the store again to buy the butter you forgot to pick up.

4. The man you met is usually more polite.

5. She bought the store she had managed for such a long time.

6. The shoppers he interviewed all preferred the new product.

7. Bob wrecked the car he rented in Las Vegas.

8. The wren you heard singing flew off.

9. I'm voting for the candidate you saw at the convention.

10. His cat caught the mouse you were trying to catch last week.

Exercise 16.10 (Chapter 4: Noun phrases)

Write the appropriate third-person pronoun above the underlined noun phrase. Use *he/she* or *him/her* for persons whose gender is not specified.

                  He/She
<u>The taxicab driver</u> had a GPS system in the cab.

1. <u>The soccer players</u> had a team meeting to discuss the loss.

2. <u>The menu from the Chinese restaurant down the street</u> lists many spicy chicken dishes.

3. <u>The history professor from Trent University</u> is also a talented opera singer.

4. Inspiration is important to <u>an artist</u>.

5. <u>Some of the highest mountain peaks on earth</u> are in the Himalayas.

6. <u>Harry and Tom</u> are my father's best friends.

7. Last Monday, <u>the electrical workers</u> went on strike.

8. <u>Aunt Sally</u> is my father's sister who lives in Canada.

9. What do you call <u>that strange-looking plant from Peru</u>?

10. She was astounded at <u>the losses projected in the company's annual report</u>.

Exercise 16.11 (Chapter 5: Possessive pronouns)

Select the proper form of the two italicized possessive pronouns by underlining the correct form.

Mary needs to see <u>her</u>/*hers* accountant about a tax matter.

1. The book that you are reading is *her/hers*.

2. I'll wait for you to finish *your/yours* coffee.

3. Is that dog *your/yours?*

4. The Wilsons lost *their/theirs* way in the woods when they were camping.

5. Did Nancy speak to *her/hers* sister yesterday?

6. They put *their/theirs* money to good use.

7. His home survived the hurricane. Did *their/theirs?*

8. Is that umbrella *your/yours* or mine?

9. She tore *her/hers* dress on that nail sticking out.

10. *Your/Yours* is a well-behaved child!

Exercise 16.12 (Chapter 5: Reflexive pronouns)

Fill in the blank with the appropriate reflexive pronoun. Confirm your answer by underlining the pronoun's antecedent. If the antecedent is understood, insert *you*.

He tends to repeat _____ .
<u>He</u> tends to repeat *himself*.

1. If you won't go to the reception with me, I'll just go _____ .

2. They had to move their offices _____ .

3. Joe built the treehouse _____ .

4. You can let _____ in if you want.

5. The students _____ conducted the debate.

6. May asked James to solve the problem _____ .

7. That computer seemed to fix _____ !

8. She didn't want to let _____ become depressed.

9. Ask _____ if you want to live like that.

10. We sewed the quilt _____ .

Exercise 16.13 (Chapter 6: Gerunds)

The base or dictionary form of verbs is listed in the first column. Opposite each verb, write the gerund (present participle) form of the verb. All of the words follow normal spelling rules.

Base form	**Gerund (present participle)**
advertise	*advertising*

1. arrange   _____

2. arrive   _____

3. attach   _____

4. bathe   _____

5. belong   _____

6. lift   _____

7. meet   _____

8. touch   _____

9. warn   _____

10. wash   _____

Exercise 16.14 (Chapter 6: Gerund phrases)

Underline the gerund phrases in the following sentences. Confirm your answers by replacing the gerund phrase with *it*.

                    it

They feared <u>taking on such a big task</u>.

1. Building a snowman is a fun winter pastime.

2. She found running a large company to be a challenge.

3. Singing in the shower is his favorite hobby.

4. The students discovered that finishing the exam took all afternoon.

5. Completing the project by Friday is their goal.

6. Seeing three movies in one day was tiring.

7. Flying south for the winter is what most North American birds do.

8. In that recipe, melting the cheese takes a long time.

9. Shivering in the stadium during the football game is not my idea of a good time.

10. The boss does not enjoy speaking to large groups of people.

Exercise 16.15 (Chapter 6: Infinitive phrases)

Underline the infinitive phrases in the following sentences. Confirm your answers by replacing the infinitive phrase with *it*.

>   It
> <u>To turn down such a generous offer</u> was a hard decision to make.

1. To sing at the Metropolitan Opera is her dream.

2. To convince the judge is your only option.

3. Tom's only goal is to elect John president.

4. To postpone the meeting now would be dangerous.

5. To sort the dirty clothes is your first task.

6. They decided to purchase their new car by the end of the month.

7. To stand up to the boss takes nerve.

8. The new law aims to prevent more road accidents.

9. Sandra refused to talk to her doctor.

10. To sleep is one thing, to sleep well is another.

Exercise 16.16 (Chapter 7: *That*-clauses)

Underline the *that* clauses in the following sentences. Confirm your answer by substituting the pronoun *it* for the *that* clause.

                    it

    I didn't know <u>that it was so late.</u>

1. That Paul would inherit the family fortune came as a horrible shock to Louise.

2. They contended that the accident wasn't their fault.

3. The plan was that we would call you when we got there.

4. The driver told us that he was out of gas.

5. That they were so late was really rude to the hosts.

6. The doctor told me that my ankle was severely sprained but not broken.

7. Their main complaint was that the restaurant closed too early.

8. Sally hated that Harry's ties were so out of style.

9. That the movie wasn't very good came as no surprise.

10. The problem is that it is getting so late.

Exercise 16.17 (Chapter 7: *Wh*-clauses)

Underline the *wh-* clauses in the following sentences. Confirm your answers by replacing the noun clause with *it*.

             It

    <u>What you are entitled to</u> remains to be seen.

1. I don't care about what he said.

2. Forgive me for what I am about to say.

3. Where they went is none of my business.

4. Did you ever notice how babies first start crawling?

5. Can you tell me how much dinner actually cost?

6. Which one we will finally pick is still up in the air.

7. I will accept whatever position they offer me.

8. Did you learn which flight they are on?

9. What shocked us the most was how much prices have gone up lately.

10. Who you know is sometimes more important than what you know.

Exercise 16.18 (Chapter 7: *Wh*-clauses)

Many of the sentences below contain *wh*- clauses that incorrectly use information question word order. Cross out these incorrect *wh*- clauses and write the corrected form in the space provided. If the *wh*- clause is correct, write *OK*.

I didn't understand ~~what were they talking about~~.
I didn't understand what they were talking about.

1. We should investigate what was that loud noise.

_____

2. I really liked what have they done to their apartment.

_____

3. They understood how much were we willing to pay.

_____

4. I wonder where should we park the car.

_____

5. How long will it take remains to be seen.

_____

6. Can you translate what did they just said?

_____

7. Do you know why are the streets so empty?

_____

8. I didn't want to ask what did she mean.

_____

9. I certainly sympathize with how are you feeling.

_____

10. They will prepare whatever would you like to eat.

_____

Exercise 16.19 (Chapter 8: Present tense)

Replace incorrect base-form verbs with third-person singular present-tense verbs. Confirm your answers by replacing the subject noun phrase with the appropriate third-person pronoun. If the sentence does not require a third-person singular present-tense verb, write *OK*.

> comes
> The cost of the houses there ~~come~~ as a complete surprise.
> It *comes* as a complete surprise.

1. The box in the hall take up a lot of space.

_____

2. What you just said about their plans convince me that they are right.

_____

3. Packing for trips make everyone crabby.

_____

4. The shopping center actually own the entire parking lot.

_____

5. What they said naturally engage our complete attention.

_____

6. The announcer on the news look like my cousin Fred.

_____

7. The size of the crowds at rock concerts make me uncomfortable.

_____

8. Knowing what to do in an emergency help me feel more secure.

_____

9. My roommate always play her iPod too loud.

_____

10. A trip to the outer islands cost nearly a hundred dollars per person.

_____

Exercise 16.20 (Chapter 8: Present tense)

Write the third-person singular form of the base-form verbs in the first column.

Base form	Third-person singular form
please	_pleases_

1. postpone   _____
2. concentrate   _____
3. develop   _____
4. try   _____
5. multiply   _____
6. boss   _____
7. tax   _____
8. mark   _____
9. nod   _____
10. match   _____

Exercise 16.21 (Chapter 8: Past tense)

Write the past-tense form of the following base-form verbs.

Base	Past tense
imply	_implied_

1. enlarge   _____
2. rope   _____
3. trim   _____

4. reply   _____

5. ship   _____

6. ban   _____

7. envy   _____

8. cause   _____

9. miss   _____

10. pray   _____

Exercise 16.22 (Chapter 8: Present participle)

Write the present participle form of the following base-form verbs.

Base form	**Present participle**
range	ranging

1. take   _____

2. arrive   _____

3. bet   _____

4. knit   _____

5. study   _____

6. cut   _____

7. leave   _____

8. perspire   _____

9. please   _____

10. win   _____

Exercise 16.23 (Chapter 8: Past and present perfect)

Select either the past-tense or the present perfect form in the following sentences.

The children ~~behaved~~/*have behaved* well since they stopped watching so much TV.

1. They *performed/have performed* that piece last week.

2. I *flew/have flown* more than 100,000 miles this year alone.

3. The owners *painted/have painted* the house in 2003.

4. She *directed/has directed* a number of independent films.

5. Last week the kids *divided/have divided* the yard into three sections.

6. I *urged/have urged* him to be more careful many times.

7. He *limped/has limped* into the meeting this morning.

8. We *examined/have examined* this issue repeatedly.

9. They *moved/have moved* to Chicago ten years ago.

10. They *lived/have lived* there ever since.

Exercise 16.24 (Chapter 9: Past and past perfect tenses)

In the following sentences, the verbs in italics are all in the base form. The verbs are used to describe two past-time events, one of which precedes the other. Change the verb whose action takes place first into the past perfect form. Change the other verb whose action takes place later into the past-tense form. Remember that the two events can occur in either order.

I *call* all my friends after I *hear* the news.
I *called* all my friends after I *had heard* the news.

1. Before I *get* two miles, I *get* a ticket.

_____

2. As soon as I *receive* the checks, I *deposit* them in the bank.

_____

3. I just *step* into the shower when the phone *ring*.

_____

4. We *have* to purchase new furniture after we *move* to Dallas.

_____

5. After I *explain* the joke to the kids, they *think* it was pretty funny.

_____

6. We *go* for a swim as soon as we *reach* the beach.

_____

7. He *lock* the barn door after the horse *be* stolen.

_____

8. They *retain* a lawyer before they *draw* up the contract.

_____

9. Naturally, I *unplug* the lamp before I *start* to rewire it.

_____

10. As soon as it *stop* snowing, we *shovel* the driveway.

_____

Exercise 16.25 (Chapter 10: Transitive and intransitive verbs)

The verbs in the following sentences are in italics. If the verb is intransitive, write *vi* above it. If it is transitive, write *vt* above it. If the verb is intransitive, confirm your answer by deleting all the material that follows the verb.

vi

Our snowman finally *melted* in the spring sunshine.
Our snowman finally *melted* ~~in the spring sunshine~~.

1. The lake *froze* earlier than usual this year.

2. I *froze* my fingers getting the ice off the windshield.

3. The water *was running* all night long.

4. Senator Blather *spoke* at great length.

5. The orchestra *was practicing* in the music room.

6. The orchestra *was practicing* their new piece.

7. The orchestra *was practicing* for their performance.

8. I *answered* the questionnaire.

9. I *answered* as honestly as I could.

10. I *answered* whatever questions were put to me.

Exercise 16.26 (Chapter 10: Separable and inseparable verbs)

Label the italicized phrasal verbs as *Sep* (for separable) or *Insep* (for inseparable). If the verb is separable, confirm your answer by moving the adverb to a position immediately after the object.

> *Sep*
> I *looked up* the answer in Wikipedia.
> I *looked* the answer *up* in Wikipedia.

1. He *turned down* the offer.

_____

_____

2. He *turned through* the pages of the book.

_____

_____

3. He *leaned against* the table.

_____

_____

4. They *printed out* the final report on Friday.

_____

_____

5. The company *hired back* the furloughed employees.

_____

_____

6. She always *laughed at* his lame jokes.

_____

_____

7. They *leaned into* the wind.

_____

_____

8. She *dressed up* the girls in their best clothes.

_____

_____

9. You must *register at* the counter.

_____

_____

10. I *looked over* today's receipts carefully.

_____

_____

Exercise 16.27 (Chapter 11: Indirect and direct objects)

Underline and label the indirect and direct objects in the following sentences. Confirm your answers by using the *to/for* paraphrase for the indirect object.

Sarah gave her daughter a surprise party.

                    IO   DO
Sarah gave her daughter a surprise party last night.
Sarah gave a surprise party **for** her daughter last night.

1. She teaches Chinese students English as a second language in Oakland.

_____

_____

2. Please order me a black coffee to go.

_____

_____

3. She showed them her engagement ring.

_____

_____

4. I made my students a traditional Korean meal.

_____

_____

5. Hand me that brush, will you?

_____

_____

6. He told us a really funny story.

_____

_____

7. Save us some dessert.

_____

_____

8. Let's give the people working in the kitchen a big hand.

_____

_____

9. We mailed the kids their Christmas presents.

_____

_____

10. I reserved them a table at the restaurant.

_____

_____

Exercise 16.28 (Chapter 11: _Bring_ and _take_)

Decide whether _bring_ or _take_ is more appropriate in the following sentences and underline the correct choice.

Can you _bring/take_ me to the airport?

1. Would you _bring/take_ me some tea?

2. What book have you *brought/took*?

3. The bus will *bring/take* you to the ferry.

4. *Bring/take* a coat if you're going outside.

5. April showers *bring/take* May flowers.

6. The employees *brought/took* their new boss to the airport.

7. My uncle *brought/took* the family photo album.

8. The tour guide will *bring/take* you through the castle grounds.

9. Anderson *brought/took* the report to the governor.

10. The governor would like Anderson to *bring/take* the report to him.

Exercise 16.29 (Chapter 11: *To*-phrase + *that*-clause)

Many of the following sentences incorrectly use objects where they should use *to* phrases instead. If the sentence is incorrect, replace the object with a *to* phrase. If the sentence is correct as it is, write *OK* above the object.

I explained my supervisor that I would be working overtime.

       to my supervisor
I explained ~~my supervisor~~ that I would be working overtime.

1. I suggested my friends that we should have dinner together.

2. We explained them that the job had to be postponed for a few days.

3. We told them that the job had to be postponed for a few days.

4. Let me prove you that you are mistaken.

5. The boss acknowledged us that he had not allowed enough time.

6. Henry showed us that there was a much simpler solution to the problem.

7. Henry proved us that there was a much simpler solution to the problem.

8. They announced everyone that they were getting married.

9. She reported us that the committee had approved our recommendations.

10. I confessed Mary that I had completely forgotten our meeting.

Exercise 16.30 (Chapter 12: Single-word adverbs)

Underline the single-word adverbs in the following sentences. Confirm your identification by deleting the adverb.

It ~~always~~ costs a fortune to eat at Gordy's.

1. I just saw the downtown bus.

2. Mary wants some cake too.

3. My mother usually sings in the church choir.

4. The twins always fight at school, and their father is angry about it.

5. The spy prudently lowered his voice.

6. The phone rang persistently for several hours.

7. Her nervous boyfriend almost forgot to shake her father's hand.

8. In January, the snow falls gently.

9. Can we go now?

10. The wolf howled frighteningly.

Exercise 16.31 (Chapter 12: Single-word adverbs)

Change the adjective in the underlined phrase into a single-word adverb. Then rephrase the sentence using the adverb in place of the underlined phrase.

honestly
He answered the question ~~in an honest manner~~.

1. He sledded down the mountain in a reckless manner.

2. The winter sun shined on the snow in a brilliant manner.

3. The teacher lectured to the students in an angry manner.

4. The drama team rehearsed in a dutiful manner.

5. They paid their restaurant bill in an immediate manner.

6. Father sighed in a moody manner.

7. The candidate walked to the stage in a hesitant manner.

8. After the presentation, the boss discussed the project <u>in an enthusiastic manner.</u>

9. The police officers questioned the guard <u>in a suspicious manner.</u>

10. The church choir sang the hymns <u>in a joyful manner.</u>

Exercise 16.32 (Chapter 12: Single-word adverbs)

In the right column, write the *-ly* adverb form of the adjective in the left column.

Adjective	Adverb
loose	*loosely*

1. dirty   _____

2. pretty   _____

3. bare   _____

4. fine   _____

5. speedy   _____

6. due   _____

7. safe   _____

8. messy   _____

9. noisy   _____

10. separate   _____

Exercise 16.33 (Chapter 13: *Yes-no* questions)

Turn the following statements into *yes-no* questions by first using the *do* insertion rule to form an emphatic *do* statement.

He shut the window.
    Emphatic *do* statement: He *did* shut the window.
    Yes-no **question:**   *Did* he shut the window?

1. She graded the exams.

_____

_____

2. Tom drove the truck.

_____

_____

3. The Adams family lived in Toronto.

_____

_____

4. The athletes lost weight.

_____

_____

5. We laughed until we cried.

_____

_____

6. The snow came down in heavy drifts.

_____

_____

7. The president toured the warehouse.

_____

_____

8. Daniel forgot his homework again.

_____

_____

9. The boxers fought ten rounds.

_____

_____

10. The dog buried his bone.

_____

_____

Exercise 16.34 (Chapter 14: Passive)

See how fast you can convert the following passive sentences to their active forms.

The manuscript was examined by an expert from the university.
An expert from the university examined the manuscript.

1. Her wedding dress was sewn by her grandmother.

2. The lecture was given by Dr. Peterson of Texas A&M University.

3. During the summer, the exams were corrected by our teacher.

4. The Montreal flight was piloted by Tom's brother.

5. Last Saturday, the guitar was played by Cindy to a rapt audience.

6. The house was inspected by the city for termites.

7. The mouse was eaten by a barn owl.

8. In Friday's game, five touchdowns were scored by the Vikings.

9. The Olympic athletes were honored by their home country.

10. The computer was repaired by a certified technician.

Exercise 16.35 (Chapter 15: Direct and indirect quotation)

Convert the following direct quotations to indirect quotations.

Sue said, "I am worried about meeting my deadline."
Sue said *that* she *was* worried about meeting *her* deadline.

1. "I'm running late for work," he said.

   _____

2. The conductor said, "The audience talked during the entire symphony."

   _____

3. We said, "The children have been doing extra chores this week."

   _____

4. Charles said, "We can't come to your party because my wife is sick."

   _____

5. The doctor said, "I need to look at your prescription again."

   _____

6. Ralph said, "I demand an explanation for what Harry did."

   _____

7. My mother said, "I liked playing soccer when I was your age."

   _____

8. The plumber said, "We will install the new sink this week."

   _____

9. Louise said, "I am having minor surgery Tuesday."

   _____

10. They said, "We were laughing at what the kids were doing."

   _____

Answer Key

Chapter 1

Exercise 1.1

1. Hamlet, play   2. Soho, neighborhood   3. Ford, car   4. Atlantic, ocean   5. Everest, mountain   6. Harrison Ford, actor   7. Dixie, song   8. Titanic, ship   9. The Ritz, hotel
10. Mercury, planet

Exercise 1.2

1. threes /z/   2. tricks /s/   3. stools /z/   4. histories /z/   5. walls /z/   6. rakes /s/   7. plays /z/   8. stoves /z/   9. coughs /s/   10. moths /s/   11. days /z/   12. notes /s/   13. delays /z/   14. hikes /s/   15. tires /z/   16. rains /z/   17. plates /s/   18. groves /z/   19. shows /z/
20. pipes /s/

Exercise 1.3

1. races /əz/   2. bays /z/   3. boxes /əz/   4. clocks /s/   5. roses /əz/   6. mists /s/   7. dishes /əz/   8. tries /z/   9. cottages /əz/   10. colleagues /z/   11. clauses /əz/   12. clashes /əz/
13. hedges /əz/   14. phones /z/   15. freezes /əz/   16. shares /z/   17. duties /z/   18. patches /əz/   19. allowances /əz/   20. sheets /s/

Exercise 1.4

1. ~~sheeps~~, sheep   2. ~~mouses~~, mice   3. ~~themselfes~~, themselves   4. ~~wolfs~~, wolves   5. ~~thiefs~~, thieves   6. ~~feets~~, feet   7. ~~sheeps~~, sheep; ~~childs~~, children   8. ~~deers~~, deer   9. ~~salmons~~, salmon
10. ~~lifes~~, lives

Exercise 1.5

1. OK; ~~fogs~~, fog 2. ~~milks~~, milk 3. ~~disappointments~~, disappointment; OK 4. OK; ~~bloods~~, blood 5. OK; ~~powers~~, power 6. OK; ~~papers~~, paper; ~~glasses~~, glass 7. ~~paints~~, paint; OK 8. OK; OK; ~~syrups~~, syrup 9. ~~fears~~, fear; OK 10. OK; ~~yeasts~~, yeast

Exercise 1.6

1. dog's, dogs, dogs' 2. horse's, horses, horses' 3. tree's, trees, trees' 4. lady's, ladies, ladies' 5. fox's, foxes, foxes' 6. tooth's, teeth, teeth' 7. play's, plays, plays' 8. worker's, workers, workers' 9. shelf's, shelves, shelves' 10. man's, men, men's 11. studio's, studios, studios' 12. place's, places, places' 13. fly's, flies, flies' 14. child's, children, children's 15. woman's, women, women's

Exercise 1.7

1. faces' /əz/ 2. bridges' /əz/ 3. foxes' /əz/ 4. chiefs' /s/ 5. boys /z/ 6. navies /z/ 7. daughters /z/ 8. carriages /əz/ 9. plays /z/ 10. colleges /əz/

Chapter 2

Exercise 2.1

1. truer, truest; **X** twoer, **X** twoest; **X** *True two* stories, *Two true* stories; The stories are *true*. **X** The stories are *two*. (marginally grammatical); true adjective: *true* 2. **X** hiser, **X** hisest; sweeter, sweetest; *His sweet* cupcakes; **X** *Sweet his* cupcakes; **X** The cupcakes were *his*. (grammatical as pronoun, not adjective); The cupcakes were *sweet*. True adjective: *sweet* 3. faster, fastest; **X** aller, **X** allest; **X** *Fast all* boats; *All fast* boats; The boats were *fast*. **X** The boats were *all*. (grammatical only if *all* is an indefinite pronoun); True adjective: *fast* 4. **X** theser, **X** thesest; hungrier, hungriest; *These hungry* cats; **X** *Hungry these* cats; The cats were *these*. (grammatical only as pronoun); The cats were *hungry*. True adjective: *hungry* 5. brighter, brightest; **X** a-er, **X** a-est; **X** *Bright a* moon; *A bright* moon; The moon was *bright*. **X** The moon was *a*. True adjective: *bright*

Exercise 2.2

1. sadder, saddest 2. more costly, most costly; costlier, costliest 3. sounder, soundest 4. more valuable, most valuable 5. more likely, most likely 6. sunnier, sunniest 7. more patient, most patient 8. more improved, most improved 9. more normal, most normal 10. bluer, bluest 11. worse, worst 12. more tiring, most tiring 13. more physical, most physical 14. stranger, strangest; more strange, most strange 15. more probable, most probable 16. more recent, most recent 17. more available, most available 18. more developed, most developed 19. shadier, shadiest; more shady, most shady 20. more fulfilling, most fulfilling

Exercise 2.3

1. capacious worn brown overcoat   2. miniature antique gold locket   3. great overripe yellow pear   4. sizeable early black and white photographs   5. long modern black desk   6. large aged grey cat   7. petite young green peas   8. bulky old pink sweater   9. immense new off-white mansion   10. slim up-to-date white drapes

Chapter 3

Exercise 3.1

1. test /ðə/   2. road /ðə/   3. action /ðiy/   4. building /ðə/   5. organization /ðiy/
6. umbrella /ðiy/   7. desk /ðə/   8. name /ðə/   9. insurance /ðiy/   10. eraser /ðiy/

Exercise 3.2

On my first trip to Manhattan, I bought *a* city map and tried to get *a* sense of its geography. I quickly discovered what every person there knows: to find out where you are, you need to know two things: whether you are facing "uptown" (north) or "downtown" (south), and whether you are facing east or west.

　　To find out, you have to go to *a* street sign. *The* street sign will tell you both street and avenue numbers. *The* numbers by themselves tell you nothing. They just define one point on *a* grid. They tell you where you are on *the* grid, but you still do not know which way you are facing on *the* grid. To know that, you have to go to *the* next street sign and compare *the* street and avenue numbers there. If *the* new street number has gotten larger, you are going north. If *the* new street number has gotten smaller, you are going south. If *the* new avenue number has gotten larger, you are going west. If *the* avenue name has gotten smaller, you are going east. If *the* avenue has *a* name rather than *a* number, then you have to take out *the* map again and compare *the* numbers and/or names of *the* two avenues. Everybody has to memorize *the* names and numbers of *the* avenues.

Exercise 3.3

1. the 2. some 3. The 4. The 5. a 6. a 7. An 8. The 9. a 10. a 11. a 12. the
13. the (<u>an</u> is also possible) 14. an 15. the 16. an 17. a 18. the 19. a 20. the

Exercise 3.4

1. the 2. a 3. the 4. the 5. The; the 6. a; some 7. The 8. An; a 9. a; the 10. The
11. the 12. a 13. the 14. the; the 15. the 16. an 17. the; a; the 18. the 19. A; the
20. the; the 21. some 22. a 23. a; the 24. the 25. the

Exercise 3.5

During *the* Christmas holidays, I flew to Los Angeles to visit with *some* friends. They picked me up at *the* airport in *an* old car one of them was leasing. Since *the* company my friend was working for required him to have *a* car, he got reimbursed for most of his driving expenses. It was *the* first car any of them had ever had. Not having *a* car in Los Angeles is not really *an* option since there is no public transportation system to speak of. As *a* result, *the* traffic is just awful.

They were renting *an* apartment in Santa Monica, *a* really nice town on *the* beach about twenty miles from *the* center of *the* city. *The* apartment building they lived in even had *a* swimming pool. We went in *the* pool every day. It was fine as long as *the* pool was in *the* sun. From *the* apartment we could walk to most of *the* stores we needed. The only thing that we had to take *the* car for was going to *the* grocery store. There was simply no place to buy groceries in *the* neighborhood.

I had hoped to go swimming in *the* ocean, but I quickly discovered that *the* water was too cold. My friends said that if I wanted to go swimming, I would have to get *a* wet suit. There is *a* current of icy-cold water that comes down *the* coast from Alaska. Even in *the* summer, *the* water is pretty cold.

Exercise 3.6

1. some   2. an   3. a   4. some   5. a   6. some   7. some   8. an   9. some   10. a   11. an   12. a   13. an   14. an   15. some

Exercise 3.7

1. ∅   2. ∅   3. the   4. ∅   5. ∅   6. ∅   7. The; the   8. ∅; an   9. the; the   10. ∅; a; ∅   11. ∅   12. ∅   13. ∅; ∅   14. the; ∅; ∅   15. ∅; a

Exercise 3.8

Travel by ∅ air has become everyone's favorite topic to complain about. We all have heard ∅ stories about ∅ passengers being stuck for hours on ∅ runways and ∅ stories about ∅ [*the* is also OK] endless lines at ∅ ticket counters. These are all true. *The* problem is that none of us is willing to pay what it would cost to fix *the* problems. None of us wants to pay *a* penny more than we have to. When ∅ airlines try to raise ∅ prices to improve their services, we all go to *the* airlines that have not raised their prices. When ∅ airports try to get approval to raise ∅ taxes to pay for ∅ airport improvements, we vote *the* [∅ is also OK] bond issues down.

Exercise 3.9

1. a   2. an   3. The; the   4. some   5. The   6. The; a; the   7. The; a; the   8. the; the   9. the [∅ is also OK];   10. the   11. a   12. some   13. a   14. The; the   15. the; a   16. some   17. an   18. a; the   19. some   20. the   21. a   22. some; the   23. ∅; the; ∅   24. a; the   25. a; the; the

Chapter 4

Exercise 4.1

1. a new statue of him; it   2. all the people who might be interested; them   3. All of the presenters who have registered; They   4. a lot more vegetables that are grown locally; them   5. ripe, locally produced organic apples; them   6. The people who live there; They   7. the documents that you requested; them   8. the new employees who were just hired; them   9. The building where I work; It   10. The last telephone number that you gave me; It   11. The new engine; any fuel that can be made into a liquid at room temperature; It; it   12. The Harry Potter books; They   13. People who drive to work every day; parking permits; the office; They; them; it   14. The new regulation; hospitals' safety records; It; them   15. a director whose movies have been very successful; him

Exercise 4.2

1. at work (place); during this difficult period (time)   2. over the weekend (time); of infection (other)   3. from California (place); about the problem (other)   4. in China (place); about the peace talks (other)   5. in the dining room (place); of paint (other)   6. despite all the odds (other)   7. by the English painter Turner (other)   8. about my chances (other)   9. to the crime (other)   10. for lying (other)   11. of the cup (other)   12. for indecision (other)   13. in the clinic (place)   14. in the city (place)   15. just after sunset (time)

Exercise 4.3

1. *The road by our house* is being paved; Adj/It   2. *The frozen chickens in the supermarket* are not very good; Adj/They   3. Breakfast will be served in the main dining room; Adv   4. *Their discovery of an error* has caused the company to restate its earnings; Adj/It   5. *A restaurant in our neighborhood* serves really good Chinese food; Adj/It   6. After much debate, we decided to consult *a specialist in toxic waste removal*; Adv; Adj/him/her   7. We finally found the book we wanted online; Adv   8. *The star of the show* was *a young singer from Australia*; Adj/It/He/She; Adj/it/he/she   9. *Ignorance of the law* is not a valid defense in court; Adj/It; Adv   10. *Visitors from China* are always welcome in our company; Adj/They; Adv   11. *The floor in the cabin* was rough, unfinished wood; Adj/It   12. *The popularity of his book* was a big factor; Adj/It   13. During the night, there was a fire that caused some damage; Adv   14. He has *the heart of a lion* and *the brain of a jellyfish*; Adj/it; Adj/it   15. At lunch time, I bought a new coat at the mall; Adv; Adv

Exercise 4.4

1. We are going to refinance *the mortgage that we have on our house*; it   2. *Most of the staff who work at my office* will be attending the office party; They   3. *The place where the pipe connects to the water line* is badly corroded; It   4. We talked to *the subjects whom we had previously identified*; them   5. *Ralph, whom you met on your last trip here*, will take you around; He   6. They

examined *the building where the meetings would be held*; it   7. That week was *a period when everything seemed to go wrong*; it   8. They asked us to redo *the tests that we had done earlier*; them   9. It was a memorial to *the pioneers who first settled this area*; them   10. We took them to *the laboratory, which is in the basement*; it   11. They took pictures of *the river where the bridge had washed out*; it   12. I didn't know *the person whom they were discussing*; him/her   13. We had *an adventure that we certainly had not planned on*; it   14. *My parents, who live in a small town,* always enjoy visiting the city; They   15. *The manager, whom we had contacted earlier,* approved our check; He/She   16. *Some fans whose enthusiasm knew no limits* climbed up on stage; They   17. *Berlin, which had been a divided city,* is now open to everyone; It   18. Our friends went to *a museum where there was free admission on Mondays*; it   19. That was *the moment when I knew we were in big trouble*; it   20. *The yogurt, which had been in our refrigerator for months,* had to be thrown out; It

Exercise 4.5

1. (anybody) who   2. (the person) whom   3. (Jason Grant's) whose   4. (the client) who
5. (the flower's) whose   6. (my husband) whom   7. (the window's) whose   8. (the president) who   9. (the employees) who   10. (the secretary's) whose   11. (the drivers) whom   12. (the waiter) who   13. (the lawyer) whom   14. (the lawyer) who   15. (the lawyer's) whose

Exercise 4.6

1. that   2. whose   3. whose   4. who   5. when   6. who   7. whom   8. whose   9. where
10. when   11. that   12. whose   13. that   14. who   15. whom   16. that   17. who
18. where   19. whom   20. whom

Exercise 4.7

1. whose enthusiasm knows no limits   2. that they were setting   3. where we were running
4. whom I had never even heard of before   5. that raises the front ramp   6. who never cut corners on anything   7. where the meeting will be held   8. that has temporarily affected his short-term memory   9. where there would be little impact on the environment   10. whose bid won the contract   11. that you can't win   12. that was given by the hosting organization   13. that the desk clerk gave us   14. whose work we consulted   15. that we went through   16. who asked not to be identified   17. whose foundation sponsored the conference   18. that you have
19. whose outcome was never in doubt   20. that we reviewed

Exercise 4.8

1. who (*that* is also OK)   2. OK   3. whom   4. who   5. whom   6. OK   7. who   8. whom
9. whom   10. who   11. who   12. whom   13. who   14. OK   15. who

Exercise 4.9

1. who create a strong sense of place in their books; OK   2. that we have today; that movie stars used to be   3. who would vote for a yellow dog before he would vote for a Republican; OK

4. ~~that~~ you can wear if it gets cold   5. ~~whom~~ the press identified as taking payoffs.   6. who were at the party; OK   7. that had passed their final exams; OK   8. who had arrived at the scene first; OK   9. ~~that~~ we saw fishing off the pier   10. ~~whom~~ we interviewed; who refereed the game; OK   11. who had already made a payment; OK   12. ~~that~~ we talked to   13. ~~that~~ we had caught.   14. who lived nearby; OK   15. ~~that~~ the speaker had named OK

Exercise 4.10

1. *whom* we all know   2. *whom* they had photographed the day before   3. *whom* he had faced
4. *whom* we saw at the beach   5. *that* they discussed during the lecture   6. *that* I was riding
7. *that* they had picked for the wedding ceremony   8. *whom* we saw at the Chinese opera
9. *that* they played during intermission   10. *whom* everyone likes at first meeting   11. *whom* I had never met before   12. *that* we should have seen coming   13. *that* I had reservations for   14. *that* I remember best   15. *whom* we admire the most now   16. *whom* we had hired
17. *that* Thomas Dewey suffered at the hand of Truman in 1948   18. *that* we had planned for ourselves   19. *that* we saw in the old movies   20. *that* the defense put forward

Exercise 4.11

1. where we had dinner last night; restrictive   2. that are made of wood; restrictive   3. whom I knew in high school; nonrestrictive   4. that grow in the Pacific Northwest; restrictive   5. that we just took; restrictive   6. that is on the Mississippi River; restrictive   7. who commutes an hour each way; nonrestrictive   8. that I use at work; restrictive   9. who works for our parent company; nonrestrictive   10. which has fluctuated wildly lately; nonrestrictive   11. that has completely blocked the tri-city bridge; restrictive   12. which crosses the James River; nonrestrictive   13. who represents our company; restrictive   14. who reports directly to the CEO; nonrestrictive   15. which he promptly wrecked the first time he drove it; nonrestrictive   16. that I could hardly refuse under the circumstances; restrictive   17. which was the coldest in twenty years; nonrestrictive   18. that were engaged in overly aggressive loans; restrictive   19. that were coming from my printer; restrictive   20. who were killed in World War I; restrictive   21. which cost me over a hundred dollars; nonrestrictive   22. that was not refrigerated right after the party; restrictive   23. where my dentist has her office; restrictive   24. that are consumed in the United States; restrictive   25. who is not noted for his sense of humor; nonrestrictive

Chapter 5

Exercise 5.1

1. It   2. them   3. They   4. it   5. He/She   6. it   7. They   8. him/her   9. It   10. them
11. it   12. him/her   13. They   14. it   15. He/She

Exercise 5.2

1. theirs   2. your   3. her   4. yours   5. yours   6. their   7. yours   8. hers   9. their
10. hers

Exercise 5.3

1. Good writers choose their words carefully.   2. Geologists spend most of their research time in the field.   3. Teachers should allow their students time to finish their work.   4. When parents arrive, ask them to take a seat.   5. We need people who will try their best.   6. All of the farmers in the neighborhood have already harvested their crops by now.   7. All painters have to learn how to keep their brushes in good condition.   8. Find some officers/the police and tell them what happened.   9. Any secretaries we hire must have Excel in their resumes.   10. Children who are invited here must mind their manners.   11. Call the hospital/the doctors and tell them we have an emergency here.   12. No CEOs would pass up an opportunity to improve their companies.   13. We cannot hire foreign citizens unless we see their green cards.   14. If visitors stop by, ask them to wait in the library.   15. No members of the Republican Party would lend their names to a cause like that.

Exercise 5.4

1. myself (I)   2. themselves (They)   3. herself (girl)   4. myself (I)   5. ourselves (we)
6. itself (trip)   7. themselves (workers)   8. themselves (pages)   9. itself (system)   10. yourself (you)   11. themselves (politicians)   12. themselves (children)   13. himself (Sam)   14. yourself (you)   15. myself (I)

Exercise 5.5

1. himself; functional   2. itself; functional   3. themselves; emphatic; They themselves saw the accident on the freeway.   4. myself; emphatic; I myself couldn't help smiling.   5. itself; emphatic; Their mortgage itself takes nearly half their income.   6. himself; functional   7. herself; emphatic; She herself proposed the idea.   8. yourself; functional   9. myself; emphatic; I myself did all the necessary paperwork.   10. themselves; emphatic; The consultants themselves were opposed to the new project.

Chapter 6

Exercise 6.1

1. amusing   2. becoming   3. choosing   4. clapping   5. dating   6. fitting   7. focusing
8. giving   9. grouping   10. judging   11. looping   12. managing   13. mining   14. modeling   15. profiting   16. researching   17. servicing   18. staying   19. traveling   20. vetoing

Exercise 6.2

1. Putting the schedule on the website   2. hearing some discussion about that   3. solving the quality control problems   4. trying to please everybody   5. cutting back on a few of our less important projects   6. Working such long hours   7. Getting it right the first time   8. having to take such a late flight   9. getting enough time to do everything   10. sliding into the ditch   11. Arriving at the airport a couple of hours early   12. ordering in pizza   13. doing the whole thing by himself   14. Acting so quickly   15. attaching such a big file to the e-mail   16. leaving early   17. Knowing the right thing; doing the right thing   18. achieving results   19. Getting off to such a bad start   20. Seeing; believing

Exercise 6.3

1. was showing; progressive; Our effort *showed* a definite improvement in sales.   2. being late for an important meeting; gerund; My worry is *it*.   3. were playing; progressive; The kids *played* in the backyard.   4. playing in the backyard; gerund; The kids' favorite activity is *it*.   5. watching football on TV; gerund; John's idea of a good time is *it*.   6. was studying; progressive; Sally *studied* classical Greek in Athens last summer.   7. studying classical Greek some summer; gerund; Sally's great ambition is *it*.   8. getting stuck in traffic on the way home; gerund; The problem was *it*.   9. losing a really close game that we could have won; gerund; The worst thing is *it*.   10. are meeting; progressive; We *meet* them at a restaurant near the station.

Exercise 6.4

1. to go to the play after having dinner in town.   2. to get an apartment somewhere in easy commuting distance.   3. To operate heavy equipment   4. to enroll in a gym or health club.   5. to get out of the contract any way we could.   6. To teach math in middle schools   7. to analyze the financial status of a small business.   8. To assume that you know what is going on   9. to fight against the zoning change.   10. To permit such dangerous behavior   11. to stop for lunch   12. To give up so easily   13. to make them an offer they couldn't refuse.   14. to stretch our legs.   15. to think about all the awful things that could happen.   16. To receive this award from you   17. to add three new positions.   18. to take a full load next semester.   19. to believe that they were telling us the truth.   20. To err; to forgive

Exercise 6.5

1. It was a great feeling to get finished on time.   2. It was Senator Blather's goal to unite the voters behind his candidacy.   3. It was totally out of character to miss three meetings in a row.   4. It was of utmost importance to make the criminals pay for their crimes.   5. It was just asking for trouble to cut too many corners.   6. It seemed terribly rude to begin eating while the hostess was in the kitchen.   7. It is the responsibility of every applicant to meet all the course prerequisites.   8. It is the gift of a great painter to see the landscape with fresh eyes.   9. It is the first obligation of a policeman to enforce the laws.   10. It seemed necessary to get a clear picture of what was going on.

Chapter 7

Exercise 7.1

1. That the movie was in French   2. that you get really exhausted after long flights   3. that it would stop raining   4. That I know all the answers   5. that we would take a trip to New Mexico this summer   6. that they should quit while they are ahead   7. that we were about 10 percent under budget   8. That we were going to be late   9. that she should jump at such a good opportunity   10. that it is a good idea to go ahead   11. that we would enter the competition   12. that we had been right all along   13. that we would be able to finish on time   14. that everything would be OK   15. that we should stick to our original plan   16. that they would be home by dinner time   17. That they loved Italian food   18. that they could rent a car when they got there   19. that we will be hearing from them any time now   20. that we were prepared and they were not

Exercise 7.2

1. It came as a big relief <u>that it was over so quickly.</u>   2. It soon became obvious <u>that the road was impassable.</u>   3. It would appear to be the case <u>that we had made a good decision.</u>   4. It seemed certain <u>that the workers would need more time.</u>   5. It was apparent to everyone <u>that they should address the problem quickly.</u>   6. It seemed increasingly likely <u>that we would have to reschedule the meeting.</u>   7. It became clear after all <u>that I would have to cancel the meeting.</u>   8. It was likely <u>that the risk was getting too great to accept.</u>   9. It became embarrassingly obvious <u>that they had forgotten to confirm our reservation.</u>   10. It was a great disappointment to all her fans <u>that she had to leave so soon.</u>

Exercise 7.3

1. that the referee had made a mistake; Noun; The coach claimed it.   2. that we are going to get a big snowstorm this weekend; Noun; Did you hear it?   3. that we had proposed; Adj; The experiment which we had proposed was finally approved.   4. that we were going to the Smiths' tonight; Noun; I almost forgot it.   5. that they took to New Zealand; Adj; They will never forget the trip which they took to New Zealand.   6. that we could all agree on; Adj; We finally picked a design which we could all agree on.   7. that the discussion had gone as well as it could; Noun; Everybody felt it.   8. that we will have this afternoon; Adj; I am very worried about the meeting which we will have this afternoon.   9. that we could not get a cab in a rainstorm; Noun; We quickly discovered it.   10. that we had ordered; Adj; The cab which we had ordered never showed up.

Exercise 7.4

1. He claimed *that* <u>he had been working at home all afternoon.</u>   2. I wouldn't have guessed *that* <u>it would have cost so much.</u>   3. His son showed us *that* <u>he could ride his bicycle without</u>

using his hands.   4. We quickly discovered *that* the roads were nearly impassable.   5. I suggest *that* we stay at the airport hotel and fly out in the morning.   6. Did you notice *that* Senator Blather was wearing one brown shoe and one black shoe?   7. They concluded *that* the proposal was going to need a lot more work.   8. The coach told the team *that* they would have to practice much harder.   9. As I have gotten older, I have found *that* I need to take better notes at meetings.   10. The defendant denied *that* he had ever been to Chicago.

Exercise 7.5

1. where all those copies of the report went; We never learned it.   2. whatever you want them to do; They will do it.   3. Why they behaved the way they did; It is a complete mystery to me.   4. whose approval was necessary for the project to get started; I wondered it.   5. where the boxes were stacked up; They parked the trucks not far from it.   6. for whom the bell tolls; Ask not for it.   7. why we did it in the first place; After all, that was it.   8. whose car was blocking the driveway? Did you ever find out it?   9. Whenever they want to start; It is OK with me.   10. how she wanted us to do it; She showed us it.   11. what the problem was; You will never guess it.   12. whatever they would pay us; We had to settle for it.   13. whomever the board appoints; The new CEO is it.   14. whatever is said at the meetings; The secretary will record it.   15. What you see; what you get; It is it.

Exercise 7.6

1. what I needed ∅   2. What we did ∅   3. why they did it ∅   4. what you actually do ∅   5. what you were trying to accomplish ∅   6. Whenever you can make it ∅   7. whose suggestion it was ∅   8. what they said ∅   9. which one they would pick ∅   10. what we should do ∅   11. Whom I voted for ∅   12. What they had to say ∅   13. where they said it would be ∅   14. what you have learned ∅   15. What John gave Mary ∅

Exercise 7.7

1. ~~were they~~; they were   2. ~~will it~~; it will   3. ~~will be the speaker~~; the speaker will be   4. ~~are we~~; we are   5. OK   6. ~~will he~~; he will   7. ~~should we~~; we should   8. ~~did she say~~; she said   9. ~~were they~~; they were   10. ~~do you feel~~; you feel   11. ~~should we~~; we should   12. ~~are you~~; you are   13. OK   14. ~~will be the next president~~; the next president will be   15. ~~where could we~~; where we could

Chapter 8

Exercise 8.1

(The sentences you write will differ from these sentences.)   1. Drive; *Be* careful when you go home.   2. help; My grandmother let the kids *be* pirates.   3. act; We asked them if they wanted to *be* in the play.   4. do; The teacher explained what they would *be* next.   5. arrive; Alice wants to to *be* on time for the party.   6. make; Please *be* as quiet as you can.   7. arrive; I thought that the train would *be* late as usual.   8. go; My dog hates it when I have to *be* away.   9. Come; *Be* here early if it is at all possible.   10. get; I love to *be* invited to these meetings.

Exercise 8.2

1. ~~meet~~; meets; The econ class; It   2. ~~be~~; is; Knowing what to do; It   3. ~~want~~; wants; My son; He   4. ~~stop~~; stops; The train on track 2; It   5. ~~make~~; makes; What the article said about the economy; It   6. ~~commute~~; commutes; My wife; She   7. ~~be~~; is; The car that he was asking me about; It   8. ~~prove~~; proves; What happened; It   9. ~~shut~~; shuts; The entire company; It   10. OK

Exercise 8.3

1. races /əz/   2. sends /z/   3. knocks /s/   4. shops /s/   5. eats /s/   6. mentions /z/   7. rushes /əz/   8. approaches /əz/   9. contains /z/   10. doubts /s/   11. causes /əz/   12. clashes /əz/   13. hedges /əz/   14. ends /z/   15. freezes /əz/   16. shows /z/   17. fails /z/   18. patches /əz/   19. allows /z/   20. signs /z/

Exercise 8.4

1. admits   2. supplies   3. goes   4. leaves   5. annoys   6. kisses   7. haves   8. matches   9. identifies   10. declares   11. reduces   12. approaches   13. destroys   14. eliminates   15. convinces

Exercise 8.5

1. defined /d/   2. washed /t/   3. shouted /əd/   4. ranged /d/   5. owned /d/   6. tested /əd/   7. granted /əd/   8. saved /d/   9. compared /d/   10. approved /d/   11. picked /t/   12. extended /əd/   13. ruled /d/   14. taxed /t/   15. permitted /əd/

Exercise 8.6

1. showed   2. denied   3. dropped   4. varied   5. occurred   6. hoped   7. permitted   8. stayed   9. applied   10. flowed   11. slipped   12. delayed   13. starred   14. enjoyed   15. dried

Exercise 8.7

1. skipping   2. crying   3. desiring   4. voting   5. phrasing   6. replying   7. spotting   8. admitting   9. shaking   10. caring

Exercise 8.8

1. had frozen.   2. had risen   3. had spoken   4. was woken   5. was hidden

Chapter 9

Exercise 9.1

1. future perfect   2. present perfect   3. future   4. present perfect   5. past   6. future progressive   7. present progressive   8. future   9. present perfect   10. present perfect   11. present perfect progressive   12. present progressive   13. future perfect   14. past perfect progressive   15. present perfect progressive   16. future perfect progressive   17. future perfect   18. present perfect   19. future perfect progressive   20. future perfect

Exercise 9.2

1. habitual   2. timeless   3. timeless   4. habitual   5. timeless   6. habitual   7. timeless   8. timeless   9. timeless   10. timeless   11. timeless   12. timeless   13. timeless   14. habitual   15. timeless

Exercise 9.3

1. left   2. has lost   3. has sung   4. has had   5. moved   6. have lived   7. lost   8. landed   9. went   10. has permitted   11. showed   12. have complained   13. fell   14. have driven   15. drove

Exercise 9.4

1. had suffered; happened   2. had received; decided   3. had made; called   4. wrote; had solved   5. had gone; got   6. had stopped; shoveled   7. had let; dashed   8. had experienced; requested   9. had written; went   10. had read; began   11. had continued; got   12. had vacationed; had   13. had waited; closed   14. were; had removed   15. settled; had offered

Exercise 9.5

1. will have hardened; get   2. will have cleared; leave/have left   3. will have starved; brings   4. will have walked; arrives/has arrived   5. will have forgotten; finishes/has finished   6. will have locked; have cleared   7. will have wondered; caused/has caused   8. will have filled; locates/has located   9. will have completed; finishes/has finished   10. will have furnished; moved/have moved

Exercise 9.6

1. is encountering   2. unlocks; stative   3. doubts; stative   4. is parking   5. costs; stative   6. deserve; stative   7. are visiting   8. is altering   9. want; stative   10. is undergoing   11. doubt; stative   12. consists; stative   13. is confirming   14. are struggling   15. belongs; stative   16. is commanding   17. is cooperating   18. suits; stative   19. is conveying   20. are waiting

Exercise 9.7

1. was baking   2. was walking   3. was grading   4. were living   5. were controlling

Chapter 10

Exercise 10.1

1. vi; *broke* ~~with a loud crash~~.   2. vt; *broke* the window.   3. vi; *melted* ~~in the toaster oven~~.
4. vi; *dripped* ~~all night long~~.   5. vi; *spoke* ~~at the meeting~~.   6. vi; *was practicing* ~~on the athletic field~~.   7. vi; *rang* ~~for several days after the accident~~.   8. vi; *will retire* ~~at the end of next year~~.
9. vi; *tore* ~~when I tried to bend it~~.   10. vi; *counted* ~~in the election~~.   11. vt; *counted* the ballots.   12. vi; *succeeded* ~~despite all of our misgivings~~.   13. vi; *have declined* ~~over the past decade~~.
14. vi; *laughed* ~~uproariously at the cartoons~~.   15. vi; *spread* ~~slowly across the floor~~.

Exercise 10.2

1. They *heard* <u>what you said</u>./it   2. The lawyers *confirmed* <u>that we needed to consult a patent attorney</u>./it   3. They *emphasized* <u>always being on time to meetings</u>./it   4. I *anticipated* <u>having to get a taxi to get to work on time</u>./it   5. We finally *chose* <u>to look for a new apartment closer to our jobs</u>./it   6. The contract *specified* <u>that all the work had to be finished by June 30</u>./it   7. We *resumed* <u>what we had been doing before we had to stop</u>./it   8. The audience *appreciated* <u>how well they had performed</u>./it   9. We *looked into* <u>taking a vacation in Mexico this summer</u>./it
10. You *need* <u>to be more careful in the future</u>./it   11. The witness *swore* <u>that the defendant had not been at the scene</u>./it   12. I couldn't *resist* <u>making fun of such a ridiculous idea</u>./it
13. Nobody could *understand* <u>his excited shouting</u>./it   14. Finally we *recovered* <u>what we had initially invested in the company</u>./it   15. Please *forgive* <u>what I said earlier</u>./it

Exercise 10.3

1. <u>my parents</u>/them; I *dropped* **them** *off* at the station.   2. <u>the message</u>/it; Jordan *wrote* **it** *down* on a slip of paper.   3. <u>the report</u>/it; He *looked* **it** *over* carefully.   4. <u>the next course</u>/it; The waiter *brought* **it** *in* promptly.   5. <u>the memo</u>/it; Susan *read* **it** *back* to me.   6. <u>the answer</u>/it; I *looked* **it** *up* on Google.   7. <u>all the complexities</u>/them; George *thought* **them** *through* very carefully.
8. <u>all the major points</u>/them; We *talked* **them** *over* before the meeting.   9. <u>my stolen bicycle</u>/it; Finally, I *got* **it** *back* from the police station.   10. <u>her troubles</u>/them; She *poured* **them** *out* to her closest friend.   11. <u>the kids' toys</u>/them; We *picked* **them** *up* quickly.   12. <u>the company's generous offer</u>/it; Albert *turned* **it** *down* regretfully.   13. <u>all the loose ends</u>/them; I *put* **them** *together* in a neat package.   14. <u>their company</u>/it; Our company *is taking* **it** *over* in a friendly merger.
15. <u>his case</u>/it; The lawyer *summed* **it** *up* simply and forcefully.

Exercise 10.4

1. Insep 2. Sep; *played* the size of the problem *down* 3. Insep 4. Sep; *split* the original team *up* 5. Insep 6. Insep 7. Sep; *pointed* all the problems *out* 8. Sep; *pulled* the red convertible *over* 9. Insep 10. Sep; *blew* a gasoline truck *up* 11. Insep 12. Sep; *paper* his involvement *over* 13. Insep 14. Sep; *pare* our expenses *down* 15. Insep 16. Sep; *set* the display tables *up* 17. Insep 18. Sep; *turned* our badges *in* 19. Insep 20. Sep; *playing* the entire conversation *over*

Exercise 10.5

1. Act; The keys ≠ the storage cabinet 2. Link; The plan = a good idea at the time 3. Act; The board ≠ the plan 4. Link; Richard = a highly successful salesman 5. Link; Her new car = a Ford 6. Link; his new mansion = a cheap motel 7. Link; Louise greatly = her sister Thelma 8. Act; Louise ≠ her sister Thelma 9. Link; The new nominee = a good choice for the job 10. Link; The housing market = a complete disaster 11. Link; My first choice = an apartment 12. Link; Albuquerque = a typical city in the 1960s 13. Link; The actor = a man in his midfifties 14. Link; My brother = a lawyer in a big law firm 15. Link; What you can see = all that we have left

Exercise 10.6

1. Link; Agnes *turned* deathly pale. Pred Adj 2. Link; The note *sounded* flat to me. Pred Adj 3. Link; George *seemed* terribly upset about something. Pred Adj 4. Link; The situation *could* easily *turn* ugly. Pred Adj 5. Link; You *look* ready to go. Pred Adj 6. Act 7. Link; Jason *looked like* a ghost of his former self. Pred Nom 8. Link; they *have grown* closer to each other. Pred Adj 9. Link; The day *was getting* terribly warm. Pred Adj 10. Link; Please *remain* calm. Pred Adj 11. Link; The wine *has gone* bad. Pred Adj 12. Link; *felt* much better after seeing the doctor. Pred Adj 13. Link; They *looked* ready to go. Pred Adj 14. Link; Our simple plan *has turned into* a huge project. Pred Nom 15. Link; All the indicators *appeared* positive. Pred Adj

Exercise 10.7

1. *Very* test: *very* frightening; Paraphrase: **X** movie *frightened* (who?); *Very* test: **X** *very* frightening the children; Paraphrase: movie *frightened* the children 2. *Very* test: *very* demanding; Paraphrase: **X** boss *demanded* (what?); *Very* test: **X** very demanding an answer; Paraphrase: boss *demanded* an answer 3. *Very* test: *very* surprising; Paraphrase: **X** suggestions *surprised* (who?); *Very* test: **X** *very* surprising everyone; Paraphrase: suggestions *surprised* everyone 4. *Very* test: *very* alarming; Paraphrase: **X** mistakes *alarmed* (who?); *Very* test: **X** *very* alarming everyone; Paraphrase: mistakes *alarmed* everyone 5. Very test: *very* accepting; Paraphrase: **X** Company *accepted* (who?); Very test: **X** *very* accepting applications; Paraphrase: Company *accepted* applications.

Chapter 11

Exercise 11.1

1. My brother *teaches* <u>college-prep high school seniors</u> (IO) <u>advanced calculus</u> (DO)   2. Please *order* <u>me</u> (IO) <u>a toasted bagel with cream cheese</u> (DO).   3. I *offered* <u>a friend</u> (IO) <u>a lift to the train station</u> (DO).   4. *Could* you *read* <u>the kids</u> (IO) <u>a bedtime story</u> (DO) before it gets too late? 5. I *did* <u>him</u> (IO) <u>a big favor</u> (DO) once.   6. *Pass* <u>us</u> (IO) <u>some plates and silverware</u> (DO), will you?   7. We *should give* <u>the people working at the desk</u> (IO) <u>a short break</u> (DO).   8. Let's *fix* <u>her</u> (IO) <u>a nice dinner</u> (DO) for her birthday.   9. Last year we *sold* <u>the Johnston company</u> (IO) <u>about a thousand laser-jet printers</u> (DO).   10. Her great uncle *left* <u>me</u> (IO) <u>a small bequest</u> (DO) in his will.   11. We *saved* <u>you</u> (IO) <u>a piece of birthday cake</u> (DO).   12. The car dealership *loaned* <u>us</u> (IO) <u>a car</u> (DO) while ours is in the shop.   13. We *should write* <u>them</u> (DO) <u>a nice thank-you note</u> (IO) for their gift.   14. Please get <u>me</u> (IO) <u>all the current invoices</u> (DO).   15. We *should show* <u>the visitors</u> (IO) <u>the new art gallery</u> (DO).

Exercise 11.2

1. My brother *teaches* <u>advanced calculus</u> **to** <u>college-prep high school seniors</u>.   2. Please *order* <u>a toasted bagel with cream cheese</u> **for** <u>me</u>.   3. I *offered* <u>a lift to the train station</u> **to** <u>a friend</u>.   4. *Could* you *read* <u>a bedtime story</u> **to** <u>the kids</u> before it gets too late?   5. I *did* <u>a big favor</u> **for** <u>him</u> once.   6. *Pass* <u>some plates and silverware</u> **to** <u>us</u>, will you?   7. We *should give* <u>a short break</u> **to** <u>the people working at the desk</u>.   8. Let's *fix* <u>a nice dinner</u> **for** <u>her</u> for her birthday.   9. Last year we *sold* <u>about a thousand laser-jet printers</u> **to** <u>the Johnston company</u>.   10. Her great uncle *left* <u>a small bequest</u> **to** <u>me</u> in his will.   11. We *saved* <u>a piece of birthday cake</u> **for** <u>you</u>.   12. The car dealership *loaned* <u>a car</u> **to** <u>us</u> while ours is in the shop.   13. We *should write* <u>a nice thank-you note</u> **to** <u>them</u> for their gift.   14. Please *get* <u>all the current invoices</u> **for** <u>me</u>.   15. We *should show* <u>the new art gallery</u> **to** <u>the visitors</u>.

Exercise 11.3

1. I *owed* it **to** him/her.   2. The real estate agent *found* it **for** them.   3. The agent *handed* it **to** them.   4. The music teacher *taught* it **to** her.   5. The wizard *granted* them **to** her.   6. Please *serve* it **to** them.   7. The owner very kindly *saved* it **for** them.   8. Throw it **to** him, will you? 9. The boss *promised* it **to** her.   10. *Would* you *read* it **to** them again, please?   11. John *bought* it **for** them.   12. We *prepared* it **for** him/her.   13. Please *give* them **to** her.   14. We *ordered* it **for** them.   15. Ship them **to** it/them.

Exercise 11.4

1. <u>myself</u> (Obj) = <u>a better person</u> (NP Comp); **X** *wished* a better person *to/for* myself   2. <u>the CEO</u> (Obj) = <u>a great natural leader</u> (NP Comp); **X** *considers* a great natural leader *to/for* the CEO.   3. <u>them</u> (IO) ≠ <u>the truth</u> (DO); *told* the truth **to** them.   4. <u>her</u> (Obj) = <u>Undersecretary</u>

of State for Latin Affairs (NP Comp); **X** *appointed* Undersecretary of State for Latin Affairs **to/for** her   5. AMPEX Corporation (Obj) = the company of the year (NP Comp); **X** *named* the company of the year **to/for** AMPEX Corporation   6. himself (Obj) = an expert on foreign affairs (NP Comp); **X** *considered* an expert on foreign affairs **to/for** himself   7. them (IO) ≠ my name (DO); *told* my name **to** them   8. them (IO) ≠ a long and happy life (DO); *wished* a long and happy life **to** them   9. him (Obj) = one of the best young golfers in the state (NP Comp); **X** *ranked* one of the best young golfers in the state **to/for** him   10. himself (Obj) = a junk-food addict (NP Comp); **X** *confessed* a junk-food addict **to/for** himself   11. her (Obj) = a rising star in the industry (NP Comp); **X** *called* a rising star in the industry **to/for** her   12. us (IO) ≠ a terrific apartment (DO); *found* a terrific apartment **for** us.   13. John (Obj) = a bit of a bore (NP Comp); **X** *found* a bit of a bore **to/for** him   14. himself (IO) ≠ a cheese sandwich (DO); *made* a cheese sandwich **for** himself   15. himself (Obj) = a first-rate bridge player (NP Comp); **X** *made* a first-rate bridge player **to/for** himself

Exercise 11.5

1. his opponents (Obj) = angry (Adj Comp)   2. the food (Obj) = cold (Adj Comp)   3. my chili (Obj) = blazing hot (Adj Comp)   4. him (Obj) = quite entertaining (Adj Comp).   5. him (Obj) = trustworthy (Adj Comp)   6. them (Obj) = ready (Adj Comp)   7. the deck (Obj) = a light blue (Adj Comp)   8. the original hypothesis (Obj) = correct (Adj Comp)   9. their food (Obj) = only so-so (Adj Comp)   10. the presentation (Obj) = light and upbeat (Adj Comp)

Exercise 11.6

1. We always *found* them (Obj) **to be** kind and considerate (Adj Comp).   2. I *believed* myself (Obj) **to be** ready (Adj Comp).   3. The jury *must presume* the defendant (Obj) **to be** innocent (Adj Comp).   4. I *consider* you (Obj) **to be** a fair person (NP Comp).   5. The treasurer *showed* himself (Obj) **to be** a wizard of financial control (NP Comp).   6. We just *assumed* the budget (Obj) **to be** a done deal (NP Comp).   7. It is a mistake to *think* him (Obj) **to be** a fool (NP Comp).   8. The court *found* the plaintiff's claim (Obj) **to be** valid (Adj Comp).   9. I always *maintained* them (Obj) **to be** one of the best companies in the business (NP Comp).   10. I *confessed* myself (Obj) **to be** totally ignorant of what they were talking about (Adj Comp).

Exercise 11.7

1. take   2. take   3. bring   4. take   5. take   6. bring   7. Take   8. take   9. took   10. brought

Exercise 11.8

1. My boss *told* me (Obj) **that** I would have to work late tonight (*that* clause).   2. We satisfied them (Obj) **that** our emergency plans met all state and federal requirements (*that* clause).   3. I *urge* the company (Obj) **that** they reconsider their decision (*that* clause).   4. We *will inform*

them (Obj) **that** the meeting has been cancelled (*that* clause).   5. The consultant *advised* the union (Obj) **that** the contract would have to be rewritten (*that* clause).   6. The salesman *assured* us (Obj) **that** the car was in perfect running order (*that* clause).   7. I'll bet you (Obj) **that** we can't get a taxi at this time of day (*that* clause).   8. *Convince* me (Obj) **that** I'm wrong (*that* clause).   9. We *instructed* everyone (Obj) **that** they would have to fill out new payroll forms (*that* clause).   10. I *e-mailed* them (Obj) **that** we would be back a day early (*that* clause). 11. *Don't remind* me (Obj) **that** this was my idea to begin with (*that* clause).   12. Man, that really *taught* me (Obj) **that** I should get everything in writing (*that* clause).   13. *Promise* me (Obj) **that** you will be careful (*that* clause)   14. My boss finally *persuaded* the company (Obj) **that** they should revise the policy (*that* clause).   15. I *warned* them (Obj) **that** they would get into trouble (*that* clause).

Exercise 11.9

1. *remarked* **to** me   2. *stated* **to** us   3. *suggest* **to** them   4. *point out* **to** the committee   5. *confessed* **to** him   6. OK   7. *acknowledged* **to** the reporters   8. *explained* **to** them   9. OK 10. *complained* **to** them   11. *will report* **to** them   12. *admitted* **to** them   13. *said* **to** me 14. OK   15. *proposed* **to** them

Exercise 11.10

1. We *expected* them (Obj) to be ready by now (Inf). (cognition)   2. The government *permitted* the project (Obj) to go ahead under certain restrictions (Inf). (permission)   3. Roberta *wanted* the kids (Obj) to go to summer school this year (Inf). (causation)   4. The coupon *entitles* you (Obj) to buy a second ticket at half price (Inf). (permission)   5. *Remind* me (Obj) to get some gas on the way home (Inf). (causation)   6. I *believed* myself (Obj) to be entirely in the wrong (Inf). (cognition)   7. They *used* the loan (Obj) to buy some much-needed equipment (Inf). (causation)   8. The news *prompted* us (Obj) to reconsider what we were planning (Inf). (causation) 9. The VP *asked* Anne (Obj) to head up the new division in Europe (Inf). (naming)   10. Please *allow* us (Obj) to help you with that (Inf). (permission)   11. His parents *encouraged* her (Obj) to apply to Duke (Inf). (causation)   12. I *knew* them (Obj) to be better players than they had first appeared (Inf). (cognition)   13. He *inspired* us (Obj) to try even harder (Inf). (causation) 14. The CEO *picked* an outsider (Obj) to head the review committee (Inf). (naming)   15. The results *forced* us (Obj) to reevaluate all of our plans (Inf). (causation)

Exercise 11.11

1. flutter   2. make   3. play   4. say   5. to be   6. discuss   7. get   8. get   9. give   10. talk

Exercise 11.12

1. finishing up   2. both   3. do   4. hiding   5. both   6. smoking   7. talking   8. both 9. both   10. worrying   11. finish   12. both   13. both   14. dozing off   15. both

Exercise 11.13

1. Obj Base; Please *let* <u>me</u> (Obj) <u>*help* you with that</u> (base form).   2. Obj Adj Comp; The test *proves* <u>the suspect</u> (Obj) <u>innocent</u> (Adj Comp).   3. Obj Pres Part; I *noticed* <u>them</u> (Obj) <u>*leaving* during the meeting</u> (Pres Part).   4. Obj NP Comp; They *appointed* <u>her</u> (Obj) <u>chief counsel</u> (NP Comp).   5. Obj Adv of Pl; He *is putting* <u>the leftovers</u> (Obj) <u>into the refrigerator</u> (Adv of Pl).   6. IO DO; My parents *sent* <u>the kids</u> (IO) <u>some books</u> (DO).   7. Obj Adj Comp; Fortunately, the board *considered* <u>my idea</u> (Obj) <u>quite promising</u> (Adj Comp).   8. Obj *That*; I *told* <u>them</u> (Obj) <u>(*that*) they needed to get prior approval before going ahead</u> (*that* clause).   9. Obj Adv of Pl; Sadly, I *put* <u>the iPhone</u> (Obj) <u>back on the counter</u> (Adv of Pl).   10. Obj NP Comp; We *thought* <u>the outcome</u> (Obj) <u>a big disappointment</u> (NP Comp), to tell the truth.   11. IO DO; Can you *give* <u>my friend</u> (IO) <u>a lift to the airport</u> (DO)?   12. *To That*; Let us *prove* <u>to you</u> (*to* phrase) <u>*that* we can do the job</u> (*that* clause).   13. Obj Adv of Pl; We *moved* <u>the kittens</u> (Obj) <u>out of the kids' bedroom</u> (Adv of Pl).   14. Obj Inf; I *wanted* <u>my parents</u> (Obj) <u>*to stay* with us this Christmas</u> (Inf).   15. Obj Adv of Pl; I *drove* <u>the car</u> (Obj) <u>over to my mother's house</u> (Adv of Pl).   16. Obj Base; I *had* <u>the waiter</u> (Obj) <u>*set* an extra place for you</u> (Base form).   17. Obj Inf; We *helped* <u>them</u> (Obj) <u>*to get* ready to leave</u> (Inf).   18. Obj *That*; I *told* <u>them</u> (Obj) <u>*that* we would be a little late for dinner</u> (*that* clause).   19. IO DO; Jane *baked* <u>Sarah</u> (IO) <u>a birthday cake</u> (DO).   20. Obj NP Comp; I *considered* <u>our project</u> (Obj) <u>a success</u> (NP Comp).   21. Obj Inf; What *prompted* <u>John</u> (Obj) <u>*to change* his mind so suddenly</u> (Inf)?   22. Obj Adj Comp; The oven *will keep* <u>food</u> (Obj) <u>hot for hours</u> (Adj Comp).   23. *To That*; She *explained* <u>to us</u> (*to* phrase) <u>*that* her parents would need to use the apartment that week</u> (*that* clause).   24. Obj Pres Part; I *caught* <u>my son</u> (Obj) <u>watching TV while studying</u> (Pres Part).   25. *To That*; I *confess* <u>to you</u> (*to* phrase) <u>*that* I am more than a little nervous</u> (*that* clause).

Chapter 12

Exercise 12.1

1. usually 2. once 3. simply 4. suddenly 5. often 6. again. 7. too. 8. well. 9. perhaps 10. always 11. already 12. probably 13. soon. 14. always 15. often

Exercise 12.2

1. safely 2. perfectly 3. warmly 4. barely adequately 5. reasonably 6. very quietly 7. capably 8. properly 9. softly 10. excellently 11. quite engagingly 12. devotedly 13. clearly 14. tellingly 15. disgustedly

Exercise 12.3

1. sleepily 2. rarely 3. needily 4. hardily 5. immediately 6. greedily 7. truly 8. sketchily 9. scarily 10. gaily

Exercise 12.4

1. sooner, soonest   2. later, latest   3. more frequently, most frequently   4. rawer, rawest
5. more firmly, most firmly   6. more brilliantly, most brilliantly   7. longer, longest   8. more
honestly, most honestly   9. more critically, most critically   10. lower, lowest   11. more bitterly,
most bitterly   12. better, best   13. more heavily, most heavily   14. tighter, tightest   15. worse,
worst

Exercise 12.5

1. in the back room; noun phrase   2. by spilling food; gerund   3. on us; pronoun   4. by simplifying the entire process; gerund   5. by how loudly he played the TV; noun clause   6. over
the holidays; noun phrase   7. after we placed an ad in the local paper; noun clause   8. near
Cleveland; noun phrase   9. by what he said; noun clause.   10. in Italy; noun phrase

Exercise 12.6

1. *in order* to save the candidate any further embarrassment   2. *in order* to reduce the risk of
infection   3. *in order* to attract a larger market   4. *in order* to pick up some things for the picnic
5. *in order* to protect my legs from the thorns   6. *in order* to minimize the possible damage
7. *in order* to file the estate papers   8. *in order* to ensure that they would have a place to stay
9. *in order* to ensure compliance with federal regulations   10. *in order* to show that there were
no hard feelings

Exercise 12.7

1. if (Sub Conj) he can (statement)   2. before (Sub Conj) it gets too dark (statement)   3. unless
(Sub Conj) there is an unexpected problem (statement)   4. when (Sub Conj) the curtain goes
up (statement)   5. after (Sub Conj) we had finished the presentation (statement)   6. as soon as
(Sub Conj) we could (statement)   7. when (Sub Conj) the waiter comes (statement)   8. after
(Sub Conj) I get back to the office on Monday (statement)   9. everywhere (Sub Conj) we looked
(statement)   10. whenever (Sub Conj) we want them to (statement)   11. if (Sub Conj) we
made a good argument (statement)   12. unless (Sub Conj) there is a good reason (statement)
13. because (Sub Conj) we had to rush the job (statement)   14. everywhere (Sub Conj) we went
(statement)   15. since (Sub Conj) they first moved to the city in the late eighties (statement)

Exercise 12.8

1. Between Christmas and New Year's, Sally *gained* five pounds.   2. Quickly, the zookeeper
replaced the cover.   3. Before I went into the meeting, I *had* everything ready.   4. To avoid the
morning rush, we *took* a later train.   5. By a rigid quarantine, the public health department *was
able to halt* the disease.   6. In the mountains to the east of us, there *is* a report of a serious forest
fire.   7. Sometime during the winter, he *will undergo* treatment.   8. After getting advice from
counsel, we *have decided* to drop the suit.   9. Whenever we get a heavy spring rain, the streets
flood.   10. Over the past six months, we *have made* significant improvements.   11. After the

last ice storm, the roads *were* nearly impassable.   12. If I got a raise this year, we *could afford* a new car.   13. To get more storage space, the company *rented* another office.   14. On nice Sunday afternoons, the family *goes* for a drive.   15. Finally, we *got* some good news.

Exercise 12.9

1. at the station (place) before getting on the train (time)   2. to find the cheapest fares (reason)   3. in the office (place) most mornings (time)   4. hard (manner) every day (time)   5. at the university (place) this spring (time)   6. quite well (manner) today (time)   7. thoughtfully (manner) for a few minutes (time)   8. today (time) because the local store didn't have it (reason)   9. carefully (manner) to make sure the rug would fit (reason)   10. this morning (time) because they couldn't go (reason)   11. recently (time) by extending the deadline (reason)   12. last week (time) because he needed it for a research project (reason)   13. noisily (manner) in the backyard (place) all afternoon (time)   14. by growling at us (manner) every time we came near him (time)   15. this morning (time) because we were all going the same place (reason)

Exercise 12.10

1. I *hurt* my knee at the gym over the weekend.   2. They *fixed* my computer this afternoon by replacing the circuit board.   3. The river *roars* loudly all the time because the flow is so restricted.   4. We *had* our sales presentation at the Marriott since our offices were being repainted.   5. He *talked* so loudly because he was calling from his cell phone.   6. We *survey* all of our customers carefully every year to keep current with their needs.   7. I *recognized* the problem at once since we had dealt with that issue before.   8. Everyone *liked* the company a lot for their generous leave policy.   9. We *investigated* the problem thoroughly before we took any action.   10. I *got* very tired at the gym this afternoon because it was so hot.   11. *Can* you *postpone* the meeting for a few minutes to give them time to get organized?   12. Our son *is taking* advanced placement courses at school every weekend.   13. Everyone *enjoyed* the lecture a great deal because the material was new to us.   14. You *must enforce* your policies seriously to get any real compliance.   15. We *tour* Italy every year to collect antiques.   16. He *understood* the idea perfectly when we explained to him again.   17. You *must solve* the problem right now in order to head off a bigger problem later.   18. They *will review* your proposal carefully since it has major cost implications.   19. Please *turn off* the lights in the office when you leave in order to save electricity.   20. *Can* I *borrow* the car tonight to take Anne to a movie?

Chapter 13

Exercise 13.1

1. Can determine; yes-no   2. did arrest; information   3. can afford; information   4. Have decided; yes-no   5. Was surprising; yes-no   6. should want; information   7. Is ringing; yes-no   8. Has been raining; yes-no   9. Must insure; yes-no   10. Will be; yes-no   11. would cost;

information   12. Will disturb; yes-no   13. should care; information   14. Has approved; yes-no   15. will be meeting; information

Exercise 13.2

1. <u>Are</u> (main verb) we <u>ready</u> to leave soon?   2. <u>Can</u> (modal auxiliary) you <u>translate</u> that into Spanish?   3. <u>Were</u> (main verb) the kids very happy with their presents?   4. <u>Should</u> (modal auxiliary) I <u>decline</u> a second helping of your terrific dessert?   5. <u>Will</u> (modal auxiliary) they <u>be</u> able to finance it by themselves?   6. <u>Have</u> (helping verb) the French filmmakers <u>influenced</u> his movies a lot?   7. <u>Is</u> (main verb) her criticism of great concern to the board?   8. <u>Am</u> (helping verb) I <u>working</u> on it?   9. <u>Should</u> (modal auxiliary) he <u>postpone</u> his trip?   10. <u>Are</u> (helping verb) they just <u>kidding</u>?   11. <u>Has</u> (helping verb) it <u>gone</u> on too long?   12. <u>Could</u> (modal auxiliary) he <u>have done</u> it differently?   13. <u>Are</u> (main verb) they in big trouble about this?   14. <u>Will</u> (modal auxiliary) that <u>stain</u> the carpet?   15. <u>Are</u> (main verb) we <u>turning</u> around at the next corner?

Exercise 13.3

1. He *did* install; *Did* he install   2. Tom *did* fall; *Did* Tom fall   3. Ralph *did* buy; *Did* Ralph buy   4. Ruth *does* swim; *Does* Ruth swim   5. The meeting *did* last; *Did* the meeting last   6. They *do* trust; *Do* they trust   7. The boss *did* quit; *Did* the boss quit   8. They *did* try; *Did* they try   9. The wind *did* damage; *Did* the wind damage   10. Bob *does* retire; *Does* Bob retire   11. She *did* loan; *Did* she loan   12. He *did* wreck; *Did* he wreck   13. She *did* get; *Did* she get   14. He *did* pay; *Did* he pay   15. She *does* still talk; *Does* she still talk

Exercise 13.4

(Only the beginning of each sentence is shown. The remainder of the sentence does not change.)   1. They <u>guessed</u>; <u>Did</u> they <u>guess</u>   2. You <u>can combine</u>; <u>Can</u> you <u>combine</u>   3. That <u>eliminated</u>; <u>Did</u> that <u>eliminate</u>   4. That <u>is</u> stretching; <u>Is</u> that <u>stretching</u>   5. They <u>will</u> hire; <u>Will</u> they <u>hire</u>   6. We <u>have</u> gathered; <u>Have</u> we <u>gathered</u>   7. You <u>can</u> get; <u>Can</u> you <u>get</u>   8. They <u>questioned</u>; <u>Did</u> they <u>question</u>   9. Ruth <u>can</u> convince; <u>Can</u> Ruth <u>convince</u>   10. The kids <u>are</u> making; <u>Are</u> the kids <u>making</u>   11. This seat <u>is</u> occupied. <u>Is</u> this seat <u>occupied</u>?   12. It <u>will</u> rain; <u>Will</u> it <u>rain</u>   13. I <u>should</u> ignore; <u>Should</u> I <u>ignore</u>   14. They <u>have</u> examined; <u>Have</u> they <u>examined</u>   15. The photographer <u>is</u>; <u>Is</u> the photographer

Exercise 13.5

(Only the beginning of each sentence is shown.)   1. Have you; Do you have   2. Has the car; Does the car   3. Have you; Do you have   4. Has she; Does she have   5. Has your cat; Does your cat have   6. Has the house; Does the house have   7. Has the picture; Does the picture have   8. Has the book; Does the book have   9. Has the letter; Does the letter have   10. Has the car; Does the car have

Exercise 13.6

1. ∅ The group working on it?   2. ∅ They redoing the office again?   3. ∅ We been opening new stores?   4. Invalid   5. ∅ The cat staring at the goldfish?   6. ∅ You been sleeping badly lately?   7. Invalid   8. ∅ Harry very upset about it?   9. ∅ There been some questions?   10. ∅ You miss me?

Exercise 13.7

1. Who; noun   2. Whom; noun   3. How much; Adv of quantity   4. Whose advice; Poss noun   5. When; Adv of time   6. Why; Adv of reason   7. Whom; noun   8. How; Adv of manner   9. Whose dog; Poss noun   10. How much longer; Adv of time

Exercise 13.8

(Only the beginning of each sentence is shown.)   1. How they *will*; How *will* they   2. Whom we *should*; Whom *should* we   3. Where they *are*; Where *are* they   4. What the matter *is*; What *is* the matter   5. How soon we *can* see; How soon *can* we see   6. How long they *are* staying; How long *are* they staying?   7. When they *had* planned; When *had* they planned   8. How long the meetings *are*; How long *are* the meetings   9. How much I *should* pay; How much *should* I pay   10. How often they *would* meet; How often *would* they meet   11. What he *had* given; What *had* he given   12. Why we *should* care; Why *should* we care   13. Where they *would* park; Where *would* they park   14. What on earth Robert *is* doing; What on earth *is* Robert doing   15. What we *should* call; What *should* we call

Exercise 13.9

(Only the beginning of each sentence is shown.)   1. How much they *claimed*; How much they *did claim*; How much *did* they *claim*   2. Whom he *demanded*; Whom he *did demand*; Whom *did* he *demand*   3. What the decision *depends*; What the decision *does depend*; What *does* the decision *depend*   4. How your cats *reacted*; How your cats *did react*; How *did* your cats *react*   5. What the kids *want*; What the kids *do want*; What *do* the kids *want*   6. Which movie you *rented*; Which movie you *did rent*; Which movie *did* you *rent*   7. When she *got*; When *she did* get; When *did* she *get*   8. Whom Roberta *picked*; Whom Roberta *did pick*; Whom *did* Roberta *pick*   9. Whose health plan you *think*; Whose health plan you *do think*; Whose health plan *do* you *think*   10. How long they *plan*; How long they *do plan*; How long *do* they *plan*

Exercise 13.10

1. When *will* the program start?   2. How *am* I doing?   3. What *have* we missed so far?   4. How much *are* they charging for it?   5. Why *did* he have so much trouble?   6. How early *could* we finish here?   7. Where *do* we sign up for the program?   8. Whose advice *are* you going to follow?   9. What song *were* they singing?   10. How many parts *should* I order now?   11. What subject *do* you teach?   12. What *was* the problem with my phone?   13. How *will* they

recognize you?   14. When *should* they take the test?   15. Why *does* the government require that form?

Exercise 13.11

(Only the beginning of each sentence is shown.)   1. Whom; They nominated whom
2. Whom; She drew a picture of whom   3. Who   4. Who   5. Whom; He had been seeing whom   6. Whom; We should send the invitations to whom   7. Whom; They will trust whom
8. Who   9. Whom; We give the money to whom   10. Whom; We have not heard from whom

Exercise 13.12

1. You should not buy   2. They are not adopting   3. We can not arrange   4. I have not driven
5. They were not upset   6. They have not ignored   7. I am not counting   8. Richard might not be   9. The replacement is not   10. I could not unlock

Exercise 13.13

1. ~~should not~~; shouldn't   2. ~~must not~~; mustn't   3. ~~will not~~; won't   4. ~~have not~~; haven't
5. ~~was not~~; wasn't   6. might not; OK   7. ~~were not~~; weren't   8. may not; OK   9. ~~would not~~; wouldn't   10. ~~can not~~; can't

Exercise 13.14

1. I do remember; I do not remember   2. You did call; You did not call   3. It did happen; It did not happen   4. He did pass; He did not pass   5. We did stay; We did not stay   6. Jim did believe; Jim did not believe   7. I did walk; I did not walk   8. They did come; They did not come   9. The manager did explain; The manager did not explain   10. The documents in question do actually exist; The documents in question do not actually exist   11. The regulations do apply; The regulations do not apply   12. They did prepare; They did not prepare   13. She did feel; She did not feel   14. Jason's family did go; Jason's family did not go   15. The SEC did stop; The SEC did not stop

Exercise 13.15

1. Shouldn't you   2. Couldn't Bob   3. Weren't they   4. Hasn't she   5. Don't you   6. Isn't she   7. Couldn't he   8. Mightn't it   9. Didn't he fill   10. Didn't you watch   11. Isn't he
12. Didn't she just buy   13. Didn't he remind   14. Don't you   15. Haven't they

Exercise 13.16

Change the period to a comma and add the following: 1. will we?   2. can't they?   3. didn't it?   4. didn't they?   5. aren't they?   6. can he?/can she?   7. doesn't it?   8. could they?
9. doesn't it?   10. was it?   11. mightn't they?   12. weren't they?   13. do they?   14. will it?
15. isn't it?

Chapter 14

Exercise 14.1

1. passive; was appointed   2. passive; was wrapped   3. passive; has been solved   4. active
5. active   6. passive; will be adjusted   7. passive; is always locked   8. passive; has been noticed   9. passive; was previously owned   10. active   11. passive; was elected   12. passive; was first sounded   13. active   14. passive; should have been recalled   15. passive; is being directed

Exercise 14.2

1. Janet *was answered* my questions; **by** Janet *was answered* my questions; My questions *were answered* **by** Janet.   2. The press office *was issued* a statement; **by** the press office *was issued* a statement; A statement *was issued* **by** the press office.   3. Everybody *was supported* the proposal; **by** everybody *was supported* the proposal; The proposal *was supported* **by** everybody.   4. A visitor *be taught* my economics class today; **by** a visitor *be taught* my economics class today; My economics class *was taught* **by** a visitor today.   5. What happened *was proved* my point; **by** what happened *was proved* my point; My point *was proved* **by** what happened.   6. Somebody *was made* a big mistake; **by** somebody *was made* a big mistake; A big mistake *was made* **by** somebody.
7. Our law firm *is represented* the union; **by** our law firm *is represented* the union; The union *is represented* **by** our law firm.   8. Many companies *are used* our software programs; **by** many companies *are used* our software programs; Our software programs *are used* **by** many companies.
9. The new process *is obtained* much better results; **by** the new process *is obtained* much better results; Much better results *are obtained* **by** the new process.   10. The government *is recognized* the problem; **by** the government *is recognized* the problem; The problem *is recognized* **by** the government.

Exercise 14.3

1. The waiter *is being calculated* the bill; **by** the waiter *is being calculated* the bill; The bill *is being calculated* **by** the waiter.   2. The police *will be solved* the crime; **by** the police *will be solved* the crime; The crime *will be solved* **by** the police.   3. The merchants *were being displayed* summer clothing; **by** the merchants *were being displayed* summer clothing; Summer clothing *was being displayed* **by** the merchants.   4. The mosquitoes *might be bothered* you this time of year. **by** the mosquitoes *might be bothered* you this time of year. You *might be bothered* **by** the mosquitoes this time of year.   5. Everybody *had been accepted* his offer. **by** everybody *had been accepted* his offer. His offer *had been accepted* **by** everybody.   6. We *are being hired* some new employees. **by** we *are being hired* some new employees. Some new employees *are being hired* **by** us.   7. The union *could have been sued* the company. **by** the union *could have been sued* the company. The company *could have been sued* **by** the union.   8. The secretary *had been delayed* the merger. **by** the secretary *had been delayed* the merger. The merger *had been delayed* **by** the secretary.   9. Jackson *should have been seen* them. **by** Jackson *should have been seen* them. They *should have been seen* **by** Jackson.

10. They *are being talked* about what happened. **by** they *are being talked* about what happened. What happened *is being talked* about **by** them.

Exercise 14.4

1. The weak response to the ads discouraged Alice.   2. A professional appraiser evaluated the estate.   3. A sensor in the lab detected smoke.   4. The maid had cleaned the hotel room. 5. The defendant's lawyer requested a new hearing.   6. The sun had badly faded the carpet. 7. A splinter had snagged the material.   8. Roberta was developing a new plan.   9. A special task force was coordinating the entire project.   10. The entire staff critiqued the idea.   11. My grandfather wound up the clock once a week.   12. A loader lifted the rocks onto the truck. 13. A team from NASA had launched the rocket.   14. Unfortunately, the previous owners had badly neglected the house.   15. A neighbor's son is cleaning the pool.

Chapter 15

Exercise 15.1

1. Alice said that the company hosted the annual meeting in Las Vegas this year.   2. Tom said that Francine had decided to move to Chicago.   3. I said that Tom would meet us as soon as possible.   4. Ralph said that everyone had enjoyed the visit.   5. The TV said that the storm might move up the coastline.   6. My mom said that everyone was looking forward to meeting Barbara.   7. Bill said that the keys were kept next to the backdoor.   8. Terry said that we could still get reservations for the weekend.   9. The contractor said that the electricians would finish the wiring Friday.   10. I said that I knew you were right.

Exercise 15.2

1. He said that they had really done a great job.   2. I said that we had been busy all afternoon. 3. Rudy said that they had seen a terrific movie Saturday.   4. Mom said that the rain had been pouring down all afternoon.   5. The mechanic said that Jack had been working on their car. 6. The bank said that the check had been deposited already.   7. Alice said that they had already made plans for dinner.   8. He said that they had helped their kids move into their new apartment.   9. Marion said that she had been watching TV when you called.   10. Francis said that Bob had pulled a muscle exercising.

Exercise 15.3

1. He said that he might be able to arrange a meeting with his manager.   2. I said that it had been a good idea to talk to him/her/you.   3. The postman said that I needed to mail my package before five.   4. Bob said that the paint in his living room was drying properly.   5. Jane said that she had just been talking to her mother.   6. He said that he would be staying at home tomorrow. 7. She told Paul that he could count on her.   8. Ruth told me that she was not ready to get rid

of her car yet.   9. Alice told her son that he had been staying up too late talking to his friends.
10. My wife reminded me that she was having dinner with her friend after work.

Exercise 15.4

1. He asked me if I would be able to come to the reception.   2. I asked the kids if they had
set the table for six people.   3. He asked if Ruth had written her essay yet.   4. They asked
Bob if it was/were true that he was moving to Dallas.   5. She asked me if I worked at J.P. Morgan.   6. They asked us if the reception was/were starting at six.   7. I asked if the coach had
announced when the game started.   8. She asked me if I would turn off the lights in my office.
9. I asked them if they had heard the news.   10. He asked if Tina was/were leaving for Seattle
Sunday.   11. The waiter asked me if I had a reservation.   12. The receptionist asked me if
they were holding my mail while I was away.   13. He asked me if I had any idea how late I was.
14. I asked Sarah if she could return the book to the library for me.   15. I asked my brother if
Mom had given him a call about the party.

Exercise 15.5

1. Sam asked Harriet when she would begin the lesson.   2. I asked him how often he went
shopping.   3. They asked me why I wanted to move back to the city.   4. She asked him where
he had parked the car.   5. I asked her whom she was looking for.   6. He asked the waitress how
long we would wait before getting a table.   7. She asked the children what story they wanted to
hear.   8. He asked us how come the class had broken up so early.   9. She asked us who knew
where the library was.   10. The cabdriver asked me where I wanted him to take me.

Chapter 16

Exercise 16.1

1. David Villa, soccer player   2. Boeing, airplane   3. Burger King, restaurant   4. Canada,
nation   5. Erie, lake   6. Simba, lion   7. Disney, company   8. Wuthering Heights, book
9. London, city   10. Schwinn, bicycle

Exercise 16.2

1. space; time   2. knowledge; electricity   3. pepper; OK   4. blood; OK   5. OK; oxygen
6. hope   7. luggage   8. wind; energy   9. cheese; milk   10. OK; justice

Exercise 16.3

1. boy's, boys, boys'   2. boss's, bosses, bosses'   3. friend's, friends, friends'   4. plane's, planes,
planes'   5. city's, cities, cities'   6. deer's, deer, deer's   7. company's, companies, companies'
8. thief's, thieves, thieves'   9. mouse's, mice, mice's   10. beach's, beaches, beaches'

Exercise 16.4

1. some 2. the 3. some 4. the 5. a 6. the 7. a 8. the 9. some 10. the

Exercise 16.5

1. an 2. some 3. an 4. a 5. a 6. an 7. some 8. an 9. a 10. some

Exercise 16.6

1. ∅ 2. ∅ 3. the 4. ∅ 5. the 6. ∅,∅ 7. ∅ 8. the 9. ∅,∅ 10. ∅

Exercise 16.7

1. I asked the new worker you hired to come to my office. (him/her) 2. The car that he wrecked is in the workshop. (It) 3. Where is the laptop that I ordered? (it) 4. My mother and her friends went to the movies. (They) 5. The mascot of that university is a tiger. (It) 6. Our office manager ordered the most expensive copy machine. (it) 7. All players, trainers, and coaches must register at the field. (They) 8. Their wildlife organization protects animals on the endangered species list. (them) 9. I am not used to driving a car that runs on ethanol. (it) 10. My aunt reads to all the little girls in her neighborhood. (them)

Exercise 16.8

1. whom 2. whose 3. who 4. whose 5. whom 6. who 7. whose 8. whose 9. who 10. who

Exercise 16.9

1. That poem *that* you memorized for class is inspiring. 2. The clothes *that* hung on the clothesline have blown away. 3. Dorothy went to the store again to buy the butter *that* you forgot to pick up. 4. The man *whom* you met is usually more polite. 5. She bought the store *that* she had managed for such a long time. 6. The shoppers *whom* he interviewed all preferred the new product. 7. Bob wrecked the car *that* he rented in Las Vegas. 8. The wren *that* you heard singing flew off. 9. I'm voting for the candidate *whom* you saw at the convention. 10. His cat caught the mouse *that* you were trying to catch last week.

Exercise 16.10

1. They 2. It 3. He/She 4. him/her 5. They 6. They 7. they 8. She 9. it 10. them

Exercise 16.11

1. hers 2. your 3. yours 4. their 5. her 6. their 7. theirs 8. yours 9. her 10. Yours

Exercise 16.12

1. myself (I)   2. themselves (They)   3. himself (Joe)   4. yourself (You)   5. themselves (students)   6. himself (James)   7. itself (computer)   8. herself (She)   9. yourself (you)   10. ourselves (We)

Exercise 16.13

1. arranging   2. arriving   3. attaching   4. bathing   5. belonging   6. lifting   7. meeting
8. touching   9. warning   10. washing

Exercise 16.14

1. Building a snowman is a fun winter pastime.   2. She found running a large company to be a challenge.   3. Singing in the shower is his favorite hobby.   4. The students discovered that finishing the exam took all afternoon.   5. Completing the project by Friday is their goal.
6. Seeing three movies in one day was tiring.   7. Flying south for the winter is what most North American birds do.   8. In that recipe, melting the cheese takes a long time.   9. Shivering in the stadium during the football game is not my idea of a good time.   10. The boss does not enjoy speaking to large groups of people.

Exercise 16.15

1. To sing at the Metropolitan Opera is her dream.   2. To convince the judge is your only option.   3. Tom's only goal is to elect John president.   4. To postpone the meeting now would be dangerous.   5. To sort the dirty clothes is your first task.   6. They decided to purchase their new car by the end of the month.   7. To stand up to the boss takes nerve.   8. The new law aims to prevent more road accidents.   9. Sandra refused to talk to her doctor.   10. To sleep is one thing, to sleep well is another.

Exercise 16.16

1. That Paul would inherit the family fortune came as a horrible shock to Louise.   2. They contended that the accident wasn't their fault.   3. The plan was that we would call you when we got there.   4. The driver told us that he was out of gas.   5. That they were so late was really rude to the hosts.   6. The doctor told me that my ankle was severely sprained but not broken.   7. Their main complaint was that the restaurant closed too early.   8. Sally hated that Harry's ties were so out of style.   9. That the movie wasn't very good came as no surprise.   10. The problem is that it is getting so late.

Exercise 16.17

1. I don't care about what he said.   2. Forgive me for what I am about to say.   3. Where they went is none of my business.   4. Did you ever notice how babies first start crawling?   5. Can you tell me how much dinner actually cost?   6. Which one we will finally pick is still up in the

air.   7. I will accept whatever position they offer me.   8. Did you learn which flight they are on?   9. What shocked us the most was how much prices have gone up lately.   10. Who you know is sometimes more important than what you know.

Exercise 16.18

1. ~~what was that loud noise~~; what that loud noise was   2. ~~what have they done~~; what they have done   3. ~~how much were we~~; how much we were   4. ~~where should we park~~; where we should park   5. ~~How long will it take~~; How long it will take   6. ~~what did they just said~~; what they just said   7. ~~why are the streets so empty~~; why the streets are so empty   8. ~~what did she mean~~; what she meant   9. ~~how are you feeling~~; how you are feeling   10. ~~whatever would you like~~; whatever you would like

Exercise 16.19

1. ~~take~~; takes; The box in the hall; It   2. ~~convince~~; convinces; What you just said about their plans; It   3. ~~make~~; makes; Packing for trips; It   4. ~~own~~; owns; The shopping center; It   5. ~~engage~~; engages; What they said; It   6. ~~look~~; looks; The announcer on the news; He   7. ~~make~~; makes; The size of the crowds at rock concerts; It   8. ~~help~~; helps; Knowing what to do in an emergency; It   9. ~~play~~; plays; My roommate; She   10. ~~cost~~; costs; A trip to the outer islands; It

Exercise 16.20

1. postpones   2. concentrates   3. develops   4. tries   5. multiplies   6. bosses   7. taxes   8. marks   9. nods   10. matches

Exercise 16.21

1. enlarged   2. roped   3. trimmed   4. replied   5. shipped.   6. banned   7. envied   8. caused   9. missed   10. prayed

Exercise 16.22

1. taking   2. arriving   3. betting   4. knitting   5. studying   6. cutting   7. leaving   8. perspiring   9. pleasing   10. winning

Exercise 16.23

1. performed   2. have flown   3. painted   4. has directed   5. divided   6. have urged   7. limped   8. have examined   9. moved   10. have lived

Exercise 16.24

1. got; had gotten   2. had received; deposited   3. had just stepped; rang   4. had; had moved   5. had explained; thought   6. went; had reached   7. locked; had been   8. had retained; drew   9. had unplugged; started   10. had stopped; shoveled

Exercise 16.25

1. vi; *froze* ~~earlier than usual this year~~.   2. vt; *froze* my fingers getting the ice off the windshield.
3. vi; *was running* ~~all night long~~.   4. vi; *spoke* ~~at great length~~.   5. vi; *was practicing* ~~in the music room~~.   6. vt; *was practicing* their new piece.   7. vi; *was practicing* ~~for their performance~~.
8. vt; *answered* the questionnaire.   9. vi; *answered* ~~as honestly as I could~~.   10. vt; *answered* whatever questions were put to me.

Exercise 16.26

1. Sep; *turned* the offer *down*   2. Insep   3. Insep   4. Sep; *printed* the final report *out*   5. Sep; *hired* the furloughed employees *back*   6. Insep   7. Insep   8. Sep; *dressed* the girls *up*   9. Insep
10. Sep; *looked* today's receipts *over*

Exercise 16.27

1. She teaches <u>Chinese students</u> (IO) <u>English as a second language</u> (DO) in Oakland. She teaches <u>English as a second language</u> **to** <u>Chinese students</u> in Oakland.   2. Please order <u>me</u> (IO) <u>a black coffee to go</u> (DO). Please order <u>a black coffee to go</u> **for** <u>me</u>.   3. She showed <u>them</u> (IO) <u>her engagement ring</u> (DO). She showed <u>her engagement ring</u> **to** <u>them</u>.   4. I made <u>my students</u> (IO) <u>a traditional Korean meal</u> (DO). I made <u>a traditional Korean meal</u> **for** <u>my students</u>.   5. Hand <u>me</u> (IO) <u>that brush</u> (DO), will you? Hand <u>that brush</u> **to** <u>me</u>, will you?   6. He told <u>us</u> (IO) <u>a really funny story</u> (DO). He told <u>a really funny story</u> **to** <u>us</u>.   7. Save <u>us</u> (IO) <u>some dessert</u> (DO). Save <u>some dessert</u> **for** <u>us</u>.   8. Let's give <u>the people working in the kitchen</u> (IO) <u>a big hand</u> (DO). Let's give <u>a big hand</u> **to** <u>the people working in the kitchen</u>.   9. We mailed <u>the kids</u> (IO) <u>their Christmas presents</u> (DO). We mailed <u>their Christmas presents</u> **to** <u>the kids</u>.   10. I reserved <u>them</u> (IO) <u>a table at the restaurant</u> (DO). I reserved <u>a table at the restaurant</u> **for** <u>them</u>.

Exercise 16.28

1. bring   2. brought   3. take   4. take   5. bring   6. took   7. brought   8. take   9. took
10. bring

Exercise 16.29

1. ~~my friends~~; to my friends   2. ~~them~~; to them   3. OK   4. ~~you~~; to you   5. ~~us~~; to us   6. OK
7. ~~us~~; to us   8. ~~everyone~~; to everyone   9. ~~us~~; to us   10. ~~Mary~~; to Mary

Exercise 16.30

1. just   2. too.   3. usually   4. always   5. prudently   6. persistently   7. almost   8. gently
9. now   10. frighteningly

Exercise 16.31

1. recklessly   2. brilliantly   3. angrily   4. dutifully   5. immediately   6. moodily   7. hesitantly   8. enthusiastically   9. suspiciously   10. joyfully

Exercise 16.32

1. dirtily   2. prettily   3. barely   4. finely   5. speedily   6. duly   7. safely   8. messily
9. noisily   10. separately

Exercise 16.33

1. She *did* grade the exams. *Did* she grade the exams?   2. Tom *did* drive the truck. *Did* Tom drive the truck?   3. The Adams family *did* live in Toronto. *Did* the Adams family live in Toronto?   4. The athletes *did* lose weight. *Did* the athletes lose weight?   5. We *did* laugh until we cried. *Did* we laugh until we cried?   6. The snow *did* come down in heavy drifts. *Did* the snow come down in heavy drifts?   7. The president *did* tour the warehouse. *Did* the president tour the warehouse?   8. Daniel *did* forget his homework again. *Did* Daniel forget his homework again?   9. The boxers *did* fight ten rounds. *Did* the boxers fight ten rounds?   10. The dog *did* bury his bone. *Did* the dog bury his bone?

Exercise 16.34

1. Her grandmother sewed her wedding dress.   2. Dr. Peterson of Texas A&M University gave the lecture.   3. During the summer, our teacher corrected the exams.   4. Tom's brother piloted the Montreal flight.   5. Last Saturday, Cindy played the guitar to a rapt audience.   6. The city inspected the house for termites.   7. A barn owl ate the mouse.   8. In Friday's game, the Vikings scored five touchdowns.   9. Their home country honored the Olympic athletes.   10. A certified technician repaired the computer.

Exercise 16.35

1. He said *that* he *was* running late for work.   2. The conductor said *that* the audience *had* talked during the entire symphony.   3. We said *that* the children *had been* doing extra chores this week.   4. Charles said *that they couldn't* come to *their* party because *his* wife *was* sick.
5. The doctor said *that he/she needed* to look at *his/her/your* prescription again.   6. Ralph said *that he had demanded* an explanation for what Harry *had done*.   7. My mother said *that she had* liked playing soccer when *she had been* my age.   8. The plumber said *that they would* install the new sink this week.   9. Louise said *that she was* having minor surgery Tuesday.   10. They said *that they had been* laughing at what the kids *had been* doing.